George
Dawson
& his Circle

N.B As well as
simplified groups/
tallys in Demourary
etc

Literary
celebrations
. world Phile.
first

BMI

1.5 hour classes in

· Philosophy
· Literature
· Stoicism

2 hour classes in
· creative Writing

½ day or
¾ day
weekends?

1 hr talks on
Philosophy 'applied Ethics' / Forum
— · — hist. etc.

Phile. of Art
~~Philosophy~~ 'Phile Fict. Book club'
(~in line two?)

To the memory of Asa Briggs

George Dawson & his Circle

The Civic Gospel in Victorian Birmingham

ANDREW REEKES & STEPHEN ROBERTS

MERLIN PRESS

First published in the UK in 2021 by
The Merlin Press Ltd
50 Freshwater Road
Dagenham
RM8 1RX

www.merlinpress.co.uk

ISBN 978-0-85036-771-3

A CIP catalogue record for this book is available from the British Library

Printed in the UK by Imprint Digital, Exeter

Contents

Introduction	9
Chapter One: George Dawson *(Ewan Fernie)*	19
Chapter Two: Joseph Chamberlain	25
Chapter Three: Arthur Ryland	33
Chapter Four: Robert Dale	41
Chapter Five: William Harris	48
Chapter Six: William Aitken	56
Chapter Seven: John Davies Mullins	64
Chapter Eight: Samuel Timmins	70
Chapter Nine: John Henry Chamberlain	79
Chapter Ten: Marie Bethell Beauclerc *(Nicola Gauld)*	86
Chapter Eleven: Henry William Crosskey and Hannah Crosskey	92
Chapter Twelve: Charles Vince	102
Chapter Thirteen: John Jaffray	108
Chapter Fourteen: John Thackray Bunce	114
Chapter Fifteen: William Kenrick	123
Chapter Sixteen: Robert Francis Martineau	131
Chapter Seventeen: Edward Taylor	139
Afterword	146
Appendix: The Institutions of Victorian Birmingham	149
Further Reading	154
Notes	155
Index	170
About the Authors	176

Acknowledgements

We are grateful to Lady Briggs and Dan Briggs for permission to dedicate this book to the memory of Asa Briggs. We are both great admirers of Asa's *History of Birmingham 1865-1938* (1952). It is truly a tour de force and indispensable reading for anyone interested in the history of Birmingham. We would also like to recognise the kindness and encouragement Asa showed to Stephen Roberts when he was writing about the Chartists.

We are indebted to Ewan Fernie and Nicola Gauld for their respective contributions to this book. To Ewan we express our thanks for the informative and enjoyable conversations and correspondence about George Dawson that we have shared in recent years. Katherine Schell kindly sent us copies of a sample of letters from Samuel Timmins to J. Parker Norris from the large collection that is deposited at the Folger Shakespeare Library and we greatly appreciate her help. Our grateful thanks go to Catherine Howe for preparing the Index. We would also like to thank Tony Zurbrugg of Merlin Press for his support for this project from the moment that it was put to him.

A number of people have answered queries and we appreciate their help: Katy Owen; Miles Taylor; and Doug Wilks. Sue Curtis carried out useful genealogical research on our behalf. Elizabeth and Jeremy Fenwick, Helen Thomson and Barnaby Reekes have offered much-needed technical support.

Thanks are also owed to the librarians and archivists at the Cadbury Research Library in the University of Birmingham; the Wolfson Centre for Archival Research in the Library of Birmingham; and the Folger Shakespeare Library in Washington DC. At the Birmingham and Midland Institute, Samina Ansari was particularly helpful.

Authors' Note

This is a collaborative work in which ideas and approaches have been shared and thoroughly discussed, but we have decided to identify the author of each chapter. The introduction, afterword and chapters 2, 3, 5, 6, 12, 14, 15 and 16 were written by Andrew Reekes. Chapters 4, 7, 8, 9, 11, 13, 17 and the appendix were written by Stephen Roberts. Chapter 1 was written by Ewan Fernie and chapter 10 was written by Nicola Gauld. We anticipate many readers will focus on particular figures in this book and for that reason there is a certain amount of unavoidable repetition. A collection of engravings and photographs relating to this book can be viewed at www.birmingham-biographies.co.uk.

Abbreviations

BDG Birmingham Daily Gazette
BDP Birmingham Daily Post
BJ Birmingham Journal
BLA Birmingham Liberal Association
BMI Birmingham and Midland Institute
NEL National Education League
NH&MS Natural History and Microscopic Society
SML Shakespeare Memorial Library

Introduction

For most of the first half of the nineteenth century, Birmingham lagged behind other great provincial towns in providing for its citizens. Forty-nine municipal gasworks across the country anticipated Chamberlain's famous take-over of the private gas companies in Birmingham in 1874; it was Glasgow which became the first British model for urban renewal; Salford and Warrington had already built municipal art galleries in the 1840s; a score of other towns took advantage of government legislation to establish free libraries, while Birmingham dithered.[1] Yet by the time it was raised by royal decree to city status in 1889, Birmingham had become a civic cynosure, widely admired as 'the best governed city in the world'.[2]

An active and interventionist town council had instigated wide-ranging municipal socialism; it had the most famous art school in the land, an enviable new museum and art gallery, the first municipal technical school, the largest and foremost provincial institute (the Birmingham and Midland Institute), and a unique memorial library dedicated to the works of Warwickshire's very own William Shakespeare. More than this, it had seized the initiative in the long-running campaign to reform elementary educational provision; the National Education League (N.E.L.) was based in Birmingham and its one hundred branches across the country looked to the town for a lead. Over forty new school board schools, built in striking Venetian gothic, were the visible expression of Birmingham's own faith in the importance of education. The turnaround from the 1850s was extraordinary. How could it be explained?

Joseph Chamberlain is popularly credited with being the architect of change. He had the drive, dynamism, and entrepreneurial know-how to re-direct the town council and make it the engine of reform. But as Asa Briggs (to whom our book is dedicated) wrote: 'the civic revolution was not the work of one man but of whole groups of men.'[3] This book is about these men and women, many of them forgotten or unregarded; across a range of social welfare reforms, of new intellectual and aesthetic organisations, 'they had the vision and the determination to push forward large schemes of city improvement,' Briggs continues. Many of them, however, looked to one source of inspiration, the prophet of that civic improvement, the minister of the Church of the Saviour, George Dawson. Chamberlain himself was clear about his importance: 'if this great town ... has special characteristics, distinguishing virtues ... these are chiefly due to the teaching of George Dawson.'[4] Dawson was a charismatic force whose 'conviction flamed into enthusiasm, (which) took shape in policy, and passed from the study and the club and the platform and the pulpit and swept through the wards of the city and fired men's minds and kindled their hearts,' as A. W. W. Dale breathlessly expressed it.[5] Perhaps the most significant of those 'special characteristics' was his framing of an overarching philosophy, the civic gospel; its intellectual coherence made Birmingham's municipal revolution quite distinctive.

The heroic mission of the civic gospel – Dawson believed – was to civilise the town dweller, a challenge preoccupying many Victorian thinkers, given the exponential and haphazard growth of industrial centres which had created an often spiritually rootless populace. Yet for Dawson the urban community 'was a society established by divine will ... for common life, common purpose,' and he saw it as the responsibility, indeed the civic duty, of its business and propertied classes to ensure that all its citizens should flourish and live life well. However,

> when we have done all we can for [the citizen's] health ... we have not ministered to all his wants ... [for] mind and spirit have needs of their own and must be satisfied. [So] the city which is a city must have its parks as well as its prisons, its art gallery as well as its asylum, its books and its libraries as well as its baths and washhouses, its schools as well as its sewers.[6]

It is the work of his disciples in setting out to realise this vision of nurturing 'the mind and spirit' of Birmingham's citizens which is our focus here. Dawson gave a strong lead. Improved educational opportunity was fundamental to everything and he was prominent at the outset in the N.E.L.; better education would not only benefit the individual but would also make for a richer public sphere, where he hoped that his own love of civilised conversation (he was one of the Victorian age's most noted and most engaging talkers) would be extended to all, to the enhancement of social life.

He frequently reiterated that 'one of the highest offices of civilisation is to determine how to give masterpieces of art and literature to the whole people'; most famously he said so at the opening of the free reference library in 1866.[7] He was at the forefront of the campaign to bring free libraries to Birmingham, because books were the means to greater knowledge, but also the key to understanding the human condition. He taught literature – to men and to women – at the Birmingham and Midland Institute, but most especially as Ewan Fernie points out, he wanted to introduce William Shakespeare into the hearts of Birmingham's working men, in the belief that Shakespeare taught 'the religion of human nature'. He had no truck with the argument that Shakespeare would be beyond their ken. In that commitment to giving 'everything to everybody' he was confident that their souls would be nourished by the human insight found in Shakespeare's plays.

Dawson started his ministry in the mid-1840s, and by 1850 his Church of the Saviour in Edward Street was attracting many of those who would shape Birmingham's renaissance over the following decades, men who feature in these pages like Arthur Ryland, William Harris, Sam: Timmins, as well as others from the Unitarian Church of the Messiah, the Chamberlains, the Kenricks and the Martineaus. He shared his civic philosophy wherever he encountered sympathetic listeners: after church, at Our Shakespeare Club, in N.E.L. committee meetings, on the free libraries committee, at the Birmingham and Midland Institute, and then again at the Arts Club on New Street, founded in 1873 explicitly to 'facilitate the social intercourse of gentlemen ... affording them the opportunity to interchange their sentiments and promote the well-being and good government of the town'.[8] Dawson was a regular attendee, animatedly discussing a range of Liberal causes with other members who comprised a roll-call of our civic gospellers: J. T. Bunce, Joseph Chamberlain, William Kenrick, Sam: Timmins, R. F. Martineau, Charles Vince, Henry Crosskey, William Harris and R. W. Dale.

The ministers here – Charles Vince, R. W. Dale and Henry Crosskey – would propagate the gospel more widely; Dale was particularly articulate on the municipal responsibility expected of the town's businessmen, with Crosskey poetically glossing Dawson when asserting 'Liberal policy was a policy of civilisation. It meant the enjoyment by the great mass of people of the blessing of a beautiful and civilised life'.[9] J. T. Bunce also reliably transmitted the gospel message across many years through the columns of the *Birmingham Daily Post*. The new civic creed gained early traction beyond the magic circle. For example, in 1864 the mayor William Holliday, not a noted Dawsonite, publicly talked of 'the duty of the municipal body to encourage everything which can tend to refine the taste and enlarge the conceptions and exalt the aims of the working-classes'. [10]

Joseph Chamberlain's municipal achievement of 'gas and water' socialism, carried through the town council between 1873 and 1876, has attracted much attention from historians, and valuable work has recently been published on a network of councillors with their consistent voting history as they sustained Chamberlain's programme.[11] Beyond that, however, it is equally clear that another under-explored network of Dawson disciples operated between 1860 and the end of the century, concerned with intellectual, literary and aesthetic development; across that period some personnel changed, of course, as a first generation (Aitken, Ryland, Vince and Dawson himself) died away in the mid-1870s, but still, it is striking how the same Dawson apostles continue to work together very regularly in different contexts and guises. All served on multiple committees. Observers like the American journalist Julian Ralph, wrote admiringly of:

> These citizens – so numerous in Birmingham, so rare elsewhere, who esteem it a privilege to deny themselves comfort and rest in the interest of the community and who work year in, year out, without pay for the town's well-being.[12]

For some of these citizens public recognition, and a sense of personal importance, the pleasure of using their power to effect change, partially explain their dedicated and prolonged service; but the predominant motive seems to have been a deeply felt obligation to participate in a quasi-religious mission to propagate the civic gospel.

Common denominators of these men were their Nonconformist background (many being Unitarian), that they were Liberal in political persuasion, and comfortably middle class, with J. T. Mullins and William Aitken being exceptions. Most were either businessmen/manufacturers or professionals (lawyers, journalists, nonconformist ministers). They were infused with that mixture of energy, ambition and that sense of all things being possible, which is so characteristic of the Victorian age. Many lived in Edgbaston; several had houses designed for them by the fashionable civic gospel architect J. H. Chamberlain, for they shared a keen interest in visual art.

We have already seen this other network in evidence at the Arts Club, and we can witness it in every *Birmingham Daily Post* notice minuting council committee business from 1860 onwards, and in its reports on the Birmingham and Midland Institute, School of Art, Technical School, Art Gallery and board school annual meetings. It can be glimpsed, for example, in the muster of those attending the ceremony to lay an inscription stone for the new Free Public Art Gallery in July 1881: those forming a concourse round the mayor, Richard Chamberlain as he did the honours, included Messrs Jaffray, Dale, J. H. Chamberlain, W. Kenrick, R. F. Martineau, Harris, Bunce and Crosskey, at an occasion which J. H. Chamberlain thought a heartening 'sign of a growing belief in Birmingham of the necessity of Art (for) the true advancement of man'.[13] Equally, this close connection of civic gospellers is apparent back in March 1870 when George Dawson, Joseph Chamberlain, John Jaffray, Frank Martineau, Charles Vince, William Kenrick, John Thackray Bunce, Henry Crosskey along with Jesse Collings and George Dixon, assembled on the platform at New Street station prior to boarding the special saloon carriage bound for London and 10 Downing Street, where the delegation would meet Gladstone to press for their brand of educational reform.[14]

Just as it was for their mentor George Dawson, a passion for extending educational opportunity in its various manifestations was common to all the subjects in this book. At its most obvious this involved the campaign to force Gladstone's government to enact free, compulsory, non-denominational elementary education. Attending the first committee meeting of the N.E.L. in Ann Street in April 1869 along with George Dawson were men featured in these essays, Harris, Kenrick, both J. H. and Joe Chamberlain, Dale, Crosskey, Vince, Jaffray, Bunce and Martineau, most of them taking executive roles in the League's management. Every one of them endorsed Dawson's sentiment that 'we all wish to lay the foundation of the national education system'.[15] Yet while it was essential better to educate the citizens of tomorrow, in the immediacy the pressing need was to civilise and elevate the town's current adult population.

This explains the importance of the Birmingham and Midland Institute, founded on the initiative of Arthur Ryland in 1854 'to diffuse and advance science, literature and the arts' among all classes. Divided into two distinct sides, the industrial department would furnish artisans with a technical and scientific grounding while the general department would offer men and women lectures and classes in the humanities and literature. From its early years this umbrella organisation hosted classes on art and design, on health education, on music and even for a while served as a patent library. Its industrial and technical side was not simply academic and theoretical in intention; for William Aitken and others the development of workmen's technical skills was vital for Birmingham's competitive future. Its fostering of science teaching would over time be augmented by other civic gospellers, notably Henry Crosskey and R. F. Martineau.

Aitken, Dawson and Timmins were engaged in the project from the outset, and Harris, Kenrick, Bunce and Aitken served on its council for many years. Two other figures profiled here, J. H. Chamberlain and R. F. Martineau, nursed it, after a sickly start, through to subsequent rude health. By 1900 the Institute had had to be extended, with in excess of 2,000 members, its lecturers and presidents were household names, and it had succeeded in raising the esteem in which cultural and intellectual interests were held in the city.

The Birmingham and Midland Institute, with its reading rooms and literature classes, reinforced Dawson's insistent message about the value inherent in books. At the opening of Birmingham's free reference library in 1866 the experience of reading was transfigured as Dawson averred that:

A great Library contains the diary of a human race ... and may be regarded as the solemn chamber in which man may take counsel of all that had been wise and great and good and glorious among the men that have gone before him.[16]

Friends and allies like W. Harris, R. F. Martineau, J. T. Bunce, A. Ryland, W. Kenrick, W. Aitken and J. A. Langford laboured to consummate his programme for free libraries, to ensure 'these treasures are brought – as it were – to the very doors of the people'; he had campaigned for a free library in 1852, with seven other members of his congregation, and for thirty-one of the thirty-three years following the creation of the council's free libraries committee in 1861, the chairmen were Dawsonites.[17] The city's eight libraries did indeed meet strong demand, such that a successful movement to open on Sundays was initiated; to illustrate that enthusiasm among all classes Birmingham's chief librarian, J. T. Mullins, painstakingly recorded borrowers' occupations each year, noting the many engineers, goldsmiths, jewellers, engravers, printers, brass founders and other workmen who patronised the central library.

When Dawson and Timmins initiated the Shakespeare Memorial Library, a distinctive entity within the reference library, they were both confident that 'the poet of the people' (as Timmins put it) had important and relevant insights into the human condition for Victorian Birmingham's citizens and that working people were interested in – and capable of understanding – this 'higher class of poetry'. The Memorial Library, along with the free libraries, was the physical embodiment of the civic gospel's aspiration to cultivate the intellectual and cultural development of all Birmingham's citizens.

In the prospectus he outlined at the reference library opening George Dawson had also talked of aesthetic education: of 'giving access to the masterpieces of art ... to the whole people.'[18] That proved to be the inspiration for a number of the civic gospellers featured here. Several thought of the cultivation of civic taste in architectural terms. Dawson often talked of emulating the history of that other industrial and commercial powerhouse, Florence; he encouraged Birmingham to imitate the Renaissance glories of its art and culture, which reflected an economic and political confidence and more than that, which distilled the whole spirit of the age. Both the Chamberlains featured here believed that the built environment expressed truths about the civic gospel. Joseph Chamberlain saw the impressive new Renaissance Council House (1874), over whose construction he presided, as symbolising 'the value and importance of (municipal institutions and) local self-government ... to the community'. For J. H. Chamberlain every new building he designed in the town was an opportunity to enrich and inform the lives of those who encountered it; his purpose was didactic, for he believed he was educating popular taste.

Many of our other civic gospellers agreed about the importance of art and design to the civilising of the city and that therefore these areas should be controlled by the municipality. J. T. Bunce, J. H. Chamberlain, John Jaffray, William Aitken and William Kenrick among others pressed for a new municipal art gallery and museum which, thanks to the generosity of Richard and George Tangye, materialised in 1881. J. H. Chamberlain spoke for all when he argued that 'Art could enlarge human life and make it wider, and brighter, and better, and give to even the poorest a greater pleasure in every hour spent'.[19] That moral, improving intent explains why Kenrick and Bunce commissioned and purchased the work of Pre-Raphaelite painters on the gallery's behalf, making Birmingham the country's leading centre for their art; the many citizens gazing on their serious works were to be elevated by the intensity of the poetic vision, to be challenged to engage with the iconography, and to admire the sheer painterly skill. More than this, the gallery and museum were to be active agents encouraging good behaviour among citizens; so, Kenrick thought it worthy of comment (when reporting to the School of Art committee) that 'order has easily been maintained and an intelligent interest shown by all classes', as if there had once been a problem in this regard.[20]

Equally, good design improved the lives of citizen-consumers, and was a commercial necessity for a manufacturing city. As J. A. Langford put it, 'to encourage the growth of taste, it is essential that those who are expected to produce the beautiful shall be surrounded by the beautiful'.[21] Edward Taylor, actively supported by William Kenrick, J. T. Bunce and R. F. Martineau, introduced executed design into the School of Art curriculum, in which students gained 'knowledge of the properties of the material and the process of execution'. (Taylor). [22] The School soon led national art education. Its focus on craftsmanship and good design reflected the involvement with the School of Walter Crane and William Morris of the Arts and Crafts movement, a relationship encouraged by civic gospellers like J. H. Chamberlain, Kenrick, Bunce and Martineau. The latter's crusade to improve technical education for Birmingham's manufacturing classes – culminating in the first municipal technical school in England in 1895 – was but one more element in the Birmingham civic gospel's aesthetic and cultural provision for its men and women.

The unignorable fact that white males dominate this book's narrative reflects an unpalatable truth about nineteenth century Britain: in Sally Hoban's words 'it is beyond argument that Victorian women were disadvantaged in terms of their legal, institutional and biological positions in society'.[23] They were excluded from almost all council meetings, most society committees, and from the masculine world of the club; they did however appear at large celebratory dinners or conversazione, generally to accompany their important husbands. A number of those men featured in these pages wished it otherwise. George Dawson set them an example being a 'firm holder of the equality of women with men'.[24] Henry Crosskey saw his wife in every way as his equal and was the most consistent suffragist of all our civic gospel advocates, being on the platform of every National Society for Women's Suffrage meeting from 1869 onwards. R. F. Martineau and William Kenrick showed a similar sympathy for the enfranchisement of women, Martineau also being active in backing Josephine Butler's campaign for the repeal of the Contagious Diseases Act. Overwhelmingly, advocates of the civic gospel in Birmingham believed in extending wider educational opportunity to girls, the better to elevate, civilise and refine the taste of all Birmingham's citizens. Hence the establishment of new Birmingham School Board schools catering for girls as well as for boys and – at the behest of Joseph Chamberlain and William Kenrick – the foundation of Edgbaston High School for Girls. Birmingham led the way too in artistic education; significant numbers of girls attended the School of Art from 1895, dominating city, and national, art competitions. Edward Taylor defied convention to allow them to attend life drawing classes, crucial to their success in draughtsmanship. [25]

It was not simply a case of what men could do for the women's cause. Female artists like Kate Bunce and Florence Camm seized opportunities for themselves to develop a reputation as practising artists after 1900. Eliza Sturge, the first Birmingham woman to be elected to the Birmingham School Board (1873) and an articulate crusader for the franchise; Hannah Crosskey, another suffrage campaigner; Louisa Anne Ryland, the philanthropist who gave Cannon Hill and Small Heath parks to the corporation and also gave £10,000 to founding a new Art school; and Marie Bethell Beauclerc, George Dawson's amanuensis (described here by Nicola Gauld) were all significant players in the civic gospel drama in Birmingham.

Chapter 1

George Dawson

Ewan Fernie

I want to start with a well-known 'General View of Birmingham' from 1893 (*see image on Front Cover*), which is included, for instance, in David Cannadine's recent history of the nineteenth century.[26] It is a picture which expresses a powerfully achieved municipal identity, with boulevards shooting out strongly from the central civic square and bisecting a cityscape dense with the smoke of industrial activity and the spires of churches. It is built around a secular spire: a flamboyantly neo-Gothic monument to Joseph Chamberlain, who put what became known as the civic gospel into practice as mayor of the town (Birmingham didn't become a city till 1889) from 1873-6. This monument was designed by the movement's greatest architect, John Henry Chamberlain. Joseph Chamberlain's contributions to Birmingham life, prior to his career as a national and imperial politician, are well known. And the Chamberlain monument still stands, in what now is known as Chamberlain Square. Nevertheless, it is hard to find the man in the monument. Chamberlain does feature, but only in a 50 cm portrait medallion by Thomas Woolner: a founding member of the Pre-Raphaelite Brotherhood, and the only sculptor of the group.

But if we refer back to the 'General View', we see that next to the Chamberlain monument there once stood another, very similar structure; indeed, at first sight, it looks like a smaller-scale copy. This memorial, too, was designed by J. H. Chamberlain. But although you can't tell from the bird's-eye perspective of the etching, in this case a full-size statue stands under the canopy: a statue of George Dawson (1821-76), also originally sculpted by Woolner, as though speaking to the people of the city. Here, the monument seems to suggest, is the lost prophet, the personal force behind Chamberlain's central but more abstract achievement in the city; the man and mind who, in the mid-nineteenth century, made not just Chamberlain but Birmingham itself possible; the man who inspired all the other subjects treated in this groundbreaking book.

According to E. P. Hennock, 'the creator of the municipal doctrine, the prophet of the new movement, was George Dawson'.[27] But Dawson's statue, unlike Prince Albert's in Kensington Gardens, memorialises not some regal superhero, but a man speaking. He was a widely celebrated talker; the best in the country, according to the Christian socialist and author of *The Water Babies* (1863), Charles Kingsley.[28] Thomas Carlyle dismissed him as 'Brumagen Dawson', adding that he was 'going all to wind (by stump-oratory) as he himself seems to be painfully aware'.[29] But that Dawson chose to speak, rather than write, tells you something important about the human contact and the impact he was seeking.

His statue seemed to be speaking under a canopy which featured four portrait medallions of its own. These represented Dawson as a man inspired by: 1. John Bunyan and reformed religion; 2. Oliver Cromwell and revolution; and 3. Thomas Carlyle and his coming-to-terms-with the contemporary 'condition of England'. But it was the fourth figure – Shakespeare – who was the key influence on Dawson, modifying and softening Bunyan's zeal into a passionate liberal humanism, answering and resolving the questions Carlyle asked of the age, and affording a more lively and joyous vision of existence than the Cromwellian interregnum. It was Shakespeare who helped Dawson to refunction Nonconformist seriousness and revolutionary drive and, consequently, propel Birmingham into a new kind of future.

It was fitting that Birmingham memorialised Dawson as a man speaking in the main square, not as a monarch, or a mortal god, like Albert in his shrine; nor as a priest or professor, set apart from other, more ordinary citizens. 'I have never been presented with an honorary degree,' Dawson said; 'and I have never been made a knight. Honours in the common sense I have never coveted, and the world has done me the credit of thinking I did not want them.' He made no pretentions to the title, 'reverend':

There were some things which he thought could be said to men and women useful to be said, and they thought he was able to say them, and that was all. He was no priest, no dignitary of the Church. He was not 'reverend' but '*reverent*'.[30]

Unlike Albert's memorial, Dawson's monument appealed for direct, personal contact with anyone who happened to look at it.

'To give everything to everybody' was his express objective.[31] He did teach, but not at a university, with an admissions requirement. Instead, he taught a literature class at the Birmingham and Midland Institute, founded in 1854, for 'the Diffusion and Advancement of Science, Literature and Art amongst all Classes'; and he pioneered education for women. Opposed to what we call 'dumbing down' – not 'afflicted' with what, in Birmingham, Dickens called 'the coxcombical idea of writing down to the popular intelligence' – he spoke at the People's Hall, and he called for a People's College.[32] At the Mechanics Institute in Manchester, he discoursed on 'Faustus, Faust, and Festus', insisting 'that the deepest mode of moving men [and women] is to deal with the deepest subjects'. [33]

Whereas the Albert Memorial elevates the Prince Consort to the heights, Dawson's statue celebrated his effort to involve the people of Birmingham in a great, pioneering recreation of culture. It was meant to express a vision of culture *as inclusive conversation* – yes, inspired by established English worthies, but animated in Dawson's dialogue with all citizens.

Joseph Chamberlain said, 'His name is written in the history of all our most cherished institutions'.[34] And if, again, we look back at the 'General View of Birmingham', it is indeed possible to trace clear lines of influence extending from him, as the man and mind most memorialised at the centre of the town, to many of the great institutions of the day.

His statue stood in front of the handsome black railings of the Birmingham Reference Library, which included the Birmingham Shakespeare Memorial Library, the first great Shakespeare library in the world, and founded for all citizens, partly at Dawson's behest in 1864. Dawson made his most famous speech outside the Reference Library in 1866. Its foundation by the corporation proved, he suggested, 'that a great town is a solemn organism through which should flow, and in which should be shaped, all the highest, loftiest, and truest ends of man's intellectual and moral nature'.[35]

Dawson's statue looked across at Birmingham's town hall, the first of the great town halls which characterise Victorian England. He spoke there on, for instance, the meaning of communism; he agitated for reduced working hours for labourers, for Polish independence, and to impeach the government who had fought the Crimean War. And, after he died, the town hall was the venue where five hundred homeless people took breakfast in his memory on Christmas Day.

Also visible in the 'General View', in the foreground of the bottom right-hand corner, is the Birmingham and Midland Institute, that pioneering proponent of Birmingham's commitment to comprehensive education, where Dawson was a lion of the lecture hall and a popular teacher. Nearer to his monument is H. R. Yeoville Thomason's Council House: 'a bricks-

and-mortar monument to the municipal gospel' Dawson preached in Birmingham, according to Tristram Hunt.[36] Its central pediment shows Britannia receiving Birmingham's manufacturers. That this, like the Chamberlain monument, features an Antonio Salviati mosaic – in the case of the Council House, of Municipality receiving figures of Science, Art, Liberty, Law, Commerce, and Industry – stresses the aesthetic as well as the moral coherence of the municipal culture which Birmingham aimed at.

Behind and to the left of the Council House is perhaps the most beautiful building in Birmingham: the first municipal art school in the country, built in warm terracotta-coloured brick, with three gables, fine masonry, naturalistic motifs, and a continuous band of colourful tiling. This handsomely proportioned building also spoke for political commitment to art in a city where Dawson lectured on Pre-Raphaelite paintings almost as they dried on the canvas. It, too, was the masterwork of the architect of both the Dawson and Chamberlain monuments, as well of Chamberlain's suburban house Highbury, the handsome board schools, and the Shakespeare Library's Memorial Room: J. H. Chamberlain.

J. H. Chamberlain was a member of Dawson's heterodox church, which is just beyond the frame of the 'General View of Birmingham', in Edward Street. Dawson had originally come to Birmingham in 1844 to take up an appointment at Mount Zion Baptist Chapel, one of those cavernous old halls which could seat up to 2,000 people. Not that anybody was coming to hear the dreary previous incumbent. Dawson filled the hall again. But he was no Baptist; he was always, as he later said, 'a free-lance', and refused to be bound by any dogma.[37] When he started giving communion to all-comers, the Baptists decided to get rid of him. But his supporters put up the money to build and retain his services for his own brand-new church, where for the rest of his life he freely preached his distinctive message of self-realisation and social commitment to a congregation of extraordinarily energetic and talented people, such as those who are represented in this book.

Municipal improvement was hardly unique to Birmingham. In his singularly productive term as its mayor, Joseph Chamberlain established gas and water as public utilities, cleared the slums, and built handsome boulevards, such as Corporation Street, which announced Birmingham as a civic power to be reckoned with, not just in Britain but across the globe (although at the same time, it is important to acknowledge, it caused serious hardship to those it displaced). But other British municipal centres outside London were transforming themselves at the same time. The construction of the Loch Katrine waterworks, for instance, commenced in 1855, creating reservoirs, 26 miles of aqueduct, 13 miles of hard rock tunnels, and almost four miles of iron pipes: an amazing feat of engineering, which delivered some fifty million gallons of fresh water to Glasgow daily, and remains the basis of its water supply today. Glasgow's Municipal Building was its answer to Birmingham's Council House, its handsome Kelvingrove Art Gallery another fruit of the movement in favour of municipal improvement, an impulse also evinced by George Gilbert Scott's magnificent infirmary, which opened in Leeds in 1869.

But, as Hennock emphasises, Birmingham's contribution was 'much more than a successful attempt to provide a rather backward borough with necessary municipal services'. 'The crucial innovation,' he suggests, 'was a new *vision* of the function and nature of the corporation.'[38] This was, above all, what Dawson provided. Matthew Arnold and other establishment authorities of the period regarded Birmingham, culturally speaking, as a sort of blank. But Dawson contended, 'The blanks of life are often handwritings upon the wall. They become places through which the eternal glory streams.' He went on, 'God makes blank the visible, in order that through it there may come the glories of the heavens.'[39] In formulating a new conception of what a great town was and could be, he broke into the blue skies of the future. 'The dreamers of society,' as he recognised, 'are the men from whom the greatest truth comes.'[40]

'Not by bread alone' was Dawson's scriptural rubric:

a city must have its parks as well as its prisons, its art gallery as well as its asylum, its books and its libraries as well as its baths and washhouses, its schools as well as its sewers; it must think of beauty and of dignity no less than of order and of health an utterance which, on its own, belies Arnold's absolute contrast between the new industrial towns like Birmingham and Oxford's 'sweetness and light'.[41]

Dawson responded magnificently to what H. J. Dyos called 'the terrible task of civilising the first nation of city dwellers', insisting that all of the tremendous force of the industrial revolution should be put to work in favour of making a more just and equal society.[42] As he reminded his auditors,

The poor will ask it before long,—whether machinery is to go on crushing them, or whether it is to set them free; whether none but the master is to be blessed by machinery; and whether the great God did not purposely intend it to bring about the last earthly millennium, when all men shall be prophets, priests, and kings, and when teaching and spiritualism, and gladness, and joy of all kinds is to be shared, as much as may be, for all and by all.[43]

Thoughts like this, which side-stepped the widespread fear of revolution in the mid-nineteenth century and embraced ambitious social change, gave Birmingham a real claim to being the world's most exciting town. As R. W. Dale put it, 'If we are true to each other and true to the town, we may do deeds as great as were done by Pisa, by Florence, by Venice in their triumphant days'.[44] Sam: Timmins suggested that Dawson had managed 'to raise the tone of life in the town—private, public, social, literary and political' and that, as a result, Birmingham was seeking to become a society made 'by the public for the public' with 'something like the discipline of naval or military life'.[45] It would be a society rich in 'libraries, and museums, and art galleries, and institutes, and parks', which would eventually realise:

> that true commonwealth which poets have sung of and prophets have foretold, 'when the lion and the lamb shall lie down together, and a little child shall lead them,' when men shall 'beat their swords into ploughshares, and their spears into pruning hooks, and shall learn the art of war no more,' but live together as one great peaceful family, enjoying the fruits in their season and the real riches which intelligence, and industry, and taste provide.[46]

No doubt this was a vision that was seriously limited by the prejudices of the time, but it was a powerful, passionate and progressive impulse, and it is one we would do well to revive, repurpose and extend in our own day.[47]

Chapter 2

Joseph Chamberlain

While George Dawson was the prophet of the civic gospel, Joseph Chamberlain (1836-1914) was its most charismatic exponent, personifying municipal ambition and evangelising Birmingham's creed. His greatest achievement was to simplify and shape the teachings of Dawson and Dale into a coherent practical programme – 'a feat of creative imagination'(Hennock) – which informed all his important actions during his legendary tenure as mayor in Birmingham (1873-76). These years established the elected council 'as the motor and repository of civic pride,' writes Tristram Hunt.[48] Chamberlain's personal ascendancy was achieved by force of personality, and also by what his foremost biographer has identified as his entrepreneurial spirit. So, his qualities as a successful businessman, habituated to driving hard bargains, to expeditious decision-making and to calculated risk-taking, shaped the council's transformative programme of social reform.[49]

Joseph Chamberlain had come to know George Dawson in the late 1850s, years before his municipal triumphs; then, he was establishing his business – Nettlefolds, the wood-screw manufacturers – as a market leader. Although he regularly attended the Church of the Messiah, rather than Dawson's Church of the Saviour, he – along with others of his Unitarian congregation like William Kenrick, R. F. Martineau, and Chamberlain's own brothers – heard Dawson talk at Sunday evening gatherings. There seems little doubt that each would have participated in the informal discussions which took place beyond chapel; talk unquestionably ranged across ideas about the civic gospel in the smoking room at Chamberlain's Southbourne home and when Dawson frequented Bryant's confectionery shop on Congreve Street. Both also belonged to the Arts Club on New Street which 'afforded members the opportunity of interchanging their sentiments and promoted the well-being and good government of the town'.[50] Chamberlain sat with Dawson at early meetings of George Dixon's Birmingham Education Society from 1867, where prominent Birmingham professionals and businessmen debated educational reform, and when in 1869 that metamorphosed into the National Education League, with Chamberlain as the chairman of the executive committee, there was George Dawson as one of his loyal committee members.

If Chamberlain hadn't been present when Dawson addressed his followers on the pressing need to tackle widespread ignorance and illiteracy ('I believe that the educational improvement of the people is a matter of paramount importance') he certainly shared his conviction; in his case, door-to-door visits in 1868 to Birmingham's slum quarters had brought in on him the extent of the squalor and ignorance prevalent in many homes.[51] Later, when the Birmingham School Board was constituted to manage the new board schools, built in the wake of Forster's 1870 Education Act, Dawson and Chamberlain served as Nonconformist representatives, with Chamberlain becoming the Board's chairman in 1873 (and with Dawson a dependable and articulate lieutenant).

Their congruity of thinking extended beyond campaigning for free compulsory education for all; in his memorable speech at the opening of the Free Reference Library in 1866 Dawson had articulated the nobility of the municipal calling when he talked of how: 'We are the Corporation who have undertaken the highest duty it is possible for us,' and when he compared the city to an organism just like a nation state.[52] Joseph Chamberlain echoed these aspirations in his rallying cry to the newly elected town council in January 1874, days after assuming office: '... he would do everything in his power to constitute these local authorities as real local parliaments, supreme in their special jurisdiction.'[53] In the years that followed, Chamberlain was as good as his word, as he employed the council's executive powers to transform Birmingham. Effectively inventing the notion of municipal socialism, he argued that 'all monopolies should be controlled by the representatives of the people, by whom they should be administered, and to whom their profits should go'. [54]

The story of Chamberlain's revolutionary mayoralty has been described exhaustively.[55] In this book, primarily concerned with the aesthetic and intellectual manifestations of the civic gospel, it is sufficient merely to sketch the outline of the reformation wrought in utilities and town planning, before then examining Chamberlain's cultural interests. Chamberlain was one of a number of Birmingham's leading manufacturers who responded to the challenge Dawson and Dale set down, to the effect that they must accept they had a moral duty to act and to put themselves at the service of the community. In the early 1860s the two ministers believed the town to be inadequately led by a council comprising small tradesmen, 'the brewer, the baker and the candlestick maker,' who were 'not accustomed to big transactions and high figures,' and who as a result were penny-pinchers lacking imagination as to how to improve Birmingham. [56] Instead, as Dale expressed it in a sermon in 1863:

(successful big Birmingham businessmen) ought to feel called of God ... they ought to be aldermen and town councillors ... they ought to be reformers of local abuses ... they ought to see to it that the towns and parishes in which they live are well drained, well lighted and well paved. [57]

These were sentiments of which Joseph Chamberlain heartily approved. Just after stepping down as mayor, to become one of the town's three MPs, he said:

I have no sympathy with those who sneer at municipal work ... In our parliament we want men of the highest ability ... If a man has leisure, and wants occupation, his taste must be difficult indeed if he cannot find some congenial employment in connection with the multifarious duties of the town council in Birmingham. [58]

He had joined the council in 1869 not simply as a response to Dawson and Dale's exhortations but because he believed – erroneously as it happened – that the Liberal government's education legislation would empower councils to administer new non-denominational schools. Chamberlain and others, such as Jesse Collings, enlisted in the council to be in the driving seat when legislation was passed; but in the event, the government insisted on ratepayers voting for candidates directly in local School Board elections. However, once on the council, Chamberlain proved himself energetic and imaginative, allying with Thomas Avery and others to tackle the town's disgraceful record on sewage disposal. Until 1873 he was not only a councillor, but a dynamic industrialist, the prominent and most belligerent member of the Birmingham School Board, as well as the driving force behind the National Education League with its one hundred countrywide branches. Then he retired from business and sold up, devoting himself to the role of mayor after his dramatic, and vigorously contested, election victory in November 1873.

He did not assume office unprepared; as in all he did, he had already mastered the detail, and had planned carefully. So he had realised how profitable would be a municipal takeover of Birmingham's two private gas companies; and having steered the policy through the council (with the assistance of his twenty or so loyal supporters) and then through Parliament, he was almost instantly able to generate such profits as to enable him to extend this policy of municipal socialism to the provision of water. All citizens, even the poorest from slum areas, hitherto condemned to taking water from disease-ridden open wells, were able to benefit from cheap, clean supplies; greatly improved mortality figures confirm this advance in public health. Chamberlain was equally active in promoting other measures to enhance the environment, insisting on the employment of more sanitation inspectors, pushing through controversial by-laws to control the quality of new house building and to insist on the provision of water closets. He was just as concerned to invest in street paving, a policy linked to the sanitation committee's strategy of clearing thoroughfares of human waste.[59]

After gas and water, the final element in the trilogy of great mayoral reforms was that of improvement. Again, the impetus was Chamberlain's, warmly supported by such as fellow councillor William White. Chamberlain's motivation was complex. He wanted to clear the insanitary slums like St Mary's in the centre of Birmingham; he sought to create a commercial centre which would benefit the town's retailers; and he dreamt of enhancing the town's prestige by opening up broad, continental boulevards which resonated with a sense of distinction and civilisation. All this did indeed come about as a result of the Improvement Act of 1876, the success, however, marred by a failure to ensure that slum dwellers, rendered homeless by the dramatic clearance of swathes of central Birmingham, were adequately re-housed. [60]

As we have seen elsewhere in this book, the civic gospel was much more than an environmental revolution. Dawson had insisted (see chapter 1) that man 'does not live by bread alone,' and as A. W. W. Dale, his biographer and Robert Dale's son, paraphrased it: '… the city which is a city must have its parks, its art gallery, its books and its libraries as well as its baths and washhouses, its schools as well as its sewers.'[61]

And Joseph Chamberlain understood this well; it was especially pertinent that Dale here should have bracketed 'schools' and 'sewers', for no man in England had greater claim to have effected a revolution in these two contrasting areas than Chamberlain, for whom they were inextricably linked. Reference has already been made to the fact that, having been awakened in the late 1860s to Birmingham's lamentable state of education, Chamberlain had conducted his own enquiry into school provision and attendance in Birmingham and had been shocked by what he found:

It seems to me that education must be a perfect farce when the instruction at the school is contradicted by the experience of home. It seems to me absurd to preach morality to people herded together in conditions in which common decency in impossible.[62]

That revelation explains his twin track approach of campaigning nationally for free compulsory education at the same time as driving his gas and water socialism through the council.

His interests weren't confined to the education of young children. He was a lifelong believer in adult education, teaching evening classes under the aegis of the Church of the Messiah, there doing what he could to feed the minds of teenage boys with English literature and stories from English history. An empathetic understanding for the work of adult education explains why he spent time when he was a busy mayor and School Board chairman to speak at Birmingham's famous Quaker Severn Street school, where he praised the fact that:

You have opened to multitudes of your fellow-townsmen, who have suffered many of them from the shameful neglect of the state – you have opened to them a new world, a land which would have been untrodden but for your guidance. [63]

That understanding lies behind his continuing interest in the work of the Birmingham and Midland Institute, founded to educate both in a broad general sense as well as in specific industrial and scientific training.

When he spoke on the occasion of the Institute's rebuilding in October 1881 he recognised how 'every year it is developing the intelligence and cultivating the taste of the community,' and he went on to say that 'for every one pupil who has made the classes of the Institute the stepping stone to his fortune there are hundreds and thousands who have had their lives developed and made happier and pleasanter by the diversity of interests which their studies have stimulated'. [64] Nurturing the cultural and intellectual interests of Birmingham's citizens was precisely the goal Dawson set in that 1866 speech. Because Chamberlain's special talent was for rigorous analysis, for creating practical solutions, he moved on in this Birmingham and Midland Institute speech to make a plea for a co-ordinated plan for Birmingham's education system from primary through to tertiary education, for an end to duplication and for technical education, hinting at the first inklings of a new approach to higher education. In under twenty years Chamberlain's vision of a great civic university in Birmingham – the country's first – would be realised; a tribute to his imagination, tenacity and capacity for persuasion.

Notions of education to some extent also informed Chamberlain's approach to aesthetics in Birmingham. He himself had refined visual senses, building a personal collection of art works which included paintings by John Singer Sargent and John Millais, the last of whom he commissioned to paint a fine portrait of his wife Mary; he also employed John Henry Chamberlain to plan and build Highbury, a model of domestic Venetian Gothic architecture.[65] When it came to art in the public domain, he sympathised with Dawson's sentiment of 1866 that 'one of the highest offices of civilisation is to determine how to give access to the masterpieces of art and of literature to the whole people'. Even before the building of Birmingham's Gallery he had given £1,000 to its predecessor for the improvement of its collection of industrial design, writing that 'I am anxious to show in some practical way my confidence in municipal institutions'.[66] Later, in 1881, he would write to the Mayor, his brother Richard Chamberlain, praising 'the progress you have made in securing the nucleus of a collection worthy of the town,' and offering two paintings by Muller.[67] He was dismissive of suggestions from such as Henry Cole, chairman of the London Society of Arts, that local museums should merely host loan exhibitions from London; Chamberlain declared in 1874 that Birmingham needed its own permanent collection of material relevant to its industries – and that admission should be free. Ever the industrialist, the exhibits would – he believed – be more than the means to civilising its citizens but also models for Birmingham's artisans, many of whom were engaged in fine metalworking.[68]

In ways that overtly linked art and architecture to the civic gospel, it is clear that Chamberlain thought of buildings as expressions of municipal aspiration. His speech when, as mayor, he laid the foundation stone of the new Council House in June 1874 reveals much about his – and his supporters' – rationale for this great Renaissance citadel. It was designed:

> to provide fitting accommodation for the deliberations of what is our greatest social representative assembly … For my part I have an abiding faith in municipal institutions, an abiding sense of the value and importance of local self-government, and I desire therefore to surround them by everything which can mark their importance, which can show the place they occupy in public estimation and respect, and which can point to their great value to the community. [69]

Here was 'a nineteenth-century Venetian palace … a bricks-and-mortar memorial to the municipal gospel'.[70] Chamberlain consciously drew a parallel with 'the old cities of the Continent – of Belgium, Germany and Italy where the free and independent burghers of the Middle Ages have left behind them magnificent palaces and civic buildings, testimonies to their power and public spirit and munificence'. He clearly thought of H. R. Yeoville Thomason's Council House as the physical symbol of Birmingham's municipal 'power and public spirit', and of its claim to improve the lives of all its citizens. Furthermore, it was a way of reinforcing, for all who looked on it, the reality of the serious and weighty responsibility borne by their elected representatives. In the large niche in its central portico is a mosaic which encapsulates civic pretensions. Here a graceful feminine figure, Municipality, is enthroned; she receives the classically attired allegories of Science, Art, Liberty, Law, Commerce and Industry, all of which submit to her.[71]

This same faith – that architecture could give visual expression to the mission of the civic gospel – is apparent in Chamberlain's approach to the new schools commissioned by the Birmingham School Board when he was chairman. At one point he told his colleagues that:

When we are dealing with what I believe to be one of the highest functions ever imposed upon a community we are bound here also to see that buildings which are the outward and visible signs of the work going on within shall not be in evident discord with the nobility of the duty we perform. If (our schools) are beautiful it is because the outline is noble, because the grouping is harmonious and pleasing and because the general appearance is graceful.[72]

It was important to him that these engines of cultural transformation should make an eloquent statement about the dignity of the instruction that went on within the walls. They well exemplify David Cannadine's memorable phrase about Birmingham's public buildings at this time, which he said 'project[ed] values into space and stone'.[73] The results certainly impressed the *Pall Mall Gazette* for it reported in 1894 that: 'In Birmingham you may generally recognise a board school by its being the best building in the neighbourhood, with its lofty towers, gabled windows, warm red bricks and stained glass.'[74] It was no accident that these buildings with their impressive ventilation towers echoed ecclesiastical architecture, for they were representing a new municipal religion. They corporally represented Dawson's belief in municipal institutions as being contemporary manifestations of the Church and the Gospel.

Satirists may have dubbed the improvement scheme's Corporation Street,

'Rue Chamberlain', mocking both its pretensions and its evident genesis in Hausmann's elegantly re-imagined Paris. These terracotta Italianate stores and offices were indeed the physical embodiment of 'Joseph Chamberlain's dream of Birmingham as a mercantile metropolis of the Midlands'.[75] Yet it was about more than the fulfilment of a businessman's commercial ambition, and more than improving health through slum clearance and street widening; John Henry Chamberlain's grand and spacious redevelopment was all about transforming a dirty, insanitary, muddle of slum housing in the heart of the town with a dignified, planned and elegant city centre to reflect Birmingham's corporate dynamism and to evoke in its people a sense of civic pride. When he looked back on the advances made Joseph Chamberlain reflected:

> Formerly the town was badly lighted, imperfectly guarded and only partially drained; there were few public buildings and few important streets ... But now, great public edifices not unworthy of the importance of a midland metropolis have risen on every side. Wide arteries of communication have been opened up. Rookeries and squalid courts have given way to fine streets and open places. The roads are well paved, well lighted, and well cleansed.[76]

George Dawson had defined the civic vocation as one which should minister to citizens' 'comfort, health and security' and, beyond that, to 'minds and spirit ... [which] had needs of their own'. Joseph Chamberlain personified that civic gospel; he did much to improve the health and physical welfare of Birmingham's people, but he appears here to have been just as concerned with advancing their cultural, intellectual and aesthetic development. The remaining board schools, Corporation Street, the Birmingham and Midland Institute, Council House and Chamberlain Square still stand today as substantial memorials reminding citizens of the halcyon days of Joseph Chamberlain's municipal revolution.

Chapter 3

Arthur Ryland

When J. T. Bunce penned his obituary in 1877, he asserted that 'there are few names better known here than that of Arthur Ryland and few Birmingham citizens who are held in greater honour'.[77] As it has transpired, posterity has not been kind. Ryland has been largely forgotten, meriting the merest mention or footnote in many Birmingham histories. Like others of his generation – men like Samuel Timmins, J. A. Langford and Charles Vince – he has suffered for not being a member of Joseph Chamberlain's inner circle. He was retired, and approaching his last years, when the municipal revolution of the early 1870s took hold. Yet Bunce was surely right in believing him to be a highly significant figure, for he was a foremost early adopter of civic gospel principles, and he did much to lay the groundwork for the golden age of municipal intervention:

> For nearly fifty years (Bunce wrote) he has been prominent in every cause and work of a character to secure freedom, personal and political; to establish and strengthen local government; to promote popular education in varied forms; and in all ways and at all times to make society better, purer and wiser. Whenever projects for social, moral, intellectual or political progress were in question, Mr Ryland was always found helping them in his own hearty, sagacious and unobtrusive manner.[78]

Whereas a number of those advocates of the civic gospel featured in this book were the sorts of wealthy businessman to whom George Dawson and Robert Dale had appealed – men like R. F. Martineau, William Kenrick and Joseph Chamberlain – Arthur Ryland was a solicitor with his own practice who established a national reputation in the legal profession ('No Birmingham practitioner was ever held in higher honour,' according to *Edgbastonia*).[79] He helped to found the Birmingham Law Society, becoming the first provincial solicitor to sit on the Incorporated Law Society in London; he was regularly called upon to give evidence to royal and parliamentary commissions on aspects of the law, for instance the laws governing partnership, trade marks and conveyancing. His legal experience was invaluable in drafting legislation – and he was central to guiding bills of incorporation for Birmingham and for the establishment of the Midland Institute through Parliament.

His personal qualities explain the success of his law practice in Birmingham. Whilst it would be palpably unhistorical to claim that all Birmingham's civic leaders of the heroic age were paragons – some were egotistical, ambitious, quick to take offence and occasionally jealous – he was an exception. The frequency with which the historian finds generous testimony for Arthur Ryland as a family solicitor and as a municipal figure is striking; he was evidently a man of great integrity, trusted for his discretion and diplomacy, and therefore much in demand in advising charities, as a solicitor to Birmingham businesses (for example, the Birmingham gun trade) and in managing donations for those who wished to remain anonymous. 'It was through him that his generous cousin Louisa Anne Ryland of Barford presented her parks to the people.'[80]

Although he built a formidable reputation as Birmingham's leading family lawyer, this was but a small part of his life. Because he was born into one of the foremost Unitarian families in the town he had been brought up with that sect's strong sense of social responsibility. He, like Thomas and R. F. Martineau, William Kenrick and Joseph Chamberlain, was a Sunday school teacher for the New Meeting Sunday (Unitarian) schools. His special interest 'was bestowed on the young and the unfortunate and for the reformation of the criminal,' wrote Bunce, and so Ryland supported or raised money for ragged schools, industrial schools, reformatories and refuges.[81] A letter from a member of the public to the *Birmingham Daily Post* on Ryland's death averred that 'he was more completely devoted to the amelioration of the condition of the working-classes than anyone I have yet known'.[82]

This interest in the lives of the working classes, and a desire to improve their lot, both ante-dated, but was then reinforced by, his friendship with George Dawson. The essence of the latter's mission was the education, elevation and improvement of all citizens. In Ryland's chairmanship of the shareholders in the Builder's Industrial Society in June 1865, for example, in which working men would help each other, and in his words, 'receive lessons in frugality, judgement and neighbourly forbearance,' he reveals his commitment to their self-improvement.[83] Again it is demonstrated in his chairmanship in 1863 of a committee formed with George Dixon, William Harris and J. A. Langford to create a club for working men in which, having set it up, the sponsors 'would help working men to help themselves,' by organising a place for recreation and social engagement.[84]

That, in the words of his obituary, Arthur Ryland 'believed it was the duty of a citizen to bear his due share in all the labours of the public good' can be seen as clear evidence of the influence of George Dawson. Wright Wilson, Dawson's biographer, tells us that 'as early as 1846 some of the men who would play a significant part in the municipal revolution joined him (at the Mount Zion Chapel, following him to his newly built Church of the Saviour) – Robert Martineau, William Harris, Sam: Timmins and Arthur Ryland'.[85] Ryland and Dawson became especially close friends, from the start of Dawson's Birmingham ministry to his untimely death in 1876, an event which devasted Ryland just weeks before he himself passed away.[86] The *Birmingham Daily Post* recorded that:

His last public appearance will be long remembered by those present when at the Dawson Memorial meeting (in January 1877) Mr Ryland said, with deep emotion and faltering voice and eyes dimmed with tears, that all that was good in his own character and life was due to the influence and the teaching of his lamented friend.

Bunce noted in 1877 that Ryland:

Took an active interest throughout his life in Dawson's church. Even when Mr Dawson and his views were far less popular than they became and when association with a teacher regarded as deeply heterodox was held to be a social sin, Mr Ryland was ever constant and ever true.[87]

One of the insistent themes in Dawson's talks at the Church of the Saviour was of the obligation of the wealthy and talented to contribute to the betterment of their city-state. Arthur Ryland needed no prompting to place his considerable gifts at the service of the municipality. He had been doing so long before Dawson came to Birmingham. In the 1830s he was involved with the Political Union; he was an articulate advocate of Birmingham's incorporation because he saw, along with other reformers, that the lack of a central authority in a town with over 100,000 souls militated against good, improving government. He completely rejected the hoary old Tory slogan enunciated by William Hutton, an early historian of Birmingham, that 'a town without a charter is a town without a shackle'.[88] In a Charter of Incorporation, largely drafted by Ryland, Birmingham gained its new municipal council in 1838. It was a by-product of the Whig government's programme of sweeping away vested borough interests; but in Birmingham it didn't finish the job, leaving the town's Street Commissioners intact alongside the new council. Comprising prominent citizens who owned property the Street Commission formed a self-elected association with authority over the town's streets, lighting and new building, responsible among other projects for the erection of Birmingham's town hall.[89] Ryland had been a Street Commissioner before incorporation, and remained one thereafter, all the while being a leading advocate of 'amalgamation', that is for uniting all municipal powers in the body of the council. He it was who drafted the report in 1851 which brought about the termination of the Street Commissioners' powers, and he was on the final arrangements committee of the Commissioners which managed their surrender to the council.

Now, with a unitary authority responsible for the growing town the prospects for its improvement, and most pertinently for solutions to its on-going sanitary problems, were much enhanced – thanks largely to Arthur Ryland.

In 1854 he was elected to the council for St Peter's ward and became one of the leading critics of the economist party on the council led by Thomas Allday, which held sway through the 1850s. An association of small tradesmen, shopkeepers and clerks, it determined to keep rates down. Their lack of vision, and prevailing preoccupation with retrenchment, explain the council's failure to take advantage of the first permissive Free Libraries and Museums Act (1850), its rejection of a bill for the municipal purchase of the Birmingham Waterworks Company (delayed twenty years until Chamberlain's advent) and, most dramatically of all, the abandonment of an improvement bill in 1855, which would have financed sewerage and street improvement, at the behest of ratepayers stirred up by Allday.[90]

It is in this context that Ryland assumes his importance. Allday's defeat in the aldermanic elections of 1859 signalled a change of mood in Birmingham. This can be seen the following year in the successful campaign led by E. C. Osborne, the Rev. Dr Miller and George Dawson in early 1860 to persuade a meeting of burgesses to adopt the Free Libraries and Museums Act of 1855. At last Birmingham would be able to levy a rate and build a municipal library which would be 'an important agent towards the mental and moral improvement of all classes of society'. Arthur Ryland represented the council on its new free libraries committee. At the same time, in 1860, he was elected mayor. This proved to be a highly significant appointment; for the first time a 'non-economist' mayor had been chosen, and Ryland's term marked the start of a new attitude to council responsibility.

One of his earliest achievements as mayor was to open the first free library in the town, that at Constitution Hill in April 1861; the overwhelming numbers queuing 'for upwards of an hour' to borrow books (108,000 loans that year) illustrated the extent of public hunger for knowledge while 'the uniform good conduct and order manifested', showed how right Dawson and his friends were to trust the good sense of the community.[91] At a banquet to celebrate his year as mayor Ryland said that above all 'he was honoured to be associated with the opening of the first free library; the movement was destined to work most happily for the good of the town'.[92] Seven other local lending libraries, as well as the Central library, were to follow by 1900.

Of still greater consequence was the fact that he presided over the passage of a new improvement act in 1861, first chairing a town meeting which by a majority of nearly two to one empowered the council to seek new powers; the Act increased the town's power to borrow for general works including sewerage, and it opened the way for the more interventionist municipal policies initially of Thomas Avery and then of Joseph Chamberlain. In keeping with this new focus on health and cleanliness, Ryland took much pleasure in opening the new public baths and wash houses in the town. In June 1861, while still mayor, he hosted the first meeting of those interested in founding a Free Hospital for Sick Children and followed this by chairing the earliest public meeting to discuss the concept. It culminated with the opening in 1862; the Birmingham Children's Hospital remains one of Britain's foremost paediatric institutions.

One of Arthur Ryland's chief recommendations for fellow councillors when choosing him as mayor in 1860 was that he had already proved he had initiative and imagination, for his great claim to fame is as the founder in 1854 of the Midland Institute, an organisation which by the end of the century 'unquestionably stood at the head of similar institutions throughout the whole kingdom'.[93] In this area, as in the empowerment of municipal government, he was giving practical expression to George Dawson's vision for the edification of Birmingham's citizens. Ryland's interest in providing opportunities for adult education was no doubt fostered by Dawson's teaching, but the form it took was determined by his own experience of a crying need for an institution which catered for those seeking technical knowledge and others simply wanting opportunities to learn more about culture and to broaden the mind. It was his time as a trustee of Birmingham's Philosophical Institution which brought these issues into focus. Founded by friends and pupils of Joseph Priestley in 1800 its object was 'to promote Literature, Science and the Arts by lectures and discussions'.[94] It became a valued place for experimental science and for science teaching, but it largely catered to the middle classes; and by the mid-1840s it was in financial difficulties.

It was Arthur Ryland who presented a vision for the future; he believed it should merge with the Polytechnic, a Birmingham institution running public classes in 'drawing, the elementary mathematics, writing and reading' with members of the working class in mind. Despite the fact that in 1844 Charles Dickens had commended its comprehensive membership – 'no sect, class or party' – the Polytechnic struggled with its debts. Even though the Polytechnic and the Philosophical Institution rejected fusion, each indicated support for a new organisation which adopted its aims. Influenced by both, Ryland was the first to visualise the shape of the future Birmingham and Midland Institute. In a memorandum of 1848-9 he wrote: 'In a philosophical institution there are two classes: one whose object is scientific and philosophical research; this is the smaller class. The other is not so advanced in knowledge and [has] to be informed in the most attractive manner of the elements and discoveries of science and the history of literature.'[95] Here was the genesis of the Institute's industrial and general departments, the former technical and scientific, the latter covering artistic, literary, linguistic and historical themes.

Ryland was now at the heart of moves to establish a new institution along the lines he had envisaged. He was one of those in 1849 who petitioned the Prime Minister, Lord John Russell, to legislate to allow town councils to provide and maintain museums, libraries and reading rooms. Spurred by the council's refusal to adopt the later Free Libraries Act, Ryland now determined to act himself and in June 1852 – as he later remembered – 'a private meeting of fifteen or sixteen gentlemen representing different political and religious opinions was held at my home ... then another [a week later] hosted by Mayor Smith at the Town Hall Committee room, and a committee was formed'.[96] Among those attending Ryland's Calthorpe Road meeting was George Dawson. Ryland was an obvious choice for the committee drawing up the proposed scheme. Evidently Charles Dickens considered him to be its prime mover for it was to Ryland he wrote in January 1853 offering to read the *Christmas Carol* for the first time in public: 'I would read the *Christmas Carol* next Christmas to the town hall folk. I should particularly desire to have large numbers of the working people in the audience, to be admitted free. I should like to do it for the benefit and advance of the Institution.'[97]

Ryland read this letter out at a public meeting just days later; it no doubt helped win support for the committee's motion 'to establish a Scientific and Literary Institution having for its object the diffusion and advancement of science, literature and the arts in this important community'. It was Arthur Ryland who drafted the bill establishing the Birmingham and Midland Institute, and he who piloted it through Parliament in 1854. He was a member of a small executive group which persuaded the town council to grant land for the building of the Institute; he was particularly important in ensuring that the Institute was made 'subject to public control, with the mayor and aldermen on the Committee of Management'. While there are many examples of similar institutions in provincial Victorian England Birmingham's Institute was the first to be thus municipalised.[98]

He was also involved in the negotiations with Birmingham's Society of Arts by which the Society and its School of Design were to be housed in the new Institute. From the outset, Ryland and his colleagues were establishing an Institute which would be an umbrella sheltering a range of cultural and scientific interests; for example, it would serve as a library hosting a significant patents collection before the Central Library was built, as Birmingham's music school, as a museum and as a centre for research on health. Once launched, the Institute became a significant part of Birmingham's life, R. F. Martineau later reflecting in 1881 that the Institute had had much to do 'with the growth of public spirit and the general development of intellectual culture [which were] essential elements in local self-government'.[99] In other words, the Institute prepared Birmingham citizens to be responsible and well informed.

The foundation stone of the impressive new Institute buildings on Paradise and Edmund Streets, incorporating a lecture theatre, a museum, reading room and library, as well as classrooms and laboratories, was laid by Prince Albert in 1855; in his speech he stressed 'the scientific objects' to be studied by 'all classes'. Ryland, appointed vice-president at the outset, certainly concurred with the aim of involving working men. It was a matter of pride that by 1869 almost half of the students in the industrial department were artisans. But the first years were not easy. As Bunce recalled four years after Ryland's death:

> The Institute was in 1854 distinctly ahead of its time. Then the bulk of the community cared little for it and the artisan class for whom the industrial department was intended was indifferent.

Numbers of students and subscribers were low in the early years; yet by 1881 'they had 2,500 members and 2,600 students attending classes'. Salvation lay in expanding the general department, establishing more classes and extending the lectures for middle classes hungry for literature, language and general science.

> They owed this success especially [Bunce continued] to Arthur Ryland who had an absolute tenderness and solicitude for the child he was helping to create, with an almost womanly affection for the working people whose lot he desired to improve.[100]

The Institute became nationally important in J. H. Chamberlain's time as honorary secretary, after those early difficulties; it attracted a succession of impressive figures as president. The only exception to the iron rule that the Institute's president should not be a Birmingham citizen was Arthur Ryland in 1860 – in a list of nineteenth-century presidents, peers and knights of the realm, privy councillors, bishops, professors and generals, plain Arthur Ryland is unique. It indicates the esteem in which he was held as founder of one of Victorian England's leading intellectual institutions. His legacy at the Institute was evidently something of which his friend George Dawson much approved; the institution manifestly furthered his goals of educating, elevating and inspiring citizens and he played his part, giving 32 lectures to Institute audiences between 1856 and 1871, teaching English literature classes with his friend Sam: Timmins, and pioneering classes for women.

The Birmingham and Midland Institute is now but a shadow of its former self; the memory of the achievements of its moving spirit, Arthur Ryland, has also dimmed. He deserves better. As both an architect and exemplar of conscientious municipal government, and as the inspiration for a transformative exercise in general adult education in Birmingham, he was a truly significant figure in the years before Joseph Chamberlain's civic revolution.

Chapter 4

Robert Dale

'Birmingham is still a remarkable place', R.W. Dale (1829-95) wrote a few years before his death, 'but it seems to me that the interesting people have gone ... There was Dawson ... Vince and John Henry Chamberlain and Harris and Joseph Chamberlain in his fresh and brilliant promise ... Joseph Chamberlain is, of course, still immensely interesting but I am not sure that he is quite as interesting as he was twenty years ago ... There was a time when I used to have a smoke with him and John Henry Chamberlain and Timmins and the rest as often as twice or three times a week.'[101]

R. W. Dale was, in the pulpit and on the platform, the most powerful advocate of the civic gospel in Birmingham after Dawson. For him it was a moral undertaking, nothing less than 'Christ's work'.[102] The two men were not close friends (of his fellow civic gospellers, Dale knew J.T. Bunce best). Their relationship was based on a shared purpose and respect for each other's talents. Dale in fact only heard Dawson preach with any regularity during the years 1847-53 when he was training to become a Congregationalist minister at Spring Hill College. From then on Dawson and Dale found themselves preaching at the same time – when Dawson was delivering a sermon at the Church of the Saviour to mark the three hundredth anniversary of the birth of Shakespeare on 23 April 1864, so was Dale, less than a mile away at the Congregationalist chapel in Carr's Lane. Listening to Dawson's sermons in those years had a deep effect on Dale – both in their ethical content and in their style of delivery. 'Dawson preaches away better than ever,' he told his parents in a letter home.[103]

Later on, his theological differences with Dawson became clearer to Dale. He also formed the opinion that Dawson was inspired chiefly by continental Liberals such as Kossuth and Mazzini and, as result, his Liberalism had 'idiosyncracies'. He declared that Dawson 'was not a good party man ... He never worked well in harness.' [104] Dale himself was a staunch member of the Birmingham Liberal Association and a great admirer of Gladstone. Yet Dale also saw the special qualities Dawson brought to Birmingham:

He had great personal force ... For many years he stood almost alone with no friends and allies but those he made for himself ... He was always aggressive. The defence of his own position never seemed to give him a moment's anxiety; his policy was a policy of attack. The courage and brilliance which year after year he carried on the war fascinated the popular imagination ... He had a remarkable power of attracting the affection of all kinds of people. It was not his personal friends alone that had a strong love for him. He drew the hearts of men and women who never saw him except on the platform ... It is little wonder that men and women loved him ... For many years ... Dawson maintained ... the vital importance of securing for municipal offices the wisest, the most upright and the most able men amongst them. He strengthened his teaching by his example. He let men see that in his case intellectual culture and literary enthusiasm did not make a man too fastidious to fight for a good candidate in a municipal contest; and that, whilst he was interested in European revolutions, he was resolved to do his best to get a good town council for Birmingham ... He lectured on a great variety of subjects ... Happily, he was born in the pre-scientific age. He ... believed that to have written 'Hamlet' was to have rendered greater service to mankind than to have discovered a new metal or a new star. He would much rather ... have been the author of *Pilgrim's Progress* than the *Origin of the Species*. He did a good work here and throughout the country in strengthening and stimulating that love of literature which is an indispensable element of true culture ... (I) never heard any man read the Bible as he read it ... His prayers were never to be forgotten. (I) remembered sitting next to him at a lunch after the ceremonial opening of some public building ... [Dawson said] 'I make it a rule never to use in prayer any word that has come into the language since the days of Queen Elizabeth'.[105]

Robert William Dale was born in Newington in London on 1 December 1829. His father sold hat trimmings and managed to send his son (Dale was ten years' older than his only sibling) to school until he was fourteen. Dale left these schools with a knowledge of grammar, arithmetic and French – and, in one case, of what poor schooling amounted to. If his schooling was preparing him for business, Dale was already forming an ambition to become a minister. He was a voracious reader, particularly of religious literature. John Angell James's *Anxious Enquirer* was a key text for him during the years he worked as an assistant schoolteacher. 'Night after night', he recalled, 'I waited with eager impatience for the house to become still that, in undisturbed solitude, I might agonise over the book which had taught so many to trust in God.' [106] During these early years Dale began to do what he was to do all his life: write and preach. He sent in essays to Nonconformist and self-improvement journals and, at the age of sixteen, published a religious tract. He preached his first sermon in Andover spring 1845, aged fifteen.

In preparation for taking on the role of a Congregationalist minister, Dale spent six years from 1847 at Spring Hill College in Birmingham. At first his expenses were paid by benefactors in Leamington – where he had moved to take up a post as an assistant to a schoolmaster – but in due course he raised his own funds from preaching during summer vacations. Not yet located in its magnificent building in Moseley, the college was situated on two sides of Dudley Road. There were around 20 other students there during Dale's time, all prohibited from speaking in public during their first two years. Not that Dale wanted to speak to any of them anyway – he formed a close intellectual friendship with one student but from the others his shyness and self-containment earned him the nickname 'the Jesuit'. Of the ministers who taught the students, Dale would remember the noted essayist Henry Rogers as having the greatest influence on him. It was Rogers who introduced him to the work of Edmund Burke, which became a life-long interest. Devoted to study, Dale secured a BA and then an MA from the University of London (and also picked up a gold medal for philosophy).

During these years Dale explored the religious and political life of Birmingham. He attended meetings at the town hall, and heard speeches from, amongst others, Arthur O'Neill, the Chartist and Baptist minister, and Edward Miall, the editor of the *Nonconformist*. Dale was to get to know both men well in later life. Dale's name appears in newspaper reports from this time as a member of the Young Men's Christian Association which existed 'to protect young men from the evils and vices of youth'.[107] He reserved Sunday evenings for Dawson's services at the Church of the Saviour, but otherwise was to be found listening to the sermons of John Angell James at Carr's Lane. 'The congregation was electrified again and again', he wrote of James. 'For an hour and a half, he poured forth a stream of argument and eloquence – always clear and majestic, sometimes swelling into a torrent.'[108] James also took notice of Dale, inviting him to dinner and, in September 1849, to preach his first sermon at Carr's Lane. It seems clear that James, who was by this time in his mid-sixties, earmarked Dale early on as his successor. Nurtured for the role as an assistant to James and soon as co-pastor, Dale was appointed pastor on James's death in October 1859. By this time, he had married Elizabeth Dowling, who herself was to become a speaker to female audiences on matters of health.[109] In the coming years

Birmingham was to hear a great deal from the man the Tories called 'the preacher of Carr's Lane'.[110]

'He had an immense belief in education', a colleague recalled of Dale, 'a wonderful enthusiasm for it, and an enthusiasm that was contagious and carried away, and carried on with him, those who were working by his side.'[111] This enthusiasm was communicated in his sermons and speeches during the tercentenary in April 1864: Shakespeare's 'wonderful creations' had 'given a measure of education to millions who, unhappily, have received no other mental discipline' and the celebrations in the manufacturing town of Birmingham 'proved ... the existence of a feeling ... that there were greater and more ennobling things than vast mills and machinery, huge steam ships and extensive and widely-diffused commercial connections ....' [112] Dales's enthusiasm was also communicated in his involvement in the Birmingham Education Society, an initiative of George Dixon's which came together in February 1867.[113] This body sought to collect evidence about the provision of schooling and to raise funds to pay the fees for working-class children to attend denominational schools. It was perpetually short of funds, and Dale had to make public appeals for donations. With even those whose fees were paid drifting away, only one quarter of the 4,720 children helped by these arrangements enjoyed any prolonged schooling. Dale's enthusiasm for education was also evident in his declaration that, after the passing of the Reform Act of 1867, branches of the Reform League (which he had joined) should become working-class institutes offering lectures and his support for evening classes at Carr's Lane which he 'took to ... with great warmth'.[114]

If Dawson 'never worked well in harness', Dale himself wasn't immune to this shortcoming. He was perfectly capable of finding a principled objection to a policy, of being 'in a miserable minority', as he called it.[115] He did not support the closure of denominational schools – if rate-aided schools were good enough, he argued, such schools would disappear of their own accord. He did not approve of the idea that rate-aided schools should be free. In consequence of these views, Dale did not attend the inaugural meetings of the National Education League, which was formed in January 1869. Well-funded by Dixon, Chamberlain and others and quickly accruing support, Dale decided to join but made clear that whilst his backing for unsectarian and compulsory schooling was 'hearty and unqualified ... on this point I must preserve my freedom'.[116] In spite of all of this, Dale emerged as a prominent figure in local – and, as he wanted, national – opposition to the Education Bill of 1870. His speeches were formidable – carefully worked out and beautifully written. He cited numerous injustices – the scope for denominational schools being supported from the rates, the arrangements for teaching religion and so on. It was a Bill which would 'surround the religious work of thousands of Nonconformist schools with new and serious difficulties ....'[117] Dale waged his campaign, with Crosskey, through the Central Nonconformist Committee, which secured thousands of signatures for the petitions it sent to chapels across the country. The two men were often in London to attend debates in the House of Commons and hatch plans with other opponents of the Bill. Though he complained about the number of meetings he attended, Dale was driven forward by a sense of the duty that befell a Nonconformist minister and also by his own egotism. In August 1871 he announced that he had received an offer to become minister of a new chapel in London and that this would guarantee him a better income and less strain; but he did not go. He declared that he had bowed to the wishes of his congregation, but it was rumoured that an agreement had also been reached that he receive all of the pew rents at Carr's Lane.

From 1870 until 1881 Dale took on the onerous responsibility of being a member of the School Board. This commitment required attendance at fortnightly meetings which went on for many hours and were held in public. There were speeches to write and also letters to the newspapers as the debates spilled out into the correspondence columns. Between 1870 and 1876 Dale missed meetings only when he was travelling in the Middle East and America – 475 meetings were called during that period and he attended 370 of them. Dale was determined that working-class children should be taught in the best buildings by the best teachers. The first election to the school board in November 1870 was mismanaged by the BLA and left the 'Bible Eight' in control. They faced, however, a formidable combination of Liberals – the ministers Dale, Dawson and Vince and Dixon, Chamberlain and John Skirrow Wright.[118] Chamberlain emerged as the coming man, forming a strong alliance with Dale. An attempt to introduce compulsory attendance which would have meant denominational schools being supported by the rates – there at that point being no board schools – was harried by these men, with Dale putting down amendment after amendment to slow down the process. In the face of this tenacious opposition, the plan was not put into operation. Dale led the resistance to the policy of permitting the reading of the Bible in board schools with an accompanying explanation. Uplifting the children of Birmingham did not mean enhancing the influence of the Church of England. The Liberal successes in the elections to the school board in November 1873 put paid to the scheme. Through the Birmingham Religious Education Society, organised by Dale and his allies, unpaid teachers drawn from Sunday Schools were deployed to provide religious instruction in board schools. However, this voluntary effort had patchy results and, in 1879, the school board made daily readings from the Bible a compulsory part of the curriculum. Dale abstained in the vote.[119]

From his pulpit, and at meetings during municipal elections, Dale provided an extremely important ethical underpinning for Chamberlain's work as mayor. He declared that the town council, in taking over the supplies of gas and water, in clearing slums and in its improvement scheme, was putting into practice Christian doctrines:

> During the last two years there had been extraordinary activity on the part of the council of a kind that deserved special recognition on the part of the Christian churches of the town ... As Christian men, it was just as much their duty to support the council in such improvements as to contribute to a hospital fund or to subscribe to a missionary society ... God's commandments ... covered their municipal life and no devoutness could be an excuse for not paying their rates, neither could it be an excuse from keeping away from the polling booth at the time of an election ... They ... committed a grave sin if they neglected using their municipal vote and as a result of that the town was badly governed ... In Birmingham ... within four years they had more than doubled the number of children attending public elementary schools ... Very soon the borough would be covered with a complete network of elementary schools and he trusted that ... every Christian man throughout the borough would pay the educational rate cheerfully ... He wished for a moment to speak more particularly to young men and women whose school days were over. There existed in the town a provision for remedying the defects of early education or for carrying their education to a still higher level of perfection such as they would discover in hardly any other town in the kingdom ... the Midland Institute. They would be guilty of great negligence, having those classes and lectures within their reach, if they did not live up to the privileges which belonged to them as inhabitants of the town.[120]

When Dale retired from the school board in November 1881, he was presented by his Liberal colleagues with a bookcase stocked with books. Dixon declared that 'they had lost not only their greatest orator but their best administrator'.[121] This moment in effect brought Dale's career as an actual enactor of the civic gospel to an end. During those years twenty-six board schools had been built across Birmingham. Dale was to remain the minister at Carr's Lane for another fourteen years but, now turned fifty and prompted by the early deaths of Dawson and Vince, he sought the time for other activities – particularly writing and travelling. By the time of his death he had added greatly to his tally of publications – no less than eight theological books and one travel book, brought out by Hodder and Stoughton, and over thirty essays in magazines. These essays dealt with his usual moral preoccupations – 'On Telling the Truth', 'Public Duty' and the like – educational questions and the Irish Home Rule crisis (which precipitated Dale's withdrawal from politics).

The end of Dale's time on the school board did not mean the end of his interventions in the affairs of that body. In December 1885 he expressed a harder position on the use of the Bible in schools, calling for teachers not to be permitted to read it at all on the grounds that they might not have strong religious beliefs themselves. 'Is it really a crime to muzzle the teacher?', he asked. [122] In November 1888 he urged the ratepayers to return the nine Liberal candidates to the school board. In his final years 'the Nonconformist Bishop of Birmingham' was only strong enough to preach one sermon a week at Carr's Lane.[123] He died on 13 March 1895; like so many of the civic gospellers, he was buried at Key Hill.[124]

For almost all of his years at Carr's Lane Dale was a member of the committee of Birmingham Library. This venerable Birmingham institution was affectionately re-christened the Old Library after the opening of the free lending and reference libraries in 1865-6, but it continued to thrive. By the mid-1880s it had a stock of about 46,000 volumes – with an emphasis on fiction, poetry, history, biography and travels – and about 1,400 members. Here, at committee meetings, Dale would regularly sit with Dawson, Bunce, William Harris, J. A. Langford, J.H. Chamberlain, Charles Vince, Charles Clarke and others.[125] In the quiet of Birmingham Library, the civic gospellers would take stock of their work.

Chapter 5

William Harris

William Harris (1826-1911) was one of the most important figures in Birmingham life in the second half of the nineteenth century; yet he remains largely unrecognised, unaccountably omitted from the *Oxford Dictionary of National Biography*. Obituarists on his death in 1911 were certainly clear about his significance. Firstly, there was his political legacy: 'he was the mainspring of the movement which brought Birmingham so prominently before the nation.'[126] A mechanical analogy is very apt for the man who conceived and constructed a Birmingham political machine which – with minor refinements – continued from 1867 to 1939 to win electoral success for its masters. Other contemporaries applied to Harris a different epithet; the (critical) *Yorkshire Post* wrote of him that 'though he was never seen or heard, he is the chief wire-puller'.[127] But tributes on his death also pointed out the extent to which he was more than simply a political operator but, instead, something of a Renaissance man. Frank Wright, the chairman of the Birmingham Liberal Association (BLA), which Harris had co-founded in 1865, concluded in 1911 that, 'he touched life at many points – in art, literature, education and municipal and national affairs and in all he took a distinguished part and rendered notable service'.[128] In that William Harris was severally an architect, journalist, historian, political theorist, Unitarian and committed civic gospeller, Wright was surely right.

The *Yorkshire Post's* comment suggests one of the reasons for Harris's anonymity. A number who observed him remarked that he was something of a mystery, a man who operated in the shadows. J. L. Garvin wrote of 'that prompting man, without the ability of speaking, he was an intent thinker, the Abbe Sieyes of Birmingham,' and the obituary writer in the *Birmingham Daily Mail* added, 'he seldom came prominently before the notice of the general public'.[129] This was partly because his particular strengths were as an analyst and problem solver with regard to political processes, and as an administrator with a superb grasp of detail. But withdrawal from the public stage was a career choice he felt called to make. In 1871 – at a time when he was simultaneously a member of the town council, an apparatchik of the National Education League, chairman of the free libraries committee and of the arts purchase committee – he suffered a paralytic stroke while addressing a council meeting. He concluded then that he needs must reduce his public commitments, and this explains, for example, his refusal to accept an offer to stand for parliament for North Birmingham in 1885.

It was not – as Garvin cruelly concluded – that he was 'without the ability to speak', for he was an articulate debater who fellow members elected president of the Birmingham and Edgbaston Debating Society, that cradle of aspirant politicians. And the fair-minded reader cannot fail to be struck by his oratorical power when he recommended John Bright's nomination for re-election in December 1868. Bright, he thundered from the platform, was:

The apostle of the gospel of peace and the advocate of such a redistribution of representation as to secure every voter in the exercise of his great duties from the tyranny of coercion, and from the degradation of bribery by the protection of the [secret] ballot.[130]

Nor was he without considerable charm and wit. R. W. Dale (chapter 4) in retrospectively lamenting that since the 1870s the 'interesting people (Dawson, Vince and J H Chamberlain) are gone,' consoled himself that, at least 'Harris remains and is as kindly and epigrammatic as ever.' [131]

It is suggestive that Dale should name-check Harris as part of that selective group of Birmingham's brightest and best; it centred on George Dawson. From the moment William Harris fetched up at Dawson's Mount Zion Baptist church in the early 1840s he fell under the minister's influence. Dawson's inspiration is evident in much of what Harris then set out to do. Dawson fell out with Mount Zion's governing body, and in 1847 William Harris joined with others like J. T. Bunce, Sam: Timmins, R. F. Martineau, J. A. Langford and George Dixon, to support and fund a new church for Dawson – the Church of the Saviour. Dawson was an articulate apologist for Lajos Kossuth, the great Hungarian radical, who came to Britain in 1851; Harris spoke eloquently in public in Kossuth's support. Dawson was an engaged and committed Liberal; Harris became a central figure in founding the Birmingham Liberal Association and was the animating genius which made it a unique success. Dawson was a fervent supporter of working-class education; Harris from 1850 was engaged in a sequence of projects aimed at achieving free compulsory education for all children. Dawson wanted to convert the public to the Liberal cause by founding a newspaper, the

Birmingham Daily Press, the first Birmingham daily after the repeal of the paper duties in 1855; Harris joined him as its co-editor. Dawson, with J H Chamberlain and Sam: Timmins, conceived of a humorous paper, the *Town Crier,* which was 'interested in good government and progress of the town and [in] putting incompetent and pretentious people [who were stumbling blocks] out of the way'.So, Harris enlisted with the team as a journalist, and he continued to pursue that profession as a regular leader writer for the *Birmingham Daily Post* for many years.[132]

In the late 1850s, Dawson and Timmins envisaged a Shakespeare Club 'to discuss and exchange views under the common bond of concern and celebration of all things Shakespearean', and Harris joined at the outset. Dawson spoke fervently of the vital importance of creating free libraries for all so that citizens could develop an understanding of the world and of civilisation; Harris was central to the Church of the Saviour clique which would dominate the management of Birmingham's municipal free libraries for over thirty years. There is, then, persuasive evidence of the extent to which William Harris was very close to Dawson and a vital component in the civic gospel project. When Dawson died prematurely in 1876, it was because 'the sword of an unusually active mind helped to wear out the scabbard of the body,' wrote Harris, who felt the blow keenly. He continued, 'to many of us who knew him most intimately and therefore loved him best – life has never seemed the same …'.[133]

It is striking how for Harris, as for George Dawson and Joseph Chamberlain after him, a personal revelation of the extent of educational deprivation in Birmingham was the initial spur to political action. Indeed, one can see the urge to transform educational opportunity as central to Dawson's ministry and as the dominant factor in Harris's public work, certainly up to the late 1870s. His anger at inadequate provision of schooling saw him in 1850 become joint honorary secretary of the Birmingham branch of the National Public School Association which – unavailingly – advocated free, compulsory, rate-aided education for all.

He went on to become a key member of the Grammar School Association. Harris – along with George Dixon, Sam: Timmins and a few others – met the governors of King Edward's Grammar School in October 1865 to demand a restructuring of the Anglican governing body, the introduction of a selective pupil entry and the opening of new foundation schools, including one for girls.[134] It was the start of a long-running, ultimately successful, campaign to break open an establishment monopoly in Birmingham. Educational opportunity for all – dissenters and working people included – was a fundamental Liberal goal, and Harris continued to pursue it, joining

Dawson as a founder member of the National Education League in 1869. Its historian, A. F. Taylor, writes that 'control of the League was in the hands of four men, Chamberlain, Bunce, Collings and Harris'. The latter was in charge of the League's finances, and he was adept at drumming up potential donors. He was also a member of the small parliamentary sub-committee which managed communications with ministers and MPs. We find Harris among National Education League delegates in 1870 travelling from New Street station to meet Prime Minister Gladstone to ask that he modify his government's education policy; that delegation comprised a roll call of Birmingham's civic gospellers – Dawson, Joseph Chamberlain, Bunce, Jaffray, Martineau, Vince among others. Harris did more still – even after that stroke he suffered in 1871 – for he chaired the League's electoral committee formed the following year to appoint and direct the work of twelve full-time agents tasked with creating new branches, arranging public meetings and canvassing their districts thoroughly.[135] The grasp of detail, the understanding of electoral methodology, is distinctively that of an acknowledged master, William Harris. Even if the League failed to win those Dawsonian goals of free, compulsory, non-denominational education, Harris had provided Chamberlain and others with a 'short model' of how to organise a political campaign.[136]

Dawson's vision was every bit as much about adult as about children's education. Many of the enterprises with which he engaged in mid-nineteenth century Birmingham were concerned with improving the quality of life for all citizens. His dream encompassed not just social reform but also the granting of opportunities to extend knowledge, learn wisdom, and cultivate discrimination, aesthetically and intellectually. Harris embraced these ideals, starting with Dawson's mission to create public (free) libraries for the use of all citizens. His friend and fellow worshipper J. A. Langford articulated the vision for Harris and others at the heart of the library campaign, in portentous prose. It was all about 'making the future life of our people nobler than the past ... remember[ing] that Ignorance is the curse of God, and Knowledge the wing wherewith we fly to Heaven', for this was 'a holy crusade against an enemy whose triumphs are crime, suffering, want and woe'.[137] Harris was there at the commencement of this 'holy crusade', being honorary secretary of the committee in 1852 which urged the council to adopt the Free Libraries Act of 1850. Undaunted by failure, he returned to the fray in 1859 and joined another founder-member of the Church of the Saviour, E. C. Osborne, in a successful campaign to persuade the council to implement the 1855 Free Libraries Act. Harris was elected to the first free libraries committee, chairing it from 1868 to 1871, years in which the town established new lending libraries.

His faith in literature, art and the extension of knowledge as essential to civilising Birmingham's citizens explains his involvement with Arthur Ryland's project at the Birmingham and Midland Institute; he was for years a valued member of its governing council. He was also a natural recruit to George Dawson and Sam: Timmins' Shakespeare Club in 1858 before it had even settled on its name. In his *History of Our Shakespeare Club,* Harris shows how the club was about much more than developing a great collection of Shakespeare works for the edification and development of Birmingham's citizens. Somewhat akin to its predecessor, the Lunar Society, it was a discussion forum where Dawson apostles promoted larger 'political and social questions affecting the intellectual and moral progress of the people' and urged 'that the welfare of a great industrial community and the elevation of its inhabitants were worthy objects of the efforts of the ablest and most highly cultivated of its citizens'. Here Harris articulates the essence of the Dawson mission: to recruit the brightest and best in the great cause of improving Birmingham's townspeople.[138]

Harris's cultural interests were not confined to literature. He was a trained architect who at one stage in the 1850s shared a practice with J. H. Chamberlain. His most notable surviving work is in Stratford upon Avon, the Old Bank designed and built in 1883 (the year of J. H. Chamberlain's death) for the Birmingham Banking Company. In its high Victorian character it is an example of Birmingham's prevailing gothic that has migrated into rural Warwickshire. Given Harris's enthusiasm for the works of Shakespeare it seems particularly fitting that this rare remaining example of his work should be decorated with fifteen terracotta panels (by Samuel Barfield) illustrating scenes from Shakespeare's plays.[139] He wanted others in Birmingham to share his passion for architecture and in 1865 was a founder member of the Birmingham Architectural Society.[140] His professional expertise was used by the town council in several ways. In 1870 Harris (as chairman of the free libraries committee) and J. T. Bunce (chairman of the Art Gallery sub-committee) were appointed to direct the expenditure of monies raised to purchase art and specimens for the town's art gallery. Langford, who records these facts, wrote that as a result 'the art gallery has never been so useful in the cultivation of art knowledge'.[141]

Harris was not just an architect, but a qualified surveyor too, and naturally enough, as a proponent of the civic gospel, was committed to improving the environmental quality of citizens' lives in Birmingham. At the council meeting of 22 May 1866 he and Richard Henshall were appointed as inspectors of nuisances 'to inspect the courts and houses in the borough and cause homes that were filthy to be limewashed, and drains and privies to be cleaned, pigs removed and smoke nuisance controlled'.[142] Harris was a member of the town council (1865-71) in those very years when Birmingham's talented businessmen began to heed Dawson's plea that they should take responsibility for municipal affairs He was engaged both as an expert, and as a councillor, as the pace of sanitary reform in Birmingham quickened, culminating in the reforms of Thomas Avery, and then Joseph Chamberlain, in the next decade.

Whilst contemporaries recognised Harris for his versatility and for his remarkable contribution to municipal affairs, what impressed them above all was his creative genius as a political manager. And although at first blush it might appear tendentious, one can cogently argue that his political work for the Liberal Party was every bit as much a part of the civic gospel story as service given to libraries and other Birmingham institutions. For the Liberal Party was the natural home for Birmingham's Nonconformists, of its reformers, of George Dawson himself, and of other leading ministers. One of them, Henry Crosskey, explained what he believed to be its relationship to the ideals of the civic gospel: 'the Liberal policy was a policy of civilisation … the enjoyment by the great mass of people of the blessing of a beautiful and civilised life.'[143] So it was axiomatic that those committed to promoting the blessing of a civilised life should also seek to further the fortunes of the vehicle most likely to realise those goals, the Liberal Party; William Harris certainly thought so.

The consistent thread running through Harris's political activities was his desire to bring about a more democratic system which would allow the participation of working people. From the 1850s, when he was in Birmingham welcoming parties for two renowned democrats, first Kossuth then John Bright, to the early 1860s when he was secretary to a committee raising funds for distressed Lancashire cotton workers, Harris was committed to Liberal causes. It was therefore inevitable that he should become a founder-member of the Birmingham Liberal Association (BLA) in 1865, established as a permanent election committee 'to maintain the Liberal representation of the borough'. It would become 'the instrument of the movement for civic betterment'.[144] In 1867 the Association was prominent and active in the campaign to elect George Dixon to Parliament at a by-election, but the impetus for a radical change came with the passing of the Reform Act in 1867.

It was Harris who recognised the importance of extending the organisation to win the allegiance of a much-extended electorate. When he succeeded Dixon as the BLA's secretary, Harris devised the system of permanent ward committees, which would send their representatives through to a central committee. This democratic system was designed to engage large numbers of working-class voters, newly enfranchised by the Reform Act; together these committees formed a large general committee of 400, later to grow to 600, which (with a smaller executive) came to dominate Birmingham politics. More than this he set out to organise how voters cast their votes. Birmingham after 1867 had three seats and each voter had two votes. Only by clear direction could an even spread of votes across the three Liberal candidates be achieved. Harris told Edgbaston Liberals that

> it was plain that with three Liberals and one Tory going to the poll, and the electors being allowed to vote for two candidates only, the nicest calculation and the utmost subordination would be necessary to carry three Liberals.[145]

Garvin later explained: 'in some wards electors were asked to vote for Bright and Dixon; in others for Bright and Muntz; in others again for Dixon and Muntz. The thing worked like clockwork.'[146]

This whole operation – with new approaches to canvassing, publicity and party direction – brought an entirely new level of discipline to British politics. The Association was dubbed 'the Caucus' by the Tory leader Benjamin Disraeli. Francis Schnadhorst, Harris's successor as BLA secretary, later boasted that 'by this process Birmingham revolutionised political organisation'.[147] Harris was its acknowledged architect, Joseph Chamberlain writing that he 'was Father of the Caucus'.[148] A generation later the founder of modern political science, Moisei Ostrogorski, credited Harris and Birmingham with having created an innovation in political management in his classic text *Democracy and the Organisation of Political Parties* (1902).[149]

Harris went on to consolidate his reputation for political inventiveness. His skills were, as we saw, channelled into organising a national campaign for the National Education League. When it was clear that it had achieved all it was ever likely to, it was Harris who converted Chamberlain and others to a new approach, that of forming 'a general political organisation ... a federation which by collecting together the opinions of the majority of people in all the great centres of political activity, should be able to speak with the full authority of the national voice'.

It would bring together single interest campaigns on education, parliamentary reform, temperance into one great umbrella organisation, the National Liberal Federation (NLF), affiliating local Liberal parties all over Britain in 1877. 'The whole credit of having initiated and carried out the new machinery belongs to my friend Mr Harris,' said Chamberlain of the first chairman of the Federation.[150] Once he had founded it, Harris then fought hard to ensure that the Federation pursued policies formulated by ordinary Liberal members from all over the country; he pioneered democratic participation in Britain. The NLF promoted many of the ideas of Joseph Chamberlain until 1886, but then the Liberal Party, divided over Gladstone's Home Rule Bill, witnessed a distressing parting of the ways. Harris ensured the Federation stayed loyal to Gladstone, while Chamberlain and other old friends, R. W. Dale and J. T. Bunce among them, steadily moved towards Unionism.

William Harris's political achievements are of a piece with the rest of his long and varied career. The aim of the caucus was both to give a voice to newly enfranchised working men and at the same time to educate them in taking political responsibility, when determining party policy and when choosing their representatives. Fostering political education was as much a part of the civic gospel's prospectus as was developing literacy, and nurturing aesthetic and literary discrimination; William Harris proves to have been a significant figure in every aspect of that crusade to widen educational opportunity.

Chapter 6

William Aitken

William Costen Aitken (1817-75) is one of the least known of the civic gospellers. He barely features in standard histories of Birmingham, for instance those towering nineteenth century works by J. T. Bunce and R. K. Dent. Sam: Timmins, however, thought very differently. He bracketed Aitken together with George Dawson and J. H. Chamberlain in his *History of Warwickshire* (1889). Aitken and Chamberlain were Dawson's 'fellow workers and devoted friends, [who] also worked in the same spirit and on the same lines but in different departments of public life'. All three were 'strangers in the gates', that is they were not Birmingham-born, with Dawson born in London, Aitken in Scotland and Chamberlain in Leicester. Timmins might have selected alternative 'strangers', for example, Bunce (from Faringdon), Collings (a Devonian) or indeed Joseph Chamberlain (London), but he particularly esteemed 'these three friends who will ever be honoured as worthies, whose full merits have never yet been adequately praised in the history of a great town'. Aitken, he elaborated, 'for forty years gave his untiring energy and splendid services to art and the industries of Birmingham'.[151] Timmins was prescient in that Aitken has even now not 'been adequately praised', perhaps at least partly because he died before the projects which absorbed him came to fruition: before Mason College opened its doors, before Taylor, Kenrick and Bunce's reforms to the School of Art curriculum were introduced, and before the Municipal Art Gallery welcomed its first visitors.

Aitken earns his chapter in this book because he has a unique place in the pantheon of Birmingham's nineteenth century improvers. Inheriting familial skills in brass-founding as a boy in Dumfries, he was a craftsman, an inventor (of new processes of nature printing for example) and for much of his working life he was a factory manager – of Hardman's new works on Newhall Hill in Birmingham, where the ancient metal working techniques demanded by their collaborator Augustus Pugin for his ecclesiastical commissions were developed. Aitken helped establish Hardman's at the forefront of decorative metal work, praised in the *Illustrated London News* at the first exhibition of industrial design in 1849 for the 'peculiar truthfulness of design and beauty of execution … eclipsing everything else in the gorgeousness of detail'.[152] Whereas Dawson's lieutenants were overwhelmingly either businessmen (Kenrick, Joseph Chamberlain, Timmins, R. F. Martineau) or professionals (Ryland, Bunce, Mathews), Aitken was a practical manufacturer himself, as well as being a foremost industrial designer. In his person he connects the civic gospel more directly to Birmingham's economic lifeblood, the metal-working industries, than anyone else, even more than his friend J. H. Chamberlain. Yet because he was welcomed into the society of wealthier Birmingham philanthropists – in a way that artists and designers were not in other provincial Victorian cities – he became a bridge between comfortable middle-class visionaries and the working men with whom he rubbed shoulders on the factory shop floor.[153]

It does not seem too fanciful to suggest that a life spent directing and managing a workforce explains those very particular character-traits highlighted by obituarists.

> His brusqueness and sometimes eccentric speech and manner caused him now and then to be misunderstood …. Though seemingly rough on occasion no man ever had a tenderer heart. [He exhibited] the most perfect frankness and plain spoken-ness when he thought friends in the wrong. [He was] a hater of shams … and the vehemence of his occasional manifestations [of outrage] only served to endear him [more].

Few of the eulogies of the Birmingham great and the good are as blunt. Aitken was evidently a man apart in this regard, but it is clear nonetheless that he was respected for being forthright and continued to be held in affection.

His contribution to Timmins' great classic of industrial literature, *The Resources, Products and Industrial History of Birmingham and the Midland Hardware District* (1866) gives proof of his encyclopaedic knowledge of metal manufacturing processes. Timmins himself prefaced a monumental work with his 'especial thanks' to a man who had 'devoted his large technical knowledge and artistic skill to the study and improvement of nearly every branch of Birmingham Art-manufacture'.[154]

> Aitken's exhaustive treatise on brass-work, a vigorous and graphic narrative, showed a perfect mastery of the history and process of the

brass-foundry trade, [concluded the *Birmingham Daily Post*] and his untiring energy and long experience, technical knowledge and artistic taste have produced papers of lasting value ... His work has vindicated the just claim of Birmingham to pre-eminence among metal-working communities.[155]

Dawson, who talked much about generating civic pride, would have welcomed such evidence of the town's growing ascendancy. Nor was Aitken's expertise confined to the written word; we find him lecturing at the Birmingham and Midland Institute on his friend, the Birmingham japanner, glass painter and engraver Francis Eginton, and at St George's Institute on *The Reproduction of Works of Art on Paper*.[156]

More importantly, Aitken saw the wider ramifications of propagating good industrial design and it was this that connected him intimately to Dawson's mission for the civic gospel. He was not a regular member of the congregation at the Church of the Saviour, but he responded to the aesthetic and cultural dimension of the message. As Roy Hartnell has written:

He recognised that Dawson's preaching was reinforcing the value of pride in individual craftsmanship. He argued persistently that improvements in the environment, the man-made world of industrial design, could only emerge through better design education.

This belief that well-designed goods, made with integrity by craftsmen, could improve society at large would – when articulated by Ruskin and Morris – be the mantra of the Arts and Crafts movement and hugely influential in Birmingham by the end of the century. 'Better standards of design in shops and homes, created by better-educated designers, purchased and appreciated by better educated consumers, would make for better and happier citizens.'[157] Aitken's lifelong preoccupation with good design was helping to achieve Dawson's vision of an elevated citizenry; just as for J. H. Chamberlain and his many buildings in Birmingham, it was but the visual expression of a more comprehensive prospectus for the civic gospel.

When his obituarist wrote in 1875 that 'his public life has long been an important part of the history of our town', he was recognising that Aitken had a broad hinterland beyond industrial design.[158] He was a member of the Birmingham Philosophical Institution in the 1840s, gifting James Watt letters to its museum.[159] Like Arthur Ryland and others, he saw the importance of integrating into one organisation middle class and mechanics alike, offering a scientific and more general education and so, 'when the Midland Institute was first spoken of Aitken was one of its warmest advocates,' talking persuasively at the town hall meeting which launched the new Institute.[160] He was one of its original council members, named in the Act of Parliament establishing the Birmingham and Midland Institute in 1854, and in 1870 and 1871 he was elected as vice-president.[161]

The common factor in much of what he did was a desire to extend educational opportunity. He made his feelings plain about the inadequacy of elementary education and the responsibility of the more fortunate. In his chapter on the brass industry he wrote that:

> It is preposterous to send children to work uneducated ... [and that] the development of God-given intelligence is a duty incumbent on those who receive benefit and profit by the labour of the uneducated.[162]

He supported the Birmingham and Midland Institute because he was committed to extending scientific education to Birmingham's workforce. He joined Dawson and Timmins in Our Shakespeare Club, attending the tercentenary dinner in 1864, not only for the stimulating company, but because like Dawson he believed all Birmingham's citizens should be able to access Shakespeare's insights into the human condition. And Josiah Mason recognised Aitken's desire to improve working-class education when he nominated him one of the original six trustees for his scientific college, a forerunner of Birmingham's university.

The greater part of Aitken's mission in life concerned the provision of good quality design education and – allied to that – the cultivation of discriminating taste. He felt that Birmingham's products were too often unimaginative and baldly utilitarian in design. Because he was famously blunt, he did not hesitate to say so. One approach to improving matters might be described as that of osmosis. His goal of educating the workman to recognise good design and then to be able to produce better finished products could be achieved through organising exhibitions whence they could absorb good practice. For, as the *Post* put it: 'he had long held that if exhibitions were to produce their proper effect the actual workmen must examine them for themselves and describe them for the benefit of others.'[163] He started in 1849, being:

> The chief promoter and able manager of the first great industrial exhibition [for the British Association for the Advancement of Science] at Bingley Hall in Birmingham ... the most important exhibition of industrial design in Britain up to that point.[164]

Aitken has a strong claim to have influenced the Prince Consort's decision to organise the Great Exhibition in 1851. Albert's visit to Bingley Hall inspired him, and he subsequently ensured Aitken was part of the management team triumphantly realising the royal vision at Crystal Palace. For Aitken the Great Exhibition was invaluable: millions of workmen could see examples of the world's best design for themselves, but equally, the poor showing of British products (with the exception of Hardman's ornamental metal work) reinforced his message of the importance of improving technical education.

He persevered in his objective, providing the impetus for another significant exhibition, that at Aston Park in 1858. Knowing his engagement with working men we cannot doubt that he endorsed the decision to form a company of workers to raise funds to purchase Aston Hall so that:

> While the beautiful grounds will afford a place of innocent bodily recreation to the artisan and his family, his mind may at the same time gather materials from the observation of nature, and the study of works of art wherewith to improve his taste, correct his design and render him both a better man and a better workman.[165]

These words of Sir Francis Scott, the workmen's amanuensis, might have been drafted by Aitken so well do they distil the essence of his mission. His contribution was central to the success of an exhibition dignified by a visit from Queen Victoria herself – securing specimens of art and workmanship, compiling the catalogue, arranging the objects and writing descriptive reports.

In 1867 Aitken took a party of 23 hand-picked artisans ('men of intelligence, knowledge of their trades, competent reporters with powers of observation') to the Paris Exhibition, arranging both to show them round the exhibits, British and Continental, as well as to take them to some French factories.[166] A retrospective years later concluded that 'Mr Aitken by his powers of organisation contributed largely to the success of this visit'.[167] What these artisans subsequently reported only echoed what Aitken had long maintained. The writer on chandeliers, for example, wrote that:

> The work people on the Continent are much better up in fine arts than our people and a very great failing with the English [is] that they are not sufficiently educated in drawing and the fine arts.

His colleague specialising in cabinet brass foundry argued that 'our great deficiency is in design. If we are to maintain our position, we must pay more attention to form and design.' James Plampin, the expert in jewellery and gift toys, reached a depressing conclusion, one which was grist to the Aitken mill:

> French superiority is in taste and taste is a matter of education – the taste of the whole nation is higher than the English. The French are taught to draw, and they [have] access to some of the finest art galleries in the world.[168]

In terms of that civic gospel ambition to elevate and educate working-class citizens, it was especially heartening that the artisans who visited the exhibition took responsibility for acting for themselves, forming the Birmingham Society of Artisans on their return from Paris. It was intended to extend technical knowledge among their peers through establishing free classes, with prizes given for model students.[169]

A more permanent solution to the challenge of illustrating excellent design and beautiful art would be to create a museum in Birmingham, continuously open to the public. Aitken had hoped Aston Hall would fit the bill, but more space was needed, in a central location, so he continued to campaign for a museum of industrial arts. His absorption in this question explains his nomination (by subscribers to the new picture gallery fund in 1871), for the Council's Art Gallery sub-committee (chaired by J. T. Bunce). Alongside prominent businessmen sat two men steeped in design, J. H. Chamberlain and W. C. Aitken. For Aitken the purchasing of art and artefacts – and here his experience of the Paris exhibition well qualified him to buy some fine Continental examples – enabled him to further his primary aim of 'cultivating art knowledge and exerting influence upon designers and workmen engaged in the manufactures of the town'.[170]

An art gallery with rooms for industrial art was one way of introducing the populace to beautiful art and artefacts. Just as important was to educate the artist and the craftsman, and Aitken frequently spoke – in his forthright way – of the need to improve Birmingham's offering. For example, at the annual meeting of sponsors at the Birmingham Society of Arts in 1863 he was a prominent speaker,

> alluding to the great improvement in art since 1851. This could be partly attributed to the new ... [government funded] schools of design. But these were in danger of changing gradually into [merely] schools of Art,

where many attended, not to apply to manufactures their knowledge and skill but, to learn to paint fine pictures ... It should never be forgotten that Birmingham was a manufacturing town and that the sale of manufactures depended on the introduction of ornament of a tasteful and artistic kind. [He concluded that] ... We ought to make use of every means in our power to educate our own youth, to cultivate their taste and elevate their minds so that they could design for the manufacturers of their own country.[171]

He continued to be involved with discussions on technical education right up to his death, being part of a special meeting of the Chamber of Commerce in 1868 to consider how Birmingham might improve in this regard. He would not live to see the establishment in the late 1870s of a specialist School of Design, later extended through the agency of R. F. Martineau and George Kenrick when it became a leader in its field. Aitken had laid the groundwork for their achievement.

William Aitken's last public appearance was at the ceremony laying the foundation stone for Josiah Mason's new college; after a few months, when he was visibly failing, he died in March 1875. Among prominent figures mourning at his funeral at Handsworth Old Church were J. H. Chamberlain, Sam: Timmins and Jesse Collings. Chamberlain designed the memorial of Portland stone, with three gables and with canopies filled with carving, foliage of English plants, the wild rose, columbine and hawthorn, in the same way that surfaces were later decorated on Chamberlain and Martin's iconic School of Art. The subject matter exemplified John Ruskin's instruction to imitate the beauty of the natural world; it also represented a practical example of high quality craftsmanship, something Aitken would indeed have appreciated. The inscription on the tomb said as much: 'He spent the best years of his life teaching men how work was rightly ennobled when thought was joined to labour and beauty to skill.'[172]

An article in the *Daily Post* nearly twenty years later, written at a time when the Birmingham School of Art and the city's technical education were the envy of the whole country, attempted to chart the journey whereby Birmingham became that model of aesthetic and cultural vitality for which George Dawson and his acolytes had worked. Back in the 1840s:

Matter of fact demand, and worship of bare utility in place of grace and elegance, prevailed. Articles of English manufacture were known everywhere for their soundness, but quite as much for their ugliness. Happily, this Spartan spirit left us, since when there has been a steady improvement in the beauty, shape and smoothness of Birmingham productions. The influence of truth in Art has penetrated deep into our commercial life.[173]

A good part of this radical transformation comprises Aitken's imperishable memory.

Chapter 7

John Davies Mullins

For 33 years, from May 1865 until June 1895, J.D. Mullins was the chief librarian in Birmingham. The central library, designed externally by E.M. Barry and internally by William Martin, was located to the west of the town hall, in Ratcliffe Place. Though his own day-to-day operations were in the reference library, Mullins also oversaw the librarians at the lending library and three lending libraries located across the town and, for a number of years, the honorary curator of the art gallery, which opened in a room in the central library in August 1867. Though he often encountered George Dawson at meetings of the free library committee, Mullins formed a particularly close association with Sam: Timmins and the two men were responsible for building up the collection of the reference library. This rose from 16,195 in 1866 to 44,519 on the eve of the great fire in 1879, which destroyed most of it. In 1869 'the ability, accuracy and patient industry displayed by Mr Mullins' led to the publication of the catalogue of the reference library.[174] After the fire Mullins was to begin again and produce – in parts – a new catalogue. With the reference and lending libraries intended to provide access for the working people of the town to any book 'of permanent value and standard interest' that they might conceivably want to read, the part played by Mullins – who is almost entirely forgotten – in translating the civic gospel from words into deeds should be recognised.[175]

John Davies Mullins was not Birmingham-born and revealed nothing about his early life apart the year and the place of his birth. He was born at 21 Capland Street in Marylebone in London on 23 November 1832 and baptised five years later. His parents were John and Susannah Mullins; his father, an omnibus driver, died in about 1841 and his mother, seemingly having left her children behind when she took up a new situation in Leicestershire, died in about 1845. Mullins managed to avoid the workhouse, but his two younger brothers did not; one of them in fact was to return in later life. It is not clear when Mullins arrived in Birmingham, but it must have been an attempt to begin a new life and in November 1854 he married a widow,

Harriet Godridge Friend, in Edgbaston. At that point he was a tailor. Mullins was clearly an autodidact and developed a deep love of books. Unlike other working men who educated themselves and became involved in literature – J.A.L. Langford, for example – this was not something Mullins wanted to talk about. Nor did he ever have any inclination to write anything himself.

In March 1858 Mullins was appointed librarian at the Birmingham Library (sometimes called the Old Library) in Union Street. He replaced William Alldritt, who had been librarian since the second decade of the century and retired with a pension of £75 per annum. The payment of this pension meant that Mullins' salary did not rise for five years from the £90 per annum on his appointment – it was increased by £25 per annum when his predecessor died in 1863. The Birmingham Library was a private institution, with its origins in the late eighteenth century, and was managed by a committee: Dawson, Timmins and Bunce were amongst those on the committee and the solicitor George Jabet was secretary (also for a time president). An annual subscription of 30s was paid by the proprietors. 'Their number, J.A.L. Langford wrote, 'was so small that they could scarcely have quarrelled had they been inclined.'[176] At the time of Mullins' arrival there were 531 proprietors – many with a habit of not returning the books they had borrowed. The committee prided itself on the quality of its reference library but knew that the number of subscriptions needed to be increased. An attempt was made – clearly somewhat reluctantly – in 1859 when a special fund was set up from which the committee was 'compelled to supply an unusual amount of light literature …'[177] The Birmingham Library remained a place 'of quietness, empty rooms and frigid gentility …'.[178]

With the prospect of competition from a public library – the town council embarked on the plan in May 1860 – and existing competition from Mudie's circulating library in New Street, the Birmingham Library decided to reorganise its operations. It absorbed a smaller library in Temple Row and created two categories of membership: subscribers paid an annual fee of one guinea and shareholders did the same but also bought shares at a cost of £2 each. This new arrangement 'saved the library'.[179] Within a year membership stood at 903 and each year continued to grow. With an income in excess of £1,000, more books could be purchased, and the committee was soon delighted that their stock amounted to 30,000.

Though Mullins did not regard his remuneration as sufficient and also disliked the accommodation provided for himself and his family in rooms below the library and moved out to a rented house, he enjoyed the work.[180] He was praised for his diligence and courtesy. 'Since Mr Mullins had filled the office,' Jabet observed, 'the library has been more successful than during the hundred years it had existed.'[181] On his departure a subscription amongst the shareholders raised enough to present him with £100 and 'a very handsome desk'.[182]

There were 32 applications for the post of chief librarian in Birmingham in 1865. These men were doubtless disappointed to find themselves described by the free libraries committee as 'not up to the standard they hoped to get …'.[183] The position offered a salary of £200 per annum, considerably more than Mullins was earning at the Birmingham Library. Three men were selected for discussion by the committee – Mullins, Edward Lings who managed the branch library opened on Constitution Hill in April 1861, and George McWhea who had been employed for six years at the Advocates Library in Edinburgh. It was an animated discussion, but Mullins' work in compiling the catalogue for the Birmingham Library proved decisive. He secured 32 votes from the committee, with Lings supported by twelve and McWhea by two. Shortly afterwards a sub-librarian and a number of assistants were appointed.

It was at the opening of the reference library on 26 October 1866 that George Dawson delivered the speech that, more than any other, defined the essential nobility of the civic gospel:

> One of the greatest and happiest things about this corporation library … [is that] … supported as it is by rates and administered by the corporation, it is the expression of a conviction on your part that a town exists for moral and intellectual purposes. A great town like this has not done all of its duty when it has put into action a set of ingenious contrivances for cleaning and lighting the streets … and has not fulfilled its highest function even when it has given the people of the town the best system of drainage …[184]

This must have been a moment of great personal pride for the tailor from Marylebone. He knew that he would be at the forefront of enacting the moral values for the governance of a town that Dawson had so brilliantly set out. From the beginning Mullins 'frequently noticed working men, fresh from labour, looking through the glass panels of the reference library with mingled admiration and wonder and then at their own persons and … go[ing] back and reappearing cleansed from the dirt the labour had left'.[185] Mullins was able to specify who was visiting the reference library. He reported, in 1870, that 1,301 engineers, 1,165 goldsmiths and jewellers, 945 engravers, 685 printers, and 628 brass founders (as well as large numbers of clerks, schoolmasters and 42 actors) had asked for books.

There were so many visitors that Mullins pressed successfully for the reference library to stay open an extra hour in the evening until 10 p.m. and also to open on Sunday afternoons and evenings. With purchases and donations (which included early editions of Don Quixote and other works by Cervantes), the stock of books in the reference library steadily increased. Within eight years, it had more than doubled, standing at 32,998 volumes by 1873. Housed in its own room, the Shakespeare Memorial Library was also expanding from its initial 1,239 volumes. The lending library was issuing over 500 books a day – with the *Memoirs of Joseph Grimaldi,* edited by Charles Dickens and *Principles of Political Economy* by J.S. Mill heavily in demand. Mullins declared that he 'supported the issue of high-class novels and intimated that, when any work got denounced in the pulpit, they had immediately to order an extra number of copies'.[186]

The most pressing task that awaited Mullins as the collection in the reference library built up was to produce a catalogue. This volume, 'most carefully and lovingly done,' appeared in April 1869, running to 380 pages, with twenty pages providing 'an excellent classification' of items relating to Shakespeare.[187] Shortly afterwards the part of the catalogue relating to the Shakespeare Memorial Library was issued separately. The catalogue was very much an expression of the civic gospel – it was 'not crowded with … special numbers useful only to the library itself', and readers were easily able to locate books by the author's name, by title and by subject area.[188] At a price of 4s to cover the cost of paper and printing, the catalogue was intended to be purchased by readers – though, as one correspondent pointed out, 'To working men 4s seems a heavy price for a mere catalogue'.[189] Mullins' catalogue received praise both local and nationally; he had, it was said, 'conferred honour on the town'.[190]

What was being done in Birmingham, Mullins believed, should be emulated in towns across the country – to assist in this, he produced *Free Libraries and News-Rooms: Their Formation and Management* (1870), his only publication.[191] Mullins was praised by the free libraries committee as 'a very excellent servant'.[192] Dawson described his management of the reference library as 'admirable … they had started this matter and Mr Mullins has carried it out'.[193] Before he left for a lecture tour in the United States in 1874, Dawson asked Mullins for a list of what he wanted and hoped that 'he might be able to bring back a good bag of honey'.[194] By 1877 Mullins' salary had reached £400 per annum – but he had lost his sub-librarian to the reference library in Glasgow. There were 'some difficulties' between him and his staff and, in December 1878, he resigned.[195] He could not be talked out of his decision but within weeks Mullins and the free library committee had something far more important to think about.

In the afternoon of Saturday 11 January 1879 – as a result of an accident whilst thawing frozen gas pipes – a fire broke out in the reference library which spread so rapidly that the destruction was extensive. The stark reality of what had happened became clear when it was discovered that only ten volumes of the 590 that made up the Cervantes collection and only 500 of the 7,000 in the Shakespeare Memorial Library had survived. About 10,000 volumes were carried out from the lending library. Neither the frantic efforts of readers handing buckets across the reference library nor, very soon after, the efforts of the fire brigade, had been able to stem the conflagration. Picking through the ruins the next day investigators came across books 'burnt almost to ashes and ... [which] fell to pieces as soon as they were touched'.[196] A devastated Mullins – who had been absent that afternoon as a result of ill health – supervised the retrieval of books that had not been lost. 'Ah, sir,' observed one workman, 'this would have broken George Dawson's heart.'[197]

The great fire of 1879 was the greatest setback the civic gospellers were to suffer – but they did not let it defeat them. The following Monday the free libraries committee announced that the library would be rebuilt 'on a scale of completeness worthy of the town' and a public subscription was launched to secure £10,000 to purchase books.[198] Immediately Joseph Chamberlain pledged £500 with another £1,000 'from a private fund at his disposal' – and donations began to flow in, amongst them collections amounting to a guinea from work people in factories.[199] Eventually the fund amounted to £15,197. An insurance payment of £20,045 met only part of the sum needed to rebuild the library, but this was not going to deter the civic gospellers. Within three months, plans for the new library had been drawn up. Mullins, no longer thinking of resigning, worked tirelessly to create a temporary home for the books that had survived in the Council House – which came into use that September. When the new library opened in June 1882, he handed the first book to be requested to the mayor Thomas Avery – a copy of the Shakespeare First Folio, purchased the previous November, and, now very appropriately stamped 'Birmingham Free Libraries'.[200]

At the heart of the revival of the reference library was Timmins. His donations and the purchase of the greater part of his collection relating to Shakespeare and Birmingham for a sum well below its worth was probably the greatest personal gesture of any of the civic gospellers. Mullins strove relentlessly to build up the Shakespeare Memorial Library, offering to exchange duplicates from the collection for items he was searching for, sending off telegrams if something important came on the market. By 1894 the collection embraced 9,302 items. Within five years the number of books in the reference library had also increased tenfold. Amongst the acquisitions were replacements for the volumes by Cervantes that had been lost in 1879. By 1889 there were 99,050 books in the reference library, almost a quarter of them donations.

Mullins set to work on compiling a catalogue – or 'index finding book', as he had taken to calling it – of the collection.[201] It required painstaking work over a number of years and was released in parts as it was completed. The section from A to C was on sale from January 1886, and the final section was published in August 1890. The entire catalogue was published as a single volume, running to 1,300 pages, in December 1890, along with a separate listing of the items in the Shakespeare Memorial Library. Mullins' work was very well received, but his health was deteriorating. In summer 1889 he took leave of absence, spending some of it in Llandudno, when his health was reported to be 'in a very unsatisfactory state'.[202] He was never to fully recover his health. In summer and autumn 1894 he was again unfit to work due to paralysis of the lower limbs. Somehow, he struggled on at the reference library for another four years, retiring with a pension in June 1898. Mullins' retirement did not last long. He died at his home in Handsworth on 27 May 1900. At his graveside the minister paid tribute to a man who had sought 'to influence for the best ... [and] direct ... the thought of the people aright'.[203] Two of his sons attended his funeral, but his wife did not; she died eight years later. Given his start in life, Mullins' rise to become chief librarian of Birmingham was by any standard remarkable.

John Davies Mullins did not preach any sermons and did not seek election to the town council. It was said that this deeply private man was not a public man,[204] but he was in the way that he wanted: he played a key role in putting into practice the civic gospel.

Chapter 8

Samuel Timmins

For almost forty years, from 23 April 1853 to 23 April 1889, fifty or so gentlemen would sit down to dinner in a hotel in Birmingham to mark the anniversary of the birth of William Shakespeare.[205] These members and guests of Our Shakespeare Club would eat their suppers, listen to glees and a speech and raise their glasses, usually in silence, to 'The Immortal Memory of Shakespeare'. On these occasions George Dawson acted as chairman and his close friend Samuel Timmins (1826-1903) acted as vice-chairman. It was the chairman – who, after Dawson's death, was Timmins – who delivered the speech. These two men were the closest of friends. A love for Shakespeare ran deep in Dawson; in Timmins it ran even deeper.

Timmins read and re-read the plays. 'The more he studied', he noted, 'the more he found to study ....'[206] To his audiences he referred to Shakespeare as 'the greatest Englishman', 'the greatest name in literature' and repeatedly as a 'genius'.[207] He was never short of things to say because 'Shakespeare's chalice was ever full ... even bubbling to the brim ... they could always find in it some of the great wine of life they delighted to enjoy'.[208] At the heart of Timmins' love for Shakespeare was that he was 'a poet of the people ... he saw more clearly and expressed more vividly than any other poet what related to the life and character and happiness of men and women ...'.[209] No man in Birmingham knew more about the work of Shakespeare and of his commentators than Timmins and it is no exaggeration to say that no man in the town loved the poet as ardently as he did.

Born in Birmingham on 27 February 1826, Samuel Timmins did not hail from a family noted for its literary interests. His father Samuel and his two uncles Richard and Joseph manufactured heavy steel 'toys' – actually tools – at premises in Hurst Street. The business had been founded in 1790 by his grandfather Richard Timmins. Sam: Timmins – as he was known to differentiate himself from his father – always knew that he would eventually join the family business. With this in mind, his father sent him to Edgbaston Proprietary School in Hagley Road when it opened in January

1838. The headmaster was John Ryall and there were seven other masters. A foundation principle of the school was that there was to be no corporal punishment, which was deemed to be 'objectionable and degrading', and the boys were managed instead by a system of 'strict moral discipline'.[210] Timmins' father paid £15 per annum for his son to be taught commerce, Greek, Latin, French, mathematics, drawing, singing and dancing. Outside his classes Timmins began to read the great works of literature. He was drawn into Burns and Byron and particularly Shakespeare. He was soon learning by heart lengthy passages from their work. For the rest of his life Timmins was able to quote from memory from all the plays of Shakespeare.

It is clear from the letters he sent to a local newspaper during a lengthy visit to Italy and Greece in 1847-8 that Timmins, at 21, was an erudite and intellectually curious young man.[211] His reports were very observational, full of detail and classical knowledge and interspersed with quotations from poetry. Crossing the English Channel, he passed through Paris, Marseilles, Genoa and Florence before arriving in Rome. With his companions he thoroughly explored the city, admiring the 'wonderful' and 'superb' art and an 'immense number of handsome women', enjoying the 'very cheap' wine and avoiding the carriages whose drivers were 'very reckless'.[212] To his delight, he met an American artist who was inspired by the work of Shakespeare. In Athens Timmins ascended the Acropolis to see the sun set and was 'powerfully excited' when he visited the cell where Socrates died; the coffee, he noted, was 'uncommonly good'.[213] Byron was on Timmins' mind in Greece, but when he returned to Venice he paid tribute to his first literary love and 'paced the very ground and breathed the very atmosphere in which Shylock moved'. [214]

The exhilaration of his youthful adventures in Italy and Greece were to draw Timmins back in future years. He gave talks relating to the places he had visited to working-class audiences at the Polytechnic Institute in Steelhouse Lane and other venues. These years of his early manhood saw him choose the life he wanted to lead. He had grown increasingly troubled by the Sunday morning visits to the Carr's Lane chapel of John Angell James that his father had introduced him to. Whilst R.W. Dale found James' preaching mesmerising, Timmins found it rigid and suffocating. Breaking free did not come without difficulty, but shortly after Dawson was installed at the Church of the Saviour in 1846, Timmins joined the congregation. It was the beginning of a friendship that was to last almost thirty years. Timmins' relationship with Dawson was founded on a deep sense of gratitude that he was allowed to think in the way that he wanted to. Timmins also decided to marry. Anne Maria Nock was the companion of one of his aunts, and their marriage took place in near secrecy in the middle of a working day in July 1848 at the Birmingham register office. The only child of the marriage, George Dawson Timmins, died 'after a few days of illness' in May 1858, aged three years.[215]

With the deaths of Samuel and Richard Timmins, Sam: Timmins and another family member Edwin Griffiths joined Joseph Timmins as partners in the steel toys business.[216] Proud of the quality of their products, everything that left Hurst Street was marked 'R.T. & Sons'. The enterprise was certainly thriving: the first decision that the new partnership made was to expand their premises into Pershore Road. Until it was sold in 1887, the business, which employed about 70 men, provided Timmins with an income that enabled him to purchase, over the years, thousands of antiquarian books. 'My new library is finished,' he later informed a friend, '& now will not hold half my books! It is vexing; I had no idea I had such a lot! They have overflowed into another room & as far as I can see they will nearly fill that.'[217] Timmins was known for his active involvement in his business, on occasion donning an apron and joining his workforce on the shop floor. He was always ready, however, to receive visitors who wanted to talk not about hammers or coal tongs but about Shakespeare.

Timmins was a talented speaker, able to tailor how he addressed an audience to suit the occasion. Like many of the civic gospellers, he honed his speaking skills at the meetings of the Birmingham and Edgbaston Debating Society at the Hen and Chickens Hotel in New Street, where the participants 'advised the municipal authorities … settled disputed points of history and … arranged the right order of rank to be taken by poets and novelists'.[218] Each November Timmins appeared on platforms to deliver powerful political punches in support of Liberal candidates. He offered this withering assessment of the Tory 'Bible Eight' who came forward in the school board elections in 1870:

Referring to the meeting held the previous evening in the town hall in support of scriptural education in the new schools, he said that, although he respected the chairman of that meeting, he could not help saying that he had contrived to talk as much illogical nonsense as he had ever seen in a single column in a newspaper … He should like to ask some of those gentlemen who talked so much about the Bible whether they had ever read it or whether they knew anything of its contents. He advised the ratepayers to keep away from the eight gentlemen who had been chosen by themselves … [they] were eight nobodies. One of them that had been selected, or who had selected himself, and whose name was Cooper had a head that seemed as empty as the barrels he made .... Some of them had talked about the part they had taken in education – they cackled like a hen with one egg.[219]

When he was speaking about Shakespeare, Timmins turned from beautiful language to energetic role play:

Besides ... [his] perfect mastery over his subject, Mr Timmins is gifted with a fluency, a vivacity and originality of idea and power of illustration seldom equalled. We observed at the commencement that he had not even a note of what he had to say and yet, during the hour and a half which his very interesting lecture lasted, in no instance did he hesitate or repeat himself .... The first division of the lecture consisted of a brief notice of all that is undisputed in the biography of Shakespeare ... [and] the second part a charming and critical review of the principal characters in [the plays] .... The glorious passage from 'The Merchant of Venice', put into the mouth of Portia, 'The quality of mercy is not strained', was rendered by Mr Timmins with true pathos and great dramatic effect; while his impersonation of Dogberry in his charge to the watch in the third act of 'Much Ado About Nothing' and of Bottom in the third act of 'Midsummer Night's Dream' was replete with vigour of conception, truth and humour.[220]

Timmins strongly believed that what he knew and what he loved should be shared with the people of Birmingham. He refused payment for any talk that he gave. From 1856 until 1866 he and Dawson taught classes on English Language and Literature at the Birmingham and Midland Institute, initially on Saturday mornings and later on weekday evenings. Timmins also contributed to the lecture programme. In 1860 he lectured on 'Childe Harold', reciting extemporaneously lengthy passages from the poem, and on the controversial John Payne Collier, who fabricated evidence about Shakespeare's life and work. In 1868, for the penny lectures series, Timmins spoke about notable figures from Birmingham's past – the antiquarian William Hutton, the schoolmaster Thomas Hill and the men associated with the famous Soho Works.[221] He was deeply interested in 'Our Old Town', urging the preservation of its records and doing much to help with this himself by building up an impressive collection of prints, drawings and maps which he put on display at his lectures. Timmins also lent his support to the Sunday Evening Lecture Society. He informed a speaker that he would act as chairman at his talk about Burns 'on condition I did not abuse the poet'. When informed that this lecture had made a profit of only 2d, Timmins cheerfully replied, 'Well, you ought to give me that for a pint'.[222]

Our Shakespeare Club grew out of the annual dinners to mark the poet's birthday that had commenced in 1853 at the Acorn Hotel in Temple Street.[223] It was formed in about 1860, though it did not immediately settle on a name. There were fifteen to twenty members in these early years, amongst them Dawson, Timmins, Bunce, Harris, J.H. Chamberlain, C.E. Matthews and Sebastian Evans. There was no subscription and funds were raised by half crown fines for non-attendance at meetings; the cost of the annual dinner was covered equally by a 'call for the reckoning'. The meetings on the first Saturday of each month were held in the smoke room of the Union Hotel in Union Street. The aim was to have a small enough membership to promote relaxed discussion – something not possible at second-hand bookshops where they often arranged to meet or at the numerously-attended events at the Birmingham and Midland Institute. It was, Dawson observed at a soiree in April 1864, 'a club probably unknown to most present'.[224]

As a student of Shakespeare, Timmins was invited to examine what was claimed to be a newly discovered portrait of the poet in the possession of the town clerk of Stratford-upon-Avon, William Oakes Hunt. Timmins' observations weren't recorded, but the portrait was soon attributed to an artist working in the eighteenth century. At this time Timmins also arranged with a local printer, Josiah Allen, to release a volume which brought together the first two editions of 'Hamlet' which were in the possession of the Duke of Devonshire.[225] Doubtless his fellow enthusiasts in the club pored over this carefully constructed volume, but their minds were also turning to how the tercentenary of Shakespeare's birth in 1864 might be marked. A dinner alone would not be good enough, and Dawson and Timmins objected in unison to a statue, 'those miserable things to which the people of Birmingham ... have been subjected,' in Timmins' words.[226] In a letter to a local newspaper in spring 1861, Dawson announced that a library consisting of all the editions of Shakespeare's plays and all works written about him and portraits of him should be established in Birmingham. Such a library, he wrote, was 'a favourite plan of mine' and he would 'make over to it the best part of my Shakesperean books'.[227] A modest man who liked to work behind the scenes, Timmins never claimed credit for what was in fact his idea – set out at the annual dinner held at the King's Head in Worcester Street in April 1858.[228]

He assured himself that he had advanced the idea in private whereas Dawson had made the public announcement – and the proposal would have more impact if it came from Dawson. In June 1862 members of the club assembled at the Greswolde Arms in Knowle to form a committee to arrange a subscription and promises of books on the understanding that the town council would provide a designated room, and a year later, at a meeting at the Philosophical Institute in Cannon Street, the fund was formally announced with Timmins and J. H. Chamberlain as secretaries and John Jaffray as treasurer. In the two years which followed, Timmins was to be involved in everything, both big and small, that led to the establishment of the Shakespeare Memorial Library.

The celebrations in Birmingham that marked the tercentenary took place over two days. Our Shakespeare Club arranged a soiree at Nock's Hotel for the evening of 22 April. As the guests arrived, they were welcomed by members of the club who were each wearing a blue ribbon embroidered with yellow silk which had been specially designed for the evening by J. H. Chamberlain. There were women present, for it would have been 'most ungracious, unthankful and barbarous' to restrict the event to men only; it was what Shakespeare would have wanted, Dawson continued, in a speech explaining how the poet was 'their best friend because he understood them better than any other man that had ever lived'.[229] The guests were able to admire an illuminated bust of Shakespeare and cartoons of many of his characters drawn by Sebastian Evans as well as savour a cantata written by Evans and Thomas Anderton and a reading of the first act of 'The Tempest' by the well-known Shakesperean actor Samuel Phelps. If Timmins went to bed at Nock's that night a deeply contented man, he woke the next morning an excited man, knowing that his long-cherished vision of bringing Shakespeare to the people was on the cusp of being realised.

At a breakfast at Nock's on 23 April the books that had been donated or purchased to form the beginnings of the Shakespeare Memorial Library along with £450 were presented to the mayor, William Holliday. It was already a considerable collection, with substantial contributions from Dawson and Timmins.[230] The greatest treasure was an edition of the Fourth Folio. The books were to be placed a room designed by J. H. Chamberlain, though its completion was slowed down by a strike by workmen. That evening's toast at the annual dinner to 'The Immortal Memory of Shakespeare' must have been all the sweeter for Timmins. In London, Glasgow, Liverpool and other places the tercentenary had been marked by performances of the plays and plans to secure a bust. In Birmingham it had been marked by the opening of a library. Timmins' achievement was declared to be 'a memorial to Shakespeare and an honour to Birmingham'.[231]

The Shakespeare Memorial Library opened on 23 April 1868. It was supported financially by the free libraries committee. However, there were also subscribers who provided between £50 and £80 annually for the purchase of books. Timmins served as secretary of the committee and had great influence over additions to the collection. In effect the final decision was his. The number of books rose steadily: 1,239 in 1868, 4,117 in 1872 and 6,279 in 1876. Timmins made use of London antiquarian booksellers to get the books he desired. In 1870 copies of the Second Folio and the Third Folio were acquired from Sotheran & Co. and Bernard Quaritch offered a copy of the First Folio for £520. 'The volume … is locked up and the key in my pocket', he wrote to Timmins. 'A volume like that cannot be shown to everybody.'[232] Though a fund to purchase this item was set up, to which Joseph Chamberlain contributed £50, it was deemed to be an excessive sum and the purchase was 'not … very urgently pressed'.[233]

Donations came in from across Europe, but Timmins believed that the links with the United States were not as strong as they needed to be. In 1873 he recruited Joseph Parker Norris of Philadelphia to promote the library and secure scarce items. Norris was not paid for his work but used a grant – £20 in 1874 – to make purchases. It became, by letter, a lengthy and close association. 'I shall be grateful if you can buy us all that you can & as soon as possible,' Timmins wrote to Norris. 'Such an addition will be a great feature in our next year's Report of S.M.L. because all will be new not only in our Library but on this side [of] the water generally.'[234] In 1883 Timmins declared himself, in the absence of an attested portrait, to be 'rather nervous' but 'strongly in favour' of a proposal from Norris that Shakespeare's tomb should be opened for photographs to be taken of his remains.[235] To Timmins' great gratification there was a regular stream of visitors from Birmingham and beyond to inspect the Shakespeare collection. He was delighted when the leading German scholar Nicolaus Delius arrived in spring 1873 and 'expressed his astonishment'.[236] When fire swept through the reference library in January 1879 consuming most of its contents, Timmins was seen sobbing; he was indeed 'the saddest man in the whole of Birmingham'.[237]

Though he was a man free from vanity, Timmins must have been moved by the acclamation that he received for his work in establishing the reference library and the Shakespeare room. With Dawson in the chair and his friends from Our Shakespeare Club in attendance, he returned to Nock's Hotel in December 1866 for a dinner at which he was presented with a portrait of himself painted by W.T. Roden, who produced many portraits of Birmingham men. When he walked into the reference library, he encountered a bust of himself. He was also elected a Fellow of the Society of Antiquaries and of the Royal Society of Literature and a member of the

German Shakespeare Society and of the Shakespeare Society of New York.

No Birmingham man knew George Dawson better than Sam: Timmins. It was an intimate friendship. When Dawson died suddenly at the end of 1876, the internment at Key Hill, as he had requested, was private. Only those who had been issued with a ticket were admitted to the cemetery. Timmins, of course, was there. Within days he let it be known that he would prepare 'some account of the public life of Mr Dawson ... a memorial volume'.[238] The book never appeared. It was later stated that the manuscript had been destroyed during a fire at the printers. For five months there was no public utterance about his friend from Timmins. He decided to wait until Shakespeare's birthday to pay tribute. Dawson's devotion to the poet, he observed, 'was founded on his love for one who loved so much. His heart, which knew no humanity, rejoiced in one so greatly human and the basis of his reverence for Shakespeare was his own reverence for man.'[239]

At the end of 1883 Timmins decided that his health would benefit if he found a quieter place to live where fewer demands would be made on him. He moved to Hill Cottage in Arley, near Coventry. It was a village with a few hundred inhabitants but did have a railway station. The man who had played such an important role in building up the reference library so that it had become 'one of the best and most admirable ... in the country, not even excepting the metropolis and the universities' arranged for 6,000 of his books about Shakespeare and the history of Birmingham to be placed in its care, accepting £1,100 in return, a price significantly below their value.[240] He also donated another 500 volumes. Timmins offered his resignation as a member of the free libraries committee, but it was refused. His links with his life's work were not entirely broken. When, in summer 1889, the executors of the will of the Shakespeare biographer James Hailwell Phillips offered to the Shakespeare Memorial Library his collection of portraits and documents for £7,000, Timmins examined them and recommended their purchase.

In the tranquillity of his cottage Timmins was able to write *A History of Warwickshire* (1889). It demonstrated the breadth of his knowledge of the county, with chapters not just on the historical story but also on topography, geology, botany and folklore. Curiously for such an erudite man, it was the only book-length study he ever wrote. Timmins preferred to answer readers' queries on historical and literary matters for local newspapers and to do editorial work – for, most notably, *The Resources, Products and Industrial History of Birmingham and the Midland Hardware District* (1866). In 1894 Timmins issued privately a short account of Our Shakespeare Club. The following year, with most of its founders now dead, he resigned as president and as a member of the club, refusing to change his mind.

In a felt hat and an Inverness cape and clutching a pipe, Timmins was a very recognisable figure in Birmingham. He was often seen making a beeline for the second-hand bookshops of the town – that of William Downing in Temple Row was an especial favourite of the civic gospellers. The man in the battered hat, Sam: Timmins, was instrumental in establishing the reference library, for which he had 'robbed his own bookshelves for the benefit of the Birmingham public', and, without him, there would have been no Shakespeare collection.[241] The journalist Eliezer Edwards observed that the town was in debt not only to 'the powerful stimulus of Mr Dawson's teaching … [but also] to Mr Timmins for giving effect to Mr Dawson's principles in a way which, from his frequent absences from Birmingham and his dislike of detail, it was impossible for Mr Dawson himself to so'.[242]

A fellow member of Our Shakespeare Club noted:

That Timmins is a very uncommon man no one who possesses the least knowledge of his ways and thoughts can deny … He is undoubtedly a great man of literature … The excellence of Timmins is marked by his modesty. Ask him for information on any point and in giving it you – for I never knew him to fail – he will make it appear as if you were already in possession of half the answer … His sense of humour is delicious … Timmins … has always a story to tell. You meet him … He does not ask you how you are, not he, he simply says abruptly, 'I say, I've such a good story' … It was a great grief to him when the local fair disappeared. The fat woman, the living skeleton, the two-headed nightingale – all visited, no opportunity for a thoughtful study despised. To this love of queer things in medicine, he has equally a sympathy with legal crookedness. Remarkable trials fascinate him, and he has power for most minute and most able dissection of circumstantial evidence.[243]

After the death of his wife in October 1901, Timmins returned to Birmingham, living in seclusion in Clarence Road in King's Heath. By this time, he was suffering from dementia. He died on 12 November 1902 and was buried in Key Hill cemetery. There were no flowers apart from a bunch of rosemary from the garden of Shakespeare's birthplace, which was placed on his grave. Attached to it was a card bearing a quotation from 'Hamlet': 'There's rosemary; that's for remembrance.'[244]

Chapter 9

John Henry Chamberlain

O nly his namesake Joseph Chamberlain did more than the architect J. H. Chamberlain (1831-1883) to implement the civic gospel in Birmingham. He gave its tenets distinctive physical form, and by the end of the nineteenth century municipal buildings from baths, fire stations and board schools to an Art Gallery and School of Art, all built in Venetian Gothic and coloured in terracotta and tile, had transformed the city. After his sudden and shocking death in October 1883, Joseph Chamberlain gave a moving tribute at a Council House meeting to discuss a memorial:

> When I first knew Birmingham it was the ugliest of provincial towns; if we have attained anything like a right conception of what is beautiful and seemly in public and corporate life we owe this appreciation very largely to this eloquent teacher, who never spared himself in telling how labour may be lightened, and life brightened by elevation, by education and by the development of the higher faculties of our nature.[245]

What he chose to emphasise about J. H. Chamberlain's legacy is highly significant, for it echoed so exactly the teaching of George Dawson. Indeed, Joseph Chamberlain goes on to underline that influence for he says that J. H. Chamberlain 'was one of those who admitted to the full obligation which a man owes to the community in which his lot is cast'. Dawson had appealed to the wealthy, the business and educated classes, to put their talents to the benefit of the whole community and the architect responded in full measure. The wider success of that appeal invigorated Birmingham's municipal government as industrialists and professionals offered themselves up to public service from the middle of the century onwards.[246]

J. H. Chamberlain joined Dawson's church congregation when he first arrived in Birmingham in 1856 aged 25, and the two men became close personal friends. From what he writes in 1879, in a very personal *Appreciation* of a recently departed George Dawson, we learn what the minister meant to him.[247] George Dawson's

> chief knowledge was the human heart and his chief delight was in humanity …. He taught from his earliest lesson to his latest breath that to each and every one there was the possibility of noble life, of brave deeds and usefulness to all.
>
> [And, germane to Chamberlain's own mission to democratise Art, Dawson had said that] beauty and Art were not the private right of the rich and powerful but ought to be common to all. He taught that Art was not a secret and its fruits could not be too widely spread or too universally enjoyed.

Here are the principles which Chamberlain's buildings would enshrine. Roy Hartnell has described how he would come to see 'every new building as an opportunity to enrich and to inform the lives of all who saw it, and that the encounter between the building and the user should be a stimulating and uplifting experience'.[248] So, Chamberlain's buildings were didactic in intention.

Dawson was a passionate, eloquent and brilliant speaker, but for Chamberlain his teaching about art and aesthetics had still greater resonance because Dawson was an enthusiastic mediator and disciple of John Ruskin, the art critic, philosopher and radical social commentator. When Dawson talked of the importance of artistic truth to nature, and of art mirroring God's glory, he was channelling Ruskin, who had been a profound influence on Chamberlain since his boyhood, long before his arrival in Birmingham. He joined Dawson's congregation already deeply in thrall to Ruskin's *Seven Lamps of Architecture*, published in May 1849, where he read that 'Architecture is the art which so disposes and adorns the edifices raised by man that the sight of them may contribute to his mental health, power and pleasure'.[249] Just as education and sanitary reforms would improve the lives of Birmingham's citizens, so he learnt that architecture could inspire and elevate them too. The impact of Ruskin and Dawson can be discerned in Chamberlain's speech at the mayoral luncheon in July 1881 which celebrated the laying of the inscription stone for the new Municipal Art Gallery:

> What Art could do (he said) was to enlarge human life, make it wider and brighter and better and to give to men and women, even down to the very poorest, a greater pleasure in every hour they spent. [250]

Ruskin gave him more than a philosophical justification for beautiful architecture. His *Stones of Venice* made of Chamberlain a life-long convert to the virtues of Gothic architecture and he travelled to Italy himself to make his own drawings of the Venetian palaces which had inspired his mentor. In so doing he came to intuit what had transported Ruskin himself, the variety, the changefulness, the naturalism, the adaptability of the Gothic form. For Ruskin had written that

> Gothic is not only the best, but the only Rational architecture, as being that which can fit itself most easily to all services, vulgar or noble. Undefined in its slope of roof, height of shaft, breadth of arch or disposition of ground plan, it can shrink into a turret, expand into a hall, coil into a staircase or spring into a tower ... subtle and flexible like a serpent.[251]

Understandably, then, Chamberlain's early commissions when he started out in Birmingham in the late 1850s were executed in Gothic form, with polychromatic surfaces, utilising coloured and patterned brickwork and encaustic tile, as for example at Shenstone House, Edgbaston (1856). And when he eventually formed a partnership with William Martin, and municipal commissions flooded in from that tight network of Liberal civic gospellers to which he belonged (see below), he found that, just as Ruskin had predicted, Gothic answered to every need.

For it proved remarkably flexible when designing buildings for which there was little precedent before the nineteenth century (baths, pumping stations, even the new board schools) and 'they were able to deploy the language of gable, buttress, lancet window, tower and apse to achieve endless variety'. Indeed, every one of J. H. Chamberlain's twenty-nine board schools was different, even if all had the characteristic ventilation towers, which added stature and presence to buildings representing in every quarter of Birmingham that serious municipal ambition to educate and improve its citizens.[252] Unsurprisingly Chamberlain found himself designing houses for members of that close Liberal clique with whom he sat on a wide variety of Birmingham committees – so he built Highbury for Joseph Chamberlain, Harborne Hall for Walter Chamberlain and The Grove for William Kenrick, each in colourful Venetian gothic with asymmetrical facades, and a wealth of naturalistic motifs. Furthermore, he would have the satisfaction of designing some of the most significant buildings to express Birmingham's civic gospel, buildings for organisations in whose governance he played an important part.

Thus, he and Martin designed the extension to his beloved Birmingham and Midland Institute in 1877, rebuilt the reference library from 1879 after the traumatic fire which destroyed the original building, also rebuilt the Shakespeare Memorial Library at the same time and, as a crowning glory, planned the new School of Art before the completion of which he died in 1883. This would be his finest achievement, still visible today on Margaret and Edmund Streets, and incorporating all Chamberlain's characteristic features of red brick, unequal gables, lancet windows, decorated tiles and carvings of acanthus and other intertwined flora. When to these significant commissions are added the board schools, the central fire station, police stations, the lunatic asylum, public baths and pumping stations, it may truly be said that J. H. Chamberlain re-shaped Birmingham's appearance in the last decades of the nineteenth century. Joseph Chamberlain's extension of municipal power and pretension in the 1870s materialised in Chamberlain and Martin's statement edifices, consciously emulating the glories of the great Renaissance republics of Florence, Siena and Venice and intended to engender a sense of civic pride, celebrating the organic unity of the whole community, just as Dawson had envisioned. That pride was the greater for the shared knowledge that in addition to the gifts of wealthy Birmingham citizens – the Tangyes and the Rylands for example who funded the School of Art – these buildings had been financed either by the subscriptions of hundreds of members (for instance the Institute) or by citizens' rates, as with the municipal facilities like baths and police stations, or the profits of municipal enterprise, in the case of the municipal Gas department's £40,000 subsidy to the building of a new Art Gallery.

Yet this was not by any means the limit to J. H. Chamberlain's contribution to the artistic expression of the civic gospel. Chamberlain quoted Dawson in his *Appreciation* as saying that:

> The root of Art lay in the power of seeing the beauty of the Universe … and that all things that are made by human hands ought to be made beautiful, and that all human work that is devoid of beauty was to some extent base and useless.

John Ruskin, too, became increasingly critical of industrial mass production and advocated a return to a golden age of individual craftsmanship, an idea he promoted in *Fors Clavigera*.[253] In 1877 he founded a quasi-medieval, co-operative brotherhood (the Guild of St George), which was to be a model of how workers could live together in a post-industrial age, removed from the pernicious influence (as he saw it) of Victorian conurbations. The concept was realised only on a small scale in the Wyre Forest community at Beaucastle, on land gifted by a Birmingham civic gospeller George Baker, and J. H. Chamberlain was an early member, joining Ruskin there at its very beginning.[254]

Chamberlain also believed that working-class life would be improved by a focus on the dignity of craftsmanship, and he set out to implement Ruskin's principles. He was in a powerful position to do so; as chairman of the School of Art he promoted the claims of Edward Taylor to be headmaster, a man committed to reforming the school curriculum to ensure artists and designers had the chance to realise their designs in practice. Even more importantly he helped bring William Morris to Birmingham to be president of the School. Morris's lectures espoused 'art made by the people and for the people'; it was to a Birmingham town hall audience in 1880 that Morris made his famous remark: 'Have nothing in your house that you do not know to be useful, or believe to be beautiful.'[255] In fact, thanks to Chamberlain and his close friend William Kenrick, Morris came to be a long-lasting and profound influence on Birmingham culture. A school of artists emerged which made the city the foremost centre of the Arts and Crafts movement.

George Dawson had talked to his followers of the need for a moral and intellectual reformation long before his famous and oft-quoted speech at the opening of Birmingham's free reference library in 1866. How J. H. Chamberlain responded to that message was every bit as important as his aesthetic contribution. From early in his time in Birmingham he had become a founder member with George Dawson, and joint honorary secretary, of the committee set up in 1863 to bring to fruition Timmins and Dawson's vision for a Shakespeare Memorial Library. It would assemble a comprehensive collection of folios and critical writings on Warwickshire's very own bard, for the benefit of all Birmingham's citizens. Chamberlain evidently subscribed to Dawson's belief 'that one of the highest offices of civilisation is to determine how to give access to the masterpieces of art and literature to the whole people'.[256] Not only was he an energetic and meticulous administrator but in his long service to the Memorial Library he also utilised his professional skills, in 1879 designing and planning the rebuilt library, as previously mentioned.

For his obituarist J. T. Bunce in October 1883 it was his eighteen years as honorary secretary of the Birmingham and Midland Institute which comprised 'the greatest labour of his life'.[257] Chamberlain joined the Institute not long after its inception, fully endorsing its Dawsonian precepts of diffusing and advancing science, literature and the arts amongst all citizens.[258] But the early momentum provided by Arthur Ryland (q.v.

chapter 3) had slowed and Chamberlain immediately brought imagination and a new drive. Indeed, he was often dubbed the Institute's 'second founder'.[259] Successive *Reports of the BMI Council presented at the Annual Meeting* record a story of unbroken growth. In the 1883 report Bunce paid tribute to the achievement of a man whose death was 'a calamity':

> His great work in education was the revival, the re-organisation, the development and the firm establishment of the Midland Institute .... He knew the working of every class and every worker and promising student in them. He inspired his colleagues with his own intense affection for the Institution, and by force of his example he compelled the labour of all to render help to the Institute.[260]

Elsewhere the report baldly noted the facts behind the 'truly marvellous development' he inspired: from 660 members in 1865 there were 2,500 in 1883; 24 classes in 1865 had become 133 in 1883; and the number of students had risen from 880 to 4,554. The Institute's annual lectures – which, Bunce averred, 'he raised from the condition of decay to one of excellence' – became a national event, given by important Victorian writers, clerics, politicians, while he also founded and popularised an annual *Conversazione*, attended by nearly 1,000 patrons, and intended both to raise Institute funds but also to instruct on scientific matters, as well as to entertain musically. He was able to secure a succession of distinguished figures to be the Institute's President, personally persuading Charles Dickens to accept the role in 1869, and proceeding to attract such as Lyon Playfair, John Morley, Dean Stanley and Charles Kingsley. In another initiative he acted on George Dawson and Samuel Timmins' suggestion in 1866 to establish morning classes for women, those for English being taught by Dawson and Timmins themselves. He was equally conscious of the need to avoid the Institute becoming a middle-class monopoly; it would have been satisfying to hear Charles Dickens in his Inaugural Address (September 1869) comment that: 'It is a cheering sign of the Institute's vigorous vitality that of its industrial students almost one half are artisans.'[261]

Dawson had taught his followers that the civic gospel involved not just a refurbishing of the environment, but the education and inspiration of all citizens; the Institute was one of the means by which Birmingham spread adult educational opportunity. The Institute building – the extension of which was the work of Chamberlain himself – housed facilities for scientific, technical, artistic, and musical as well as general education. J. H. Chamberlain established it as the most famous institution of its kind in Victorian England. He was equally significant in his chairmanship of the School of Art committee charting a new course in which it became the first and foremost municipal art school in the land. His dynamism inspired its growth (in terms of student numbers), and he was furthermore a powerful advocate for its transfer from the Institute's buildings to its own site. Inevitably he was on the committee which planned and executed the erection of a great new Municipal Art Gallery opening in July 1881 and no doubt to his satisfaction realising George Dawson's vision, enunciated in 1866, that 'the moment you put great works of Art into the hands of the corporate body like this you secure permanence of guardianship ... [to open] precious collections to the multitude'.[262]

When J. T. Bunce wrote in 1883 that 'there is hardly a department of our Birmingham life in which for nearly thirty years we fail to find traces of him', he was thinking not just of his considerable aesthetic contribution, and that to the BMI, but also of his service as a Justice of the Peace, as a long-standing Vice-President of the Society of Artists, a trustee of Ruskin's Guild of St George, as local Secretary of the British Association for the Advancement of Science, and as Professor of Architecture at Queen's College. His obituary hinted that his workload contributed to his early death: 'the strenuousness ... gave [him] no time for repose.'[263] It was especially poignant that he should have died of a heart attack minutes after the exertion of delivering a lively and well-received talk on 'Exotic Art' at his beloved Institute.

Making every allowance for Victorian sentimentality it is clear from the 'imposing character ... the great crowd assembled ... the thronged streets' on the occasion of his funeral that J. H. Chamberlain was widely esteemed and, among the inner circle who formed a memorial committee immediately after (including Bunce, Joseph Chamberlain, Kenrick, R.F. Martineau, Timmins, Harris, Dale, Jaffray and Richard Tangye), held in great affection for (in Joseph Chamberlain's words) 'his brilliancy of conversation, tenderness of wit, and self-devotion', and as a recognition of his enormous contribution to evangelising the civic gospel's mission in Birmingham.[264] William Harris put it very well in his tribute to J. H. Chamberlain in his *History of Our Shakespeare Club*, of which he and Chamberlain were both members:

His special function and duty was the promotion – one might always say creation – in the town of a love of Art and of an appreciation of its influence in the refinement, culture and elevation of character and thereby in the extension of the highest kind of enjoyment in all classes of society. With what incessant zeal he prosecuted this purpose is a part of the history of this town.[265]

Chapter 10

Marie Bethell Beauclerc

Nicola Gauld

Marie Bethell Beauclerc (1845-1897) is rightly credited as an important member of the Dawson circle and was integral to the recording of George Dawson's lectures, sermons and prayers, but she was also highly significant in her own right, a woman who, against all the odds, went on to become an early proponent and pioneer of Pitman shorthand in Birmingham, a popular and well-liked educator of adults and children, and arguably the first female reporter in England. Not only were her notes from the Dawson lectures essential to their preservation, but the quality was of the highest level, confirmed by one of her editors: 'When a lecture is reported by Miss Beauclerc ... we have a near approach to fullness and accuracy.'[266] In her teaching at the Birmingham & Midland Institute, she:

> identified herself ... from the beginning with so rare a self-devotion, and so complete an absence of all thought for her own leisure or convenience, that they can never be quite the same to any who had the privilege of being counted among her students and her friends.[267]

Beauclerc was dedicated, diligent and motivated, popular and highly respected by colleagues. Her talents ensured that she achieved great career success at a time when that was not expected of women.

Born Maria Bethell in the St Pancras area of London on 10 October 1845, Beauclerc showed early signs of intelligence and dedication. Beauclerc's father, Richard, a merchant, was able to send his daughter and her two siblings to Mr Browning's Boarding School at Weston near Bath. A newspaper advert from 1857 shows that for the annual fee of £20 parents could expect 'the highest intellectual advantages ... combined with careful and moral training and superior domestic arrangements. The premises are spacious, and the situation is beautiful and healthy.'[268]

There is some confusion around the addition of the name 'Beauclerc', which appears to have been added when she was an infant. This may be connected to a tragedy which befell the family when she was only five years old: the death of her father. Unfortunately, Richard Bethell had left little provision for his family. Beauclerc's mother, Elizabeth, made attempts to earn money from shopkeeping but things were very difficult for the family, resulting in Beauclerc leaving school at the age of nine in order to assist her mother in the family business. In 1859, Beauclerc and her mother moved to Birmingham, possible to capitalize on the town's rapid growth, where Beauclerc continued to work for her mother, initially in a grocer's shop and then later as a retail stationer. Although she had been forced to leave school at a young age, Beauclerc was privileged to have received this level of education at a time when it was not compulsory, enabling her to develop good reading and writing skills; according to the *Phonetic Journal*, which published a portrait of Beauclerc in 1891, she showed early signs of being a gifted writer, composing short stories for other children when she was only eight years old.[269]

Beauclerc's first encounter with phonography came at the age of twelve when, according to the *Phonetic Journal*, she was sorting some wastepaper and came across an old copy of Sir Isaac Pitman's book *The Phonographic Teacher*. She took an immediate interest in this and so she began studying the system, setting the course of her life. Although largely self-taught, she did seek help from the Phonetic Society in Bath and from a family member who was also learning the system. Unfortunately, the majority of her family were unsupportive of Beauclerc learning this new skill and in the portrait that was published in *Birmingham Faces and Places* in 1892 we learn that 'she had no word of encouragement from anyone in her self-imposed studies, on the contrary, it was thought she "was wasting her time" over a useless pursuit'.[270] Pitman shorthand was first presented by Sir Isaac Pitman in 1837. An English language teacher in Bath, Pitman was an advocate of spelling reform, which led to his creation of the shorthand system. A phonetic system whereby symbols do not represent letters but rather sounds and words are written as they are spoken, the system was immediately popular and is still used today. The system was also suitable for distance learning: texts that had been transcribed into shorthand would be sent to students who would then return the edited text for correction. By the age of eighteen Beauclerc was so proficient in the system that she was able to secure some work with an American lecturer on phrenology, Alfred Hagarty, who visited Birmingham in 1865 and required an amanuensis, or note-taker, during his two-month stay.

Soon after, Beauclerc began teaching shorthand to an interested group, based at the Church of the Saviour. A 'Free Christian' church, situated on Edward Street in the town centre, it was founded in 1846 for George Dawson and was instrumental in the development of ideas around the civic gospel with its aim of improving the conditions and lives of ordinary working citizens. Beauclerc was already a member of the congregation and used Dawson's sermons as material to help her practice shorthand. We learn from *The Institute Magazine* that

> In connection with the Church of the Saviour under the ever-memorable leadership of Mr. George Dawson, a strong educational impulse always existed, and to the educational work of the Church Miss Beauclerc contributed as her share a shorthand class, held in the vestry; the first of a long series of successful classes of which she has been the guiding spirit.[271]

In 1871 Dawson started a radical newspaper, the *Birmingham Morning News*, and employed Beauclerc as a shorthand amanuensis to report on public meetings, conferences and lectures in Birmingham and in other towns in the Midlands, giving her a claim to being the first female reporter in England, and she was certainly the first woman to work on a daily newspaper. Although a strong advocate for equal opportunities for women, in his lecture 'National Education', Dawson was scathing about women's educational abilities: 'ladies' spelling is always pretty feeble. It has never been a strong point with women. Even out of 100 educated women 99 will spell independent with 'a' dant'.' There were no doubts as to Beauclerc's spelling abilities, however, and she went onto work for Dawson over the next five years. After his sudden death in 1876, her verbatim notes of his lectures were used for the published collections of his works. Without these notes the lectures would have been lost. Her reports were credited by Dawson's wife, Susan Dawson, and Dawson's assistant minister and successor, George St Clair (both of whom edited the works) as 'better than the best', indeed, 'so great was her contribution that she was given a share of the royalties from the publication of Dawson's work'.[272]

Other meetings that Beauclerc would have reported on would have included those of the Birmingham Women's Suffrage Society: in 1871, at least one of these meetings was chaired by George Dawson, and Susan Dawson was an executive member of the BWSS. As part of the Dawson circle, Beauclerc would have mixed with other leading members of the suffrage campaign in Birmingham, including the Crosskeys but also the Sturge family (Eliza Sturge, niece of Joseph Sturge, the anti-slavery campaigner, was secretary of the BWSS until the 1880s), and William and Caroline Taylor, who had established the BWSS in 1868. It is very possible that Beauclerc was also involved with the suffrage society in some capacity.

In September 1887 Beauclerc was invited to give a lecture, 'Phonography in Birmingham', at the London International Shorthand Congress and Phonographic Jubilee. Here she reflected on her time working with Dawson:

> Another way by which, by the aid of Phonography, I have been able to do some lasting service, has been in the recording the eloquent utterances of one of the world's most gifted teachers – George Dawson M.A., of the Church of the Saviour, Birmingham. For many years I reported from week to week, those high discourses, and those tender impassioned, soul inspiring prayers, which touched the hearts of all who heard them, and which, but for Phonography, would have been entirely lost to the world. But by my knowledge and practice of this glorious art, I was able to record those precious utterances as they fell from his lips, which records have since been published, and may now be found in thousands of homes, serving in large measure, 'to comfort those whom here he comforted', until like Abraham, 'he went forth whither he knew not,' nevertheless without fear, to serve his God elsewhere.

After Dawson's death, Beauclerc went on to work for two other preachers, one of Dawson's successors at the Church of the Saviour, James Christopher Street, and the American Unitarian clergyman and lecturer, Robert Collyer, who visited Birmingham in 1883 and engaged Beauclerc to report and edit his sermons delivered at Newhall Hill Church.

While still working for Dawson, Beauclerc secured another position, this time in education. In 1874 she was appointed teacher of shorthand at the Perry Barr Institute and then started teaching classes at the Birmingham & Midland Institute in 1876. The BMI was established in 1854, founded by an Act of Parliament for the 'Diffusion and Advancement of Science, Literature and Art amongst all Classes of Persons resident in Birmingham and Midland Counties', by way of the 'penny lecture', and was originally located next to the Town Hall on Paradise Street (the building was demolished in 1965). The Perry Barr Institute, an offshoot of the BMI, was founded in 1874. The move to Birmingham in 1859 transpired to be a very fortunate one for Beauclerc, enabling her to live in a progressive town in terms of education and opportunities for women. During the nineteenth century, Birmingham played an important role in education and in developing ideas around the civic gospel, plus it was significant in that it had one of the first suffrage societies in England (after Manchester and London). Indeed, as Ruth Watts suggests, 'it was actually in the struggle for a national system of education that Birmingham first emerged as an enlightened leader,' 'characterized [by] the idealism promulgated by Nonconformist ministers such as … Dawson … and Henry Crosskey'.[273] Birmingham was also the birthplace of the National Education League, developed from the Birmingham Education Society. While the aim of the league was to secure the education of every child in the country, these progressive ideas extended to adult education.

By the 1880s the ability to use shorthand was invaluable for 'literary and mercantile purposes' and classes were in great demand.[274] In 1887 Beauclerc established a Shorthand Writers Association, 'with its library, and its lectures in which some of the best in our town were proud to assist her work, stood as a monument to her self-sacrificing energy'.[275] At the inaugural lecture given by Thomas Reed, President of the Association, at the BMI in October 1887, he stated: 'Shorthand might be a mechanical occupation, but if intelligently and zealously pursued it would stimulate the mental faculties, and serve important education purposes.'[276] Beauclerc estimated that since shorthand classes began she had taught over 4,000 pupils, and as well as teaching at the BMI she taught at other institutes and educational establishments across the region – that she was so much in demand during this period is testament to her popularity and expertise and she was credited with running 'by far the largest and most successful branch of the Institute School of Commerce'.[277] Now at the forefront of her profession, Beauclerc embraced new advances in her field and new technologies by introducing typewriting to Birmingham, again of huge influence across commerce: 'her activity in this direction has no doubt been a principal cause of the very extensive adoption of the typewriter in our local professional and commercial offices.'[278]

After breaking barriers in journalism and adult education, perhaps the natural next move for Beauclerc was teaching in schools and so in 1888 she achieved another first when she was appointed as teacher of shorthand at Rugby School. This was the first time that shorthand had been taught in an English public school and, more importantly, the first time a female teacher had been employed at an English boys' public school. She taught at the school for four years and 'her success was as great here as elsewhere'.[279] During this period, she also taught boys at the Birmingham Blue Coat School. Shorthand was not the only subject that Beauclerc taught however; the 1881 census shows that she also taught dance and calisthenics, a gentle form of physical exercise similar to gymnastics, which was deemed appropriate for young women of the upper and middle classes. In 1892 Beauclerc was forced to retire due to ill health and died five years later, on 19 September

1897, at the age of 51.

Marie Bethell Beauclerc is buried at Key Hill Cemetery, close to George Dawson's grave. The inscription on her headstone reads: 'This stone was erected by the members of the Church of the Saviour, Birmingham. In grateful recognition of her services, by which many of the prayers, sermons and lectures of the late George Dawson, MA have been preserved.' While Beauclerc is rightly recognized as being central to recording Dawson's work, which would have been otherwise lost, she is deserving of much greater recognition in her own right – as a reporter, an educator, and a pioneer of shorthand. Disadvantaged through gender and class, she worked hard for her success. The *Phonetic Journal* perhaps provides a more fitting epitaph: Marie Bethell Beauclerc was 'a pioneer of shorthand in Birmingham ... a successful teacher of other subjects and is a standing witness to the power of perseverance and hard work'.

Chapter 11

Henry William Crosskey
and Hannah Crosskey

When Henry Crosskey, the Unitarian minister of the Church of the Messiah in Broad Street, died in October 1893, the men who had worked alongside him for a quarter of a century to see their town improved were not to be found stinting in their praise. R.W. Dale wrote:

> Dr Crosskey came to Birmingham at a very felicitous time. The town was feeling the breath of a new spring ... To Dr Crosskey the atmosphere that he found among his immediate friends was exhilarating – almost intoxicating. November after November in the municipal contests, and all year through, whenever there was a chance of preaching the municipal gospel, he pleaded with pathetic earnestness and with passion for the new policy. When the contests were on, he went to two or three meetings night after night in the obscurest parts of the town and appealed, as if for his own life, for the return of the right man. His intensity was astonishing. He spoke as if the whole fate of the town depended on the result of a ward election.[280]

George Dixon, who worked with Crosskey to secure educational improvement, had this to say:

> His desire was that the only objective to be sought in the education of children should be something higher than the mere attainment of such knowledge as would enable them to become better workmen and gain larger wages. He wished to raise them to a higher level in which the pleasures of literature, science and art might be opened out to them.[281]

In August 1869, when Henry Crosskey arrived at the Church of the Messiah, he brought with him many years of experience as a Unitarian minister. He had spent four years as a minister at Derby and seventeen years as a minister at Glasgow. Immediately Crosskey joined the Birmingham Liberal Association and its offshoot the National Education League; 'in becoming a minister', Crosskey observed, 'I did not cease to be a citizen.'[282] He was impressed by Joseph Chamberlain's argument that the BLA should organise municipal meetings and not concentrate solely on parliamentary elections. 'The Liberal policy,' Crosskey believed, 'was a policy of civilization. It meant the enjoyment by the great mass of people of the blessing of a beautiful and civilised life.'[283] This firm belief even led him at one point to advocating the ambitious proposal that a rate-supported college teaching Latin and Greek should be established in Birmingham for young working-class men of real intellectual ability.

During the lengthy illness that culminated in his death Crosskey compiled two volumes of notes about his life. A man who does this clearly believes what he did is worthy of being remembered and expects a biography to be written. Crosskey recalled – a story he doubtless told on many occasions – how his grandfather deposited in a pond a squire who had insulted him. It is difficult to imagine Crosskey behaving in this way, but he did describe himself as 'a man with a highly nervous temperament' and did seem to enjoy the controversies he sometimes stirred up.[284] Crosskey's religious and political affiliations and sense of public duty were all derived from his father. William Crosskey was in business in Lewes in Sussex and played a leading part in the governance of the town. Born in Lewes on 7 December 1826, the oldest of five children, Crosskey was sent to three schools run by Unitarians. He acquired a knowledge of grammar – his grammar book 'had to be learnt from end to end' – spelling, arithmetic and Latin.[285] He remembered being so delighted by *Arabian Nights* that he perused it surreptitiously when he was meant to be doing arithmetic; pausing on walks in the countryside to read Virgil; watching a master impersonating Falstaff 'in which he appeared stuffed out to due rotundity to our intense delight'; and playing chess against another master who 'always lost his temper and used rather violent language whenever he was beaten'.[286] In 1843 Crosskey went From Lewes to Manchester New College to study theology, with some history, literature and classics. The Unitarian ministers who taught there exercised a profound influence on him. With the Revd J.G. Robberts he and his fellow students became 'as familiar with Shakespeare as with the Bible ... to our great advantage ... subsequently as preachers'.[287] Through her husband, the Revd W. Gaskell, he met Elizabeth Gaskell, enjoying conversations with her on walks and during the evenings. At one of these evening discussions he was introduced to Thomas Carlyle who observed that 'the lad has ideas'.[288] But the greatest influence on Crosskey was the brother of Harriet Martineau and uncle of R.F. Martineau (see chapter 16), the philosopher James Martineau. He deeply influenced Crosskey's theological thinking and he remained in touch with Martineau for the rest of his life, often referring admiringly to him in conversations. In 1848 Crosskey left Manchester New College without a degree, but there he had met the daughter of the assistant secretary, Hannah Aspden. They both became involved with the Anti-Corn Law League and married in September 1852. It was a union, Crosskey later wrote, with a woman 'in every way my superior' and which provided him with 'at least two thirds of my power to be of the slightest service either to the religious interests committed to my charge or to the community in which I lived ....'[289]

The years that Crosskey spent as a Unitarian minister in Derby and Glasgow were often punctuated by controversy. In these places he remained something of an outsider and, at public meetings, was shouted down when he set out the case for unsectarian schooling. Though there were also to be collisions with opponents in Birmingham, he undoubtedly fitted in more, and his opinions and campaigns found ready ears. The congregation in Derby was small – though it was to increase during his pastorship – and he was provided with an annual salary of only £70. Typical of the hostility Crosskey encountered was a claim by an Anglican clergyman that he based his sermons on the verses of Byron rather than the Bible – a charge which Crosskey, whilst admitting a liking for Byron, firmly denied. There were many battles against Anglicans in Glasgow – and Crosskey admitted to relishing them. He doubtless enjoyed the fury that his dedication of his tract *A Defence of Religion* (1854) to George Jacob Holyoake provoked. Yet in Derby and Glasgow we see the gestation of the work that he sought to bring to fruition in Birmingham. He allied himself with middle-class advocates of household suffrage like Sir Joshua Walmsley – who he brought to both Derby and Glasgow – and by the 1860s, with his wife Hannah, he was advocating extending the vote to women. In Derby Crosskey set up a working men's institute at which he read aloud Shakespeare's plays. In 1851 he also joined the National Public School Association, which campaigned for compulsory, free and secular schooling; his great memory of his involvement was shaking the hand of Richard Cobden. In Glasgow Crosskey set up, for working men associated with his chapel, mutual improvement classes and encouraged them to write essays. He also taught geology classes at the Mechanics Institute – geology became his great intellectual interest after a holiday on the Isle of Arran in 1855 and he went on to publish many papers on glaciation in Scotland.

Crosskey was a preacher who his congregations did not want to let go: in 1864 his Glasgow congregation presented him with 400 guineas. He turned down an invitation to become the Unitarian minister in Newcastle-upon-Tyne but, when a deputation of Arthur Chamberlain (brother of Joseph), Timothy Kenrick, and Follett Osler from the Church of the Messiah in Birmingham visited him to express the wish of the congregation that he succeed the stricken Samuel Bache, he knew that was the place he wanted to be. That feeling had doubtless been fostered in November 1867 when George Dawson had delivered three lectures at Crosskey's chapel. The two men had met before, but in Crosskey's home they were now able to talk at length. Crosskey had no doubts that they were of one mind in their belief that, when religious men preached, they preached to get things done. Soon he had taken a house in George Road in Edgbaston.

The Church of the Messiah had opened in Broad Street in Birmingham on 1 January 1862. It was built over the Birmingham to Worcester Canal and supported by arches embedded in the sandstone over each side of the water. The chapel provided seating for 600, but only those in the first third of the chapel could hear the sermon. For those who could hear them Crosskey's sermons were 'always extremely rich in lofty and beautiful thought', but another member of the congregation observed that 'we could very often hardly hear a word of them … but … we felt the better just for seeing him'.[290] For those who were oblivious to what was being said, Crosskey ensured that his most important sermons went into print.[291]

At the rear of the church there were rooms for its educational activities. There were morning lectures for female members of the congregation – an indication of Henry and Hannah Crosskey's strong belief in the educational rights of women – and Joseph Chamberlain, who attended the chapel, took an interest in an improvement society for working men. There was also a Sunday School and day schools for boys and girls. In December 1869 these pupils were, at two sittings, 'regaled with a bountiful tea' before receiving 'a few words of friendly advice' from Crosskey.[292] In 1875-6 there were 149 on the books of the boys' school (with an attendance rate of 87 per cent) and 157 on the books of the girls' school (with an attendance rate of 86 per cent). Crosskey himself took a monthly teachers' class. The pupils were encouraged to cultivate window boxes and each year were provided with plants; in 1873 William Kenrick, another prominent townsman who was a member of the congregation, distributed 187 fuchsia for this purpose. These schools ceased to operate after the building of board schools began across the town.

The National Education League, established in February 1869, in effect revived the campaigning of the now-defunct National Public School Association. It sought to make elementary education unsectarian, free and compulsory. The message was spread by postal communications and a team of lecturers, and soon the NEL had enrolled thousands of supporters from across the country. Crosskey became part of its core leadership along with Joseph Chamberlain, George Dixon, Jesse Collings, Willam Harris and J.T. Bunce. Speaking at meetings on behalf of the NEL, he declared that 'he hoped they would see the necessity of making unsectarian education free as the air of heaven'.[293] The children of the working class deserved nothing less than to be 'given an opportunity of passing from cottage to college … it was no idle matter but a question of raising people in the social scale, of removing them from tyranny, of giving them nobler tastes …'.[294] Through the NEL and the Central Nonconfomist Committee, founded in March 1870 and of which he and R.W. Dale were joint secretaries, Crosskey played a prominent part in the agitation against W.E. Forster's Education Bill. The campaign believed that the Bill would reinforce the power of Anglicans over the elementary school system. When Chamberlain led a large delegation to London to meet Gladstone in March 1870, Crosskey was amongst them. A decision that there should be no distinctive denominational teaching in board schools and a number of other concessions did not appease Crosskey and his allies and the campaign continued. A few years after the Bill had been passed, Crosskey described it as 'a collection of contradictory policies, so blended that, in its working, the balance of power is always struck in favour of an ecclesiastical interest … The Church of England seized upon the golden opportunity and has covered the country with its schools.'[295] At the Church of the Messiah in Birmingham, the minister continued to demand the abolition of denominational schools and the creation of a universal system of free, unsectarian, rate-supported schools.

When the elections for the school board took place in Birmingham in November 1870, Crosskey was more than willing to offer himself as a candidate. He had only been a resident in the town for little more than a year, however, and his offer was not universally welcomed in the BLA. 'His nomination looks like a little bit of a hole-in-the-corner work,' one Liberal complained. 'Why should gentlemen like Arthur Ryland, Sam: Timmins and Dr Freeman be supplanted by newcomers? These three gentlemen are well known as old educationalists … It is shameful to see a clique riding roughshod over some of the most respected and honoured men of Birmingham.'[296] Despite such protestations, Crosskey did go forward – to defeat. With only six of the fifteen seats on the School Board, the Liberals suffered a serious setback. When, three years later, the BLA managed to return all eight of its candidates, Crosskey had stood aside and it was not until November 1875 that he secured election to the School Board. 'The Board', he would often say, 'is bound not to be content with giving a poor education to poor people'; indeed, its purpose should be ensuring 'opportunities for receiving the largest culture and enjoying the best results of science and art brought by corporate action within the reach of the greatest possible number'.[297]

'To conduct the religious services such as those demanded from Sunday to Sunday,' Crosskey observed, 'was in itself a task he could not discharge to his own satisfaction.'[298] His election to the school board greatly added to his responsibilities, but Crosskey informed his congregation that it was 'not only in harmony with his duties as their minister but a part of those duties themselves'.[299] From 1876 until 1881, he was chairman of the sites and building committee. In Crosskey's evaluation the urgent need to push back denominational schools could only be achieved if more board schools were built, and he relished the role. During his tenure sixteen new board schools opened, providing places for 17,329 working-class children; the smallest school at Oozells Street (1878) and the largest school at Hope Street (1880) catered for, respectively, 807 and 1,445 pupils. For a few years, even the schoolrooms at the Church of the Messiah were taken over by the School Board.

From 1881 to 1892 Crosskey was chairman of the school management committee. He did not recoil from his hostility to denominational schools, branding them 'an educational failure'.[300] Inevitably he found himself in conflict with Anglican members of the board, who accused him of submitting resolutions of 'appalling length', of his opposition to denominational schools being 'a standing joke' and being 'in educational matters ... a showman and an actor'.[301] When, in 1879, his Liberal colleagues agreed that the head teacher in a board school should be able to read the Bible without comment, Crosskey declared that 'it was a disappointment to see an ideal broken' and only gave way in the face of considerable pressure.[302] That year, on Crosskey's initiative, lessons on morality – obedience to parents, honesty, truthfulness, industry, frugality and the like – were introduced into board schools.

Himself possessed of a keen interest in science, Crosskey unsurprisingly urged that the subject be taught in board schools by trained demonstrators. In 1880 William Jerome Harrison, an enthusiast for geology and photography, was appointed chief science demonstrator and provided with six assistants. Harrison believed that science 'should be taught practically and the children should actually see the effects and not merely be told about them'.[303]

Scientific demonstrations were provided either weekly or fortnightly, with the apparatus pushed in hand carts from board school to board school by youths. Another change that Crosskey oversaw was tying the salaries of teachers to the standard of their teaching. There were complaints from ratepayers, but Crosskey observed that 'a bad teacher was dear at any price and to retain a good teacher was the best economy'.[304]

It was for his efforts in seeking to secure the best schooling possible for working-class children that Crosskey made his mark as a civic gospeller. Yet this was not the only concern of this energetic and high-minded man. He also became an important ally of the campaign for women's suffrage in the town. He held a deep belief that men and women were equal in all respects. He was on the platform at every meeting of the local branch of the National Society for Women's Suffrage from his arrival in the town until his death. It appeared to him, he declared, 'that in every direction it was for the good of man that woman should enter into his loftiest aims and be his companion and comrade in the work of life'.[305] It was a line of argument he was to reiterate, observing on another occasion that, as a result of the Reform Act of 1867, 'many men had been wakened into intelligence …. He believed the effect would be still greater in many homes when women obtained the suffrage.'[306]

In this campaign Crosskey worked in partnership with his wife. Hannah Crosskey was prominently involved in the local branch of the Women's Liberal Federation and the ladies' committee of a charity which provided instruction on domestic service for working-class girls. She had thought deeply about the role of a woman. 'If domestic duties be discharged with intellectual energy, guided by a deep sense of moral responsibility, they will not be found antagonistic to the fullest intellectual cultivation,' she wrote.[307] In February 1881 Hannah Crosskey agreed to chair a suffrage meeting at the town hall. Crosskey wrote to a friend:

Mrs Crosskey is in agonies of preparing a speech … Women are to come in their thousands free – a few poor men are to get in at 2/6 each. Such are man's rights when women ask for the suffrage! Imagine men calling a meeting and admitting men free and women at 2/6. It is to show that women are prepared to ask for votes for themselves – & they can manage affairs as well as their tyrants.[308]

Hannah Crosskey's speech was highly effective:

She earnestly desired to see women freed from the vexatious and unjust laws affecting their property and the custody of their children. They believed that the laws affecting women unjustly would not be altered until the women had a voice to influence the lawmaker. They had laws in existence that would never be repealed unless attention was directed on them by women, for only they knew where the shoe pinched ... It was useless for men to maintain they were legally protected to the same extent men were. They only had to look at police reports to see the laws in some recognised women as only on about a level, or inferior to, their goods and chattels. In one case reported in the *Daily Post* last week a man was sentenced to a month's imprisonment for a brutal assault on his wife, another man received a month for stealing a gun and a third was sentenced to six weeks imprisonment for stealing three chairs. By those decisions it followed that knocking down a woman was of rather less importance in the eyes of the law than taking three chairs and about equal to the theft of a gun ... Notwithstanding all that was said of the courtesy and deference shown by all well-bred men towards women, there was a tacit understanding that they were to consider themselves as inferior to men. Was there not a glow of secret satisfaction in the heart of every man, from the most cultivated gentleman down to the most incapable youth that ever existed, that he was lucky in not having been born a woman? ... She advocated the extension of the franchise to women because she believed that home life would be better ... that women's whole nature would be benefitted and, with women's elevation men always rose too ....[309]

In fact the Church of the Messiah provided many of the leading supporters of the local campaign for women's suffrage, including Caroline Kenrick, who was elected to the school board in 1876, and Catherine Osler, 'the Crosskeys' most consistently energetic colleague in local feminist ventures'.[310] Under Crosskey's leadership, it led the way in seeking to advance this aspect of the civic gospel.

Crosskey's commitments as a minister, administrator and agitator left him exhausted. He recovered his strength and spirits in his garden and by fishing expeditions (always taking a volume of Shakespeare's plays with him when he went). In the winter he enjoyed skating. Each August Crosskey and his large family would escape to an isolated location in the west of Scotland. Here he could indulge in his great passion for geology. It was an interest he shared with his wife – they often discussed the subject in their courtship correspondence. It was whilst reading Andrew Ramsay's book about the geology of the Isle of Arran in summer 1855 during a holiday there that Crosskey's interest deepened so that he went on to become one of the best-known amateur geologists of his day. He joined the Geological Society in Glasgow and the Geological Section of the British Association and, in August 1867, visited Norway with another self-taught geologist, David Robertson. From 1863 onwards Crosskey published, sometimes in collaboration with Robertson, papers on glaciation every year until almost the end of his life, usually in the proceedings of the societies he belonged to.

In Birmingham Crosskey's enthusiasm for geology found expression in the Natural History and Microscopical Society and the Philosophical Society (NH&MS). He became president of both societies. At the meetings of these societies Crosskey regularly read papers with titles such as 'On Some Phenomena of the Glacial Epoch' and 'Notes on the Post-Tertiary of Norway' and displayed the extensive collection of shells which he had built up himself. With his fellow members, he went out on local expeditions – in September 1870 to a gravel and clay pit near Harborne and in May 1875 to inspect a boulder in Cannon Hill Park, which had to be fenced off after being kicked and hit with sticks by locals. The two societies had small memberships. In 1870 there were 187 on the books of the NH&MS, but many were in arrears and attendance at its weekly meetings was usually 20-30. Henry Lapworth, professor of geology at Mason College from 1881, recalled Crosskey's ability to make his talks understandable to those who were not geologists, and Crosskey did seek to widen the appeal of scientific study. With Hannah's encouragement, he arranged for women to attend the annual meetings of the NH&MS, and he also argued that it could recruit many more members if it embraced a wider selection of scientific subjects. It was extremely important to Crosskey to go out regularly with his hammer. 'Dr Crosskey did not, I think, care very much either for theology or philosophy,' Dale recalled. 'It was a relief to him to get away to questions about the boulders and the glaciers of Switzerland and Scotland.'[311]

The week before he died Crosskey had joined in cricket and leapfrog at the annual picnic of his Sunday School. He had, however, only recently resumed his duties after a long absence. Advised by doctors to rest, he had spent time on the continent and at a hydropathic establishment. 'I have been chiefly resting and loafing, resting and loafing and doing nothing,' he reported from Monte Carlo, 'and am certainly the better for it.'[312] Crosskey died on 1 October 1893; Hannah was to live for another eleven years. His successor at the Church of the Messiah, L.P. Jacks, undertook to continue to deliver sermons that were calls for action.

When the trustees of the Church of the Messiah were looking for a new minister in 1859, the appointment they wished to make was a man who could match George Dawson. Certain in his religious and political convictions, animated and undaunted, Crosskey established the Church of the Messiah as a bastion of progressive thought and action in Birmingham. Truly he could be called 'one of the leading men amongst the leading men of the town'.[313]

Chapter 12

Charles Vince

The Baptist minister Charles Vince (1823-74) was the first of the civic gospellers to die. George Dawson was on a lecture tour in the United States, but otherwise Vince's funeral was attended by all the civic gospellers. Joseph Chamberlain, J. H. Chamberlain, J.D. Mullins, Samuel Timmins, John Jaffray, J.T. Bunce, Henry Crosskey, William Harris, Robert Martineau and other figures of note were at Mount Zion chapel in October 1874 to hear R.W. Dale pay tribute to a man who had lived according to the highest standards of Christian duty. This show of support was a tribute to both the public man and the private man. Vince was an eloquent advocate of the civic gospel, but his geniality, courtesy and sense of humour also made him a much-loved figure. He was not a man of great means, and the immediate concern of his congregation and friends was to make provision for his wife and seven children. By the end of the year subscriptions had raised over £5,000, and the civic gospellers then turned their attention to a memorial. Within the stipulated year, enough had been subscribed to erect an impressive monument at Key Hill.

Vince was working class by birth. He believed that this provided him with a better understanding of the lives of working people than that possessed by the middle-class men he was associated with – for example, he expressed support for limited opening hours for shops on Sundays so that the men and women who were employed for ten hours a day in the factories of the town could buy the provisions their hours of work prevented them from doing during the week. Vince's personal knowledge of the people was certainly recognised by Chamberlain: the two men often met privately to discuss questions relating to the working class. Vince served as minister of only one Baptist chapel – Mount Zion in Edmund Street for more than two decades. Though born in Farnham in Surrey in 1823, Vince was, in the words of his friend J.S. Wright, 'a true lover of their town … he felt himself to be a Birmingham man'.[314]

At a school run by the nephew of William Cobbett in Farnham – one of his earliest memories was of a day's holiday to commemorate Cobbett's first election to Parliament – Vince acquired the basics of reading, writing and arithmetic. His father was a carpenter and Vince entered the trade, acquiring skills he practised later in life for pleasure. In his spare time, he studied. The depth of his reading enabled him to begin to give lectures at the Mechanics Institute in the town and to draw his own conclusions about his religious affiliation. Vince ceased to attend the Congregationalist chapel of his parents and became instead a Baptist. He developed the habit of going out in the villages around Farnham and delivering short sermons. Vince's piety and the pleasure he got from speaking to audiences made clear what he would do in life: he would become a minister.

In 1848 Vince sought to become a student at Stepney College, which prepared young men to become Baptist ministers. He submitted a letter setting out his suitability and sat a written examination. He was expected to be competent in Latin and Greek. He was admitted, and began four years of study which embraced theology, philosophy, history, mathematics, science, Latin, Greek and Hebrew and the responsibilities of a minister. A contemporary recalled how Vince 'gave himself to the work of the student with great ardour and devotion'.[315] He passed his annual examinations but did not remain for a final year to secure a degree from the University of London. The principal recommended him to Mount Zion Chapel in Birmingham, which had for some time been without a permanent minister. It was Vince's desire to live amongst the working people of a manufacturing town, and he had already rejected overtures to take charge of a number of Baptist chapels in London. In October 1852 he was installed as the new minister at Mount Zion.

Mount Zion was one of the largest chapels in Birmingham. It was able to seat 2,500 people, and its school rooms could accommodate 500 pupils. It was often used for public events – religious discussions in the 1820s and anti-slavery meetings in the 1830s. Erected in 1824, this huge chapel had bankrupted its builder, been occupied by a small congregation loyal to the Scottish preacher Edward Irving and was standing empty when, in 1827, it was put up for auction. It was acquired by the Baptists, with Thomas Thonger and then James Hoby serving as minister.[316] When Hoby decided to step down in October 1844, he was succeeded by a young man who had only just begun his career as a preacher. His name was George Dawson.

Dawson filled the role of Baptist minister at Mount Zion for little more than a year. His sermons soon won him many admirers amongst the congregation who, in September 1845, presented him with a set of the *Penny Cyclopaedia*, published by the Society for the Diffusion of Useful

Knowledge, and a purse of one hundred guineas. These people were also inspired to reduce the chapel's debt, raising by subscriptions £500. In February 1846, however, negotiations began for Dawson to resign as minister. The cause of this parting of the ways was the form of worship. Dawson believed that he was in danger of being minister of 'a sect' whereas what he wanted was that he and his congregation 'would be bound only by their own free will'.[317] To be able to preach as he pleased, Dawson wanted his own chapel. 'As long as you stay with me,' he informed his admirers, 'I shall stay with you. If you build a chapel, I remain. If not, I consider you have no claim on my services.'[318] An agreement with the trustees of Mount Zion was reached. Dawson did not need to 'get tents' and was permitted to continue preaching at Mount Zion until June 1846.[319] Until the Church of the Saviour was opened in August 1847, he conducted his services at other halls in the town centre. At Mount Zion, meanwhile, a subscription was raised to repair the galleries, which were in danger of collapse, and in due course a new minister, J. Mortlock Daniel, was appointed. By the time of the religious census of March 1851, he was gone and about 700 were attending morning and evening services on Sundays.

It was on the recommendation of the principal of Stepney College that Dawson had arrived in Birmingham. It is likely that Vince had come across him during the years he was training to be a minister, but he was certainly meeting him periodically, privately and at committees, soon after taking up his position. Like Dawson, he was unable 'to believe in a man's Christianity who prays at prayer meetings unless he is scrupulously upright and downright in all his business transactions and withal carries himself kindly towards his brother – the poor and needy'.[320] Vince joined Dawson as one of the most powerful preachers in the town. Repudiating the title of reverend, he usually preached three times each Sunday and once during the week. He emphasised duty and laced his sermons with humour and references to the beauty of the world. It was noted that Sunday after Sunday Vince spoke in the pulpit with the same vigour he demonstrated on the platform. At first, he made notes for his sermons, but on one occasion, 'getting, as he told a friend, "into a mess", he threw the ill-fated scrap on the pulpit floor …'.[321] Thereafter he preached without notes and his sermons were described as being 'remarkable for their variety and freshness … singularly devoid of cant and cant phrases … I have never heard him preach without coming away refreshed and thanking God for such an able minister of the New Testament.'[322] After his death a selection of Vince's sermons, based on notes made by a member of his congregation as they were being delivered, were published as *The Unchanging Saviour* (1875).

It is little wonder that the number of people attending Mount Zion grew steadily, and they took Vince's calls for action seriously; in 1857, after the rebellion in India, they arranged for a petition to be presented in the House of Commons calling for an end to oppression and self-government in the country. Vince's growing popularity did not go unnoticed by the Anglicans of the town. When an Anglican clergyman met a member of Vince's congregation, he made this enquiry: '"Does he teach religion?" The woman replied, "You had better come and hear him." He said, "Well I know that Mr Vince favours the Romanists a great deal."'[323]

The return of John Bright as an MP for Birmingham brought Vince into local politics. Vince's son recalled that his father was 'a hero-worshipper. The faith in which I was nurtured was that Gladstone was all very well, but that the real savour of Liberal doctrines was to be found in the speeches of Bright.'[324] Vince began to address meetings regularly, often several times a week at election times. 'His enjoyment of political work was keen and intense,' his son noted, 'he was never happier than addressing an audience of Birmingham artisans.'[325] A speech at a lunch on the day of the opening of the reference library in October 1866, when he censured the mayor Edwin Yates for his regular visits to the Woodman public house, brought Vince into the local spotlight. Like Dawson, Vince believed that the town councillors should be different sorts of men.[326] Vince was nominated as first president of the Birmingham Liberal Association, but, for the Tories, this very effective speaker became a marked man and, during a by-election campaign in 1867, was subjected to 'gross attacks' and 'a scurrilous advertisement'.[327]

It was sure to happen that a working-class autodidact like Vince would become deeply committed to improving the educational opportunities for the poor and their children. 'If God had not intended the child to be educated,' he observed, 'He would not have given it a mind that needed education.'[328] He began this work immediately. Vince chaired a meeting of working men at Mount Zion in March 1854 to support attempts to raise subscriptions for the Birmingham and Midland Institute. Though he himself was to deliver his lectures to working men on history and literature outside the Institute, he recognised its immense value to the town. He was also a member of the free libraries committee. 'He knew nothing like a taste for reading,' he commented, 'which enabled a man to spend his leisure hours in a manner honourable and profitable to himself.'[329]

Vince lent his support to the Birmingham Scholastic Institution for the Sons of Ministers. This Baptist enterprise was established in a mansion in Smethwick in 1851 with the aim of providing schooling for the sons of ministers who were, in general, not well off. In fact, it admitted boys from all denominations and did not require them to be the sons of ministers. Some were boarders. It was funded by an annual fee of at least ten guineas, supplemented by donations and profits from fundraising bazaars. Within a few years there were between 30 and 40 boys in the school, studying a wide range of subjects; Vince acted as examiner for theology. Boys from Vince's own congregation attended the school, and a day school and a Sunday School at Mount Zion provided instruction for many others. The latter was a big operation, with 780 pupils and 90 teachers in 1859. Vince was also involved in the Nonconformist school in Severn Street, which had a large attendance and provided lessons in reading, writing and arithmetic; a former pupil remembered him visiting and urging the older boys to set up adult early morning schools across the town.[330]

These local initiatives led Vince inexorably into the national campaign for unsectarian, free and compulsory elementary education that spread out from Birmingham. 'They wanted a system,' he informed a meeting to much laughter, 'which would not be dependent for revenues to educate the poorer children on the money derived from bazaars, fancy fairs and Christmas trees ... but ... a truly national system.'[331] He was elected to the national executive of the National Education League, and he became a tireless lecturer on behalf of the organisation across the country. He knew that, with the Anglican church blocking the way, it would be a long and difficult struggle. 'It would be a glorious object to give to every child whom God had blessed with a mind that knowledge which was the glory of the mind,' he told an NEL meeting. 'It would be a great thing to live to see it; but there was something even better than that in working, working, working to bring it to pass.'[332]

For the Education Bill of 1870, which appeared to bolster the Anglican grip on schooling, Vince had hard words: it was 'obnoxious', 'a virtual revival of church rates,' 'gross ecclesiastical favouritism' which 'the whole of the Nonconformist portion of the Liberals must fight to the death against'.[333] It seemed almost a betrayal of the great efforts that Nonconformists had put in to return the Liberals to power. 'It would be bad enough that one had to leave his proper and more congenial work to resist the wrong expected from the hands of an adversary,' he lamented. 'It was worse still, however, to sustain a wound in the house of one's friends.'[334]

At the School Board elections in November 1870 the Liberals suffered an unexpected body blow. With 15,943 votes, Vince himself was elected but he was one of only six Liberals and the 'Bible Eight' took control. Vince described this defeat as 'temporary' and attributed it to 'a great many honest members of the Liberal Party ... who were not able to see clearly the great principles of the education question'.[335] In seeking to frustrate the victors at the fortnightly meetings of the School Board, Vince left it to Chamberlain and Dale to take the lead. He believed that the School Board was pushing ahead too quickly in seeking to identify sites and build schools. 'The necessity for the schools existed, but the demand did not,' he told one meeting, 'and to create it they must make a social revolution in the habits of the people.'[336] On the question of religious instruction in board schools, Vince was clear. The Bible should be read each day, but without commentary, which should be left to voluntary teachers. He observed that 'he could not see anything very horrible in teaching little boys the multiplication table without their learning the Church Catechism or in the teaching little girls to read without teaching them the names of the twelve tribes of Israel or the twelve Apostles'.[337] At the school board elections of November 1873 Vince's strategy was to poke fun at his opponents before sharply turning on them for 'fanning ... the spirit of bigotry'.[338] Vince was returned, and the Liberals secured control of the school board.

Vince rarely turned down invitations to speak at Baptist chapels across the country. 'He was a favourite with London audiences,' a fellow preacher recalled, 'the announcement that he would preach at Bloomsbury Chapel brought lawyers from the neighbouring Inns as well as young men from that city.'[339] He not only regularly travelled to address Baptist congregations, he liked to take his holidays on the Continent. The travelling and all his work in Birmingham took its toll. In autumn Vince fell ill and withdrew from preaching and left Birmingham to recuperate. He never fully recovered and for most of the last year of his life rarely returned to the pulpit.

It was reported in 1891 that at a meeting in support of Liberal candidates for the school board, 'one of the most interesting faces on the platform, for those who recognised it, was the widow of Mr Charles Vince'.[340] It was a public endorsement of what her husband had fought for. Not that Vince had been forgotten in Birmingham. For many years after his death he would be recalled in the same breath as George Dawson.

Chapter 13

John Jaffray

'John Jaffray ... cannot walk down New Street,' it was observed a few years before he retired as senior partner in the proprietorship of the *Birmingham Daily Post*, 'without a good many, especially of the older people, recognising his compact and well-knit form and decided gait ....'[341] For forty years John Jaffray (1818-1901) played a prominent part in promoting the educational, cultural and charitable institutions of Birmingham. He was 'wrapped up in everything that was for the welfare of ... Birmingham', and in August 1892 was rewarded with a baronetcy for his public work.[342] An Anglican, Jaffray was not one of the men who emerged from the Church of the Saviour determined to improve the town, but he admired George Dawson as much as they did and worked with great energy and belief alongside them. His newspaper became not just the voice of Birmingham Liberalism but the voice of Birmingham. Jaffray sat on committee after committee – for example, he came forward to raise funds to help the families of the twenty people killed in an explosion in a munitions factory in Whittall Street in September 1859. He also served as secretary of the Birmingham and Midland Institute and treasurer of the Shakespeare Memorial Library. Jaffray derived only a small part of his income from the *Daily Post* – he also had sizeable stakes in banking, the manufacture of metal sheathing for ships' hulls, the leasing of railway wagons and, especially, in collieries.[343] The considerable wealth he accrued enabled him to purchase a country mansion and to build up a fine collection of paintings. A favourite story of Jaffray's was that when he arrived in Birmingham he had just £20 in his pocket. However, when he died he left a personal estate of £555, 521 13s 8d.

Jaffray is amongst those many men from nineteenth century Birmingham who one wishes had written a memoir. His grandfather was the remarkable William 'Citizen' Jaffray, a sympathiser with the French Revolution who paid for the vaccination of thousands of children across Stirlingshire against smallpox. His example must surely have had a deep influence on Jaffray's view of the world. Jaffray was born into a middle-class family in Stirling on 11 October 1818. His father, also John, was a weaver and dealer in spirits and his son completed his education at the prestigious Glasgow High School. In his early twenties Jaffray was offered a post as a reporter by a relative on a newspaper in Shrewsbury. He re-located to Birmingham in 1844 after replying to an advertisement for assistance in reviving the *Birmingham Journal,* a Liberal weekly that, with each issue selling little more than 1,000 copies a week, was 'in a sadly decrepit state'.[344] The advertisement had been placed by John Frederick Feeney, who had arrived in Birmingham from Sligo in 1835 and was employed as a reporter for the *Midland Counties Herald*. Feeney acquired the paper cheaply and he and his new colleague put in very long hours to revive its fortunes – Jaffray would later recall often writing and then setting up the type for the same article. Within a few years of these new arrangements being put in place, sales of the *Journal* had soared to 12,000 a week. Jaffray's reward was to become a partner in the business. The *Journal* was once again being widely talked about in the town – and receiving bitter complaints of contributions being refused on partisan grounds and on occasion threats of libel actions. Jaffray's decided views were evident in his strong condemnation of the wave of anti-Catholic feeling in the country in 1850. For his positioning of the *Journal* on this matter, he was presented with an address and the works of Samuel Taylor Coleridge on behalf of subscribers by George Dawson. Jaffray never forgot this moment, proudly showing visitors to his house the inscription Dawson wrote in the first volume: 'To John Jaffray, who saw Truth when fear and passion made many blind; loved the Truth when its lovers were but few; and taught the Truth when to teach it brought no profit and small praise.'[345] Those unable to get to Dawson's lectures found them fully transcribed in the pages of the *Journal*. The success of the partnership between Feeney and Jaffray in resuscitating the *Journal* provided them with the ambition and the funds to launch a daily newspaper. The *Birmingham Daily Post* made its debut on 6 December 1857. Within a year, sales had risen from 4-5,000 copies each day to 10,000. J.T. Bunce was soon brought in as editor and was utterly trusted by the proprietors. With his views almost indistinguishable from Jaffray's, Bunce was allowed considerable editorial freedom.

Feeney remained a newspaper proprietor until his death in May 1869 but played no part at all in public life. In contrast Jaffray immersed himself in what was going on in the town. With a deep interest in art, he became secretary of the Fine Arts' Prize Fund Association. Also involved were Arthur Ryland and the landscape painter F.H. Henshaw, and these years saw the beginnings of long associations with these men. This initiative, launched in June 1852, sought to build up a fund from subscriptions so that the best paintings could be put on display at exhibitions in Birmingham. For Jaffray art was not just for private enjoyment and he believed that such a scheme would raise taste in an industrial town. A prize of £60 was put forward and eighteen paintings were submitted for consideration, with E.M. Ward's 'Last Toilet of Charlotte Corday' being selected for inclusion in an exhibition organised by the Society of Artists. A few years later the focus was on local artists, with a prize of £50 being offered. Jaffray's commitment to opening up access to high-quality art extended beyond this scheme. As secretary of the Birmingham and Midland Institute, he strongly urged that it establish a 'Gallery of Art'. Portraits by John Watson Gordon of David Cox and Arthur Ryland and four landscapes by local artist J.V. Barber were acquired. In a real coup in November 1863, Jaffray put together a bid to secure for the Institute over 60 drawings of historic and rural scenes in Warwickshire by Peter De Wint, David Cox and others. They were displayed in the busiest part of the Institute, the newsroom.

In the early 1860s the civic gospellers were coming together and edging towards their first steps. Jaffray was a member of the free libraries committee and saw a public art gallery as a natural auxiliary to a public library, but he knew that many councillors would object strenuously to purchasing paintings from the rates. Progress was as slow as he expected. In November 1864 Jaffray, on behalf of a list of subscribers, sought to begin a collection with an offer to the town council of 'Dead Game' by the local artist Edward Coleman. This was his final act as a member of the free libraries committee. It was not until August 1867 that a room with 56 paintings, mostly borrowed from the Society of Artists and the Birmingham and Midland Institute, was opened in the central library. It was declared to be 'an event of great importance'.[346] Local people flocked to see paintings they would otherwise have had little opportunity to view – at a rate of 267 a day in the first few months. The arrival of a statue of Prince Albert – Jaffray had been intimately involved its commissioning – and loans of new paintings and of armour and jewellery resulted in even greater interest the following year, with almost 200,000 visitors. A public subscription in 1870 raised £1,100 – Jaffray himself donating £100 – to purchase fabrics, metal work and other items of Indian origin. The expansion of displays of industrial art was overseen by W.C. Aitken (see chapter 6), who had a background in the brass trade.[347] Still the people came, and the gallery was opened on Saturday evenings and Sunday afternoons. In 1874 a collection of etchings attracted immense interest. 'It is usually supposed that works of this character are interesting to only a comparatively small and educated class,' it was reported, 'but the thousands of visitors who have been attracted by them and who have diligently gone through the collection, catalogue in hand, proves that art of a refined and suggestive nature is as keenly enjoyed by the great body of visitors as by the educated few.'[348]

With the removal of the art gallery to Aston Hall in 1878, the number of visitors began to decline significantly, and the *Daily Post* began to campaign for a new building in the middle of the town. The offer by Richard and George Tangye to provide £5,000 for the purchase of items for a new art gallery, with a similar sum promised if the original donation was matched by a public subscription, spurred the town council into action. Plans were soon drawn up to build an art gallery above new offices of the highly profitable gas department.[349] Jaffray's part in this important development in the story of Birmingham's civic gospel was to play a leading role in an art gallery purchases committee. With a sum of £17,000 at their disposal, the committee – which also included Timmins, Harris, Martineau and Kenrick – invested in paintings by, amongst others, W.J. Muller, Frederick Leighton, A. W. Hunt, Dante Gabriel Rossetti, and Edward Burne Jones. The art collector J.C. Robinson travelled to Italy on behalf of the committee, returning with such treasures as a Greek terracotta figure of a female, a Greek painted vase and two marble statuettes. So pleased were the committee that they sent Robinson back, and he acquired about another hundred items. The paintings, statues, vases, metal work, embroideries, carved furniture, medals and much else was stored in the basement underneath the Council House until, in November 1885, the Art Gallery opened. On that first day 25,630 local people passed through the turnstiles.

For Jaffray the civic gospel embraced the humanitarian principles he had learned from his grandfather. He was also a staunch supporter of the charitable institutions of the town. He became a governor of four hospitals: the General Hospital in Summer Lane, the Queen's Hospital in Bath Row, the Free Hospital for Sick Children in Steelhouse Lane and the Hospital for Women in the Crescent. Dawson and a few other civic gospellers also lent their support to the hospitals of the town but were not involved to the extent that Jaffray was. Immediately after joining the board of the General Hospital in 1863, Jaffray, ever a reformer, secured and then chaired a committee of inquiry into its management and financial position, which, after fifty sittings, issued a detailed report in July 1864. There were objections to proposals for democratising the board and reducing the debt, but in time they were largely adopted. An important source of funds for the General Hospital was the musical festival held every three years in the town, and the energetic Jaffray eventually became, unsurprisingly, chairman of

the committee that organised these events. He had a great love for music –
portraits of Dvorak and the French soprano Marie Roze were on the walls
of his house in Edgbaston – and he had plenty of ideas about who should be
invited to perform. Jaffray asked the performers at these festivals to sign his
programmes, which he then had bound.

Jaffray knew as much about the state of the hospitals as any man in the
town. He was concerned that patients with chronic illnesses were not being
as well catered for as they might be. His solution was to prove one of the
greatest acts of philanthropy in nineteenth century Birmingham. Having
already purchased a site and had plans drawn up by the leading local architect
H.R. Yeoville Thompson, he proposed to the committee of the General
Hospital that he fund entirely the building and equipping of a suburban
hospital. He expected the hospital to be maintained by subscriptions:

> I cannot help believing that there are many persons who, having benefitted
> by the prosperity of the town [he wrote in his letter], feel that they owe
> a duty to the community and will gladly embrace this opportunity of
> discharging at least some portion of their obligation.[350]

This evocation of the principles of the civic gospel resulted in the
endowment fund reaching £21,297 3s 6d within three months; Jaffray did
not disclose how much he had laid out. The four acre site was in Gravelly
Hill, and the foundation stone was laid in June 1884. A central section
provided offices for the staff and two wings, one for male and one for female
patients, accommodated fifty patients in four wards. The Jaffray Hospital
was opened in September 1885 by the Prince of Wales, who heaped praise
on its founder before disappearing inside to enjoy a cup of coffee and a
cigar.

At all the great Liberal meetings in Birmingham Jaffray had been on the
platform and had often stepped forward to make a speech. He was part of
the deputation that invited John Bright to stand for Birmingham in August
1857, and in February 1865 he played a leading part in the formation of the
Birmingham Liberal Association, of which he became treasurer. Echoing
Dawson's views, he declared that the new organisation should embrace
Liberals of all hues and that it should exist to do more than seek to return
Bright at each parliamentary election. Jaffray had ambitions of his own
to enter the House of Commons, though he recognised that, with Dixon,
Muntz and Bright firmly installed, it would not be in Birmingham. He
received deputations from Liberals from other towns in the Midlands –
from Bewdley in 1868, for example – but, it was not until summer 1873 that

he came forward. He addressed numerous meetings during the by-election in East Staffordshire and was confident that he would emerge the victor. He was, however, resoundingly beaten by the Tory brewer Samuel Allsopp.[351] It was a shock to a man who did not usually encounter setbacks, and it brought to an end any interest he had in fighting election campaigns, even in Birmingham. Jaffray remained active in the BLA up until the rupture over Irish Home Rule in 1886. At that point, like a number of other Birmingham Liberals, he chose to withdraw from active involvement in local politics.

Jaffray had married Hannah Morton in Manchester Cathedral in February 1850, and the couple had two sons and a daughter. The family lived in Edgbaston from 1867 at Park Grove on Bristol Road, 'a low, white house, half-hidden amidst the trees and shrubs which encircle it'.[352] Visitors admired a magnificent collection of paintings – for example, in the drawing room a dozen landscapes by David Cox. In fact, Park Grove was as much an art gallery as it was a home and Jaffray had so many paintings that in 1899 he issued a catalogue. In the garden Jaffray was able to inspect his hothouses and peach houses and stroll around a pool. Not far from Park Grove was Edgbaston Pool, where he found plenty of ducks to shoot. Jaffray also owned a country house – The Skilts, set in an estate of 1,166 acres in Studley, which he bought at auction for £59,000 in May 1876. During August of each year he was to be found in neither place – he was at Remony in Perthshire for the grouse shoots.

The death of his wife in February 1893 and his withdrawal from involvement with the *Daily Post* later that year brought about the drawing-to-a-close of Jaffray's lengthy career in public life. He severed his last connection, as treasurer of the Shakespeare Memorial Library, in 1900. John Jaffray died at Park Grove on 4 January 1901. A few days later the man who had promoted the civic gospel through making art available to all, extending hospital provision and lending the support of his newspaper to Dawson's vision was interred in a vault with his wife at Edgbaston Old Church 'with the clergy and mourners standing bare-headed in the thickly falling snow'.[353]

Chapter 14

John Thackray Bunce

Great revolutions have their Tocquevilles and their Jeffersons to record and to draw out the significance of an historic upheaval. Birmingham's civic transformation was no different; here John Thackray Bunce (1828-1899) played a central role, both as a journalist and as the official historian, recounting and interpreting the story of the town's golden years. Nor was this by any means all he contributed. Birmingham owed its Art Gallery and School of Art to his advocacy, he was prominent in the fight to reform education both locally and in the country at large, he was a central figure in the Birmingham and Midland Institute, Our Shakespeare Club, the Old Library and the free libraries committee, and as a friend of Josiah Mason, a valued trustee of Mason College. His breadth of interest, versatility and sheer stamina across more than forty years of public service is striking. Still, while others featured in this volume would emulate that all-roundedness, with regard to his literary output he remains singular. From the first inklings of the caucus in 1867 through Chamberlain's gas and water socialism and on to the cultural and aesthetic efflorescence which followed, Bunce played a unique role for the propagators of the civic gospel. He was their influential cheerleader, chronicler and commentator in his editorial columns of the *Birmingham Daily Post,* while his *History of the Corporation of Birmingham* celebrated their considerable achievements.

Born in Oxfordshire the son of a watchmaker, then educated at the Gem Street school in Birmingham (part of the King Edward's foundation), Bunce – though an Anglican and initially a Tory – became a close friend of George Dawson and his immediate circle. Their views came to affect his political affiliations and his adherence to programmes of civic and educational renewal. He underwent a printing apprenticeship at the *Midland Counties Herald* before becoming first a reporter with *Aris's Birmingham Gazette,* and then its editor. Within two years (in 1862) he had been appointed to edit the *Birmingham Daily Post,* one of a number of new Liberal-leaning provincial dailies summoned into existence by Gladstone's abolition of paper duties in 1855.[354] It was a portentous moment and he would go on to hold this influential position for 36 years. As R.W. Dale put it:

> The new (civic) movement was fortunate in securing from the first the able support and wise guidance of the *Daily Post*. Mr Bunce was the trusted friend and adviser of the leaders, and the intimate personal friend of the most important of them. Through the columns of the most powerful newspaper in the Midland Counties the new ideas about municipal life were pressed on the whole community.[355]

Bunce was much more than a mere observer of unfolding events. He was himself an active Liberal, accorded considerable editorial latitude by his proprietors, John Jaffray and John Feeney, who allowed him to express his own opinion on public affairs. His personal engagement at the heart of the emerging caucus is seen, for example, in his chairing of the Birmingham Liberal Association (BLA) meeting which selected the three candidates for the 1868 election and in then seconding the historic resolution whereby the BLA endorsed William Harris's ingenious plan to distribute votes across those three candidates. Nearly twenty years later, when still prominent in the BLA, he presided at the management committee on that fateful evening in April 1886 when members divided acrimoniously over whether to support Gladstone on Home Rule, or their own Joseph Chamberlain, now the Prime Minister's greatest critic.[356] Equally, he was a committed campaigner; he was invaluable when running the National Education League's publishing committee after 1869, working with Joseph Chamberlain on the text, layout and marketing of pamphlets, and acting as the inspiration for 'a stream of pamphlets, leaflets, verbatim reports of debates, and off-cuts of parliamentary speeches' in advancing the principles of this national pressure group, which he helped control.[357]

The *Daily Post* reflected Bunce's support for the reformists' programme, sometimes in the sheer weight of column inches devoted to council affairs, and on other occasions through a more overt prejudice, well-illustrated in its coverage of the early years of the Birmingham School Board, an innovation for which Bunce and his reforming allies had such high hopes in 1870. His disgust at the School Board election results in November 1870, when poor Liberal management enabled Anglicans to top the poll, pervades the editorials and the reporting. He railed alike at the (unfair) cumulative voting system and at 'the Conservative canvassers and agents for falsifying voting papers'.[358] Though defeated, and in a minority on the School Board, Liberal members (Chamberlain and Dale) later (in 1873) relentlessly exposed the impossible position for teachers entrusted with delivering biblical exegesis in the classroom; Bunce devoted four column inches to an exhaustive, verbatim report of their demolition at the hands of their inquisitors.[359] The corollary was that in victory, after the Liberals' emphatic win in the November 1873 School Board elections, Bunce's editorial crowed 'that all men of Birmingham could rejoice at an exhibition of political strength'.[360]

Joseph Chamberlain valued Bunce for just those qualities William Harris would illuminate in his sketch of Bunce in his *History of the Shakespeare Club*: he relied on 'the clearness of his intellect', the quality of 'his literary style'. Time and again he would get him to redraft League literature or to pen a supportive commentary.[361] 'I wish to heaven I had a few of you fellows in London and the House,' he wrote to Bunce in 1877, after finding the metropolitan press unbiddable. In 1880 he was writing: 'thanks for an admirable article in the *Post*.'[362] Bunce was Chamberlain's sounding board for ideas on Ireland; he was his chairman of the publishing committee of the National Liberal Federation after 1877; he leaked minutes of Gladstone's cabinet discussions to help Chamberlain appeal to radical supporters in the country at large in 1881; and he was his saviour when in April 1886 Bunce overruled Gladstone supporters to ensure a fair hearing for Chamberlain at that BLA ruling council meeting. After agonies of indecision Bunce followed Chamberlain out of the Liberal Party; by 1888 the *Post* was robustly championing Chamberlain's imperial policies.

For over thirty years Bunce ensured that the *Post* was much more than a champion of Joseph Chamberlain; he provided comprehensive coverage of Birmingham's metamorphosis. He did not confine those column inches to political or environmental matters; he gave generous space to reports of art, library, debating, Shakespearean and institutional meetings and activities. Municipal matters received close attention, so the decision to ask Bunce to write a *History of the Corporation of Birmingham* seemed an obvious one. George Dawson had spoken of the importance of engendering a sense of pride in one's town and so Bunce was very much on message when he aspired in his *History* to educate all citizens about Birmingham's singularity. Chamberlain, who in 1876 presided over the council's general purposes committee that engaged Bunce to write the *History*, saw this as the way of shaping the civic gospel's narrative for posterity: 'I am very anxious you should undertake to develop the Birmingham theory of municipal government,' he would write.[363] Bunce needed no persuasion, for he truly believed in the municipality's power for good – 'it should completely grasp the life of the community' – and (in the spirit of Dawson) that 'such a community needs the help of its best men'.[364]

Bunce's narrative remains influential after more than a century. Employing vivid *chiaroscuro*, he contrasts the then and the now. The years before the civic gospellers got to work were dark ages: 'the central district of Birmingham was so poor and neglected that Birmingham people, jealous of the credit of their town, were ashamed to show it to visitors.' On the council this was the era of the economists, led by Joseph Allday, whose policies 'excited a strong feeling of hostility, personal, political and municipal [for] he was violent of speech, and prone to ... engage in personal attack'. The entire council in these years (the 1850s) was, it seems, of a 'disorderly character'.[365] Now Birmingham, a generation later, has witnessed the lambent dawn of a new age:

[It was] like a feat of the imagination, so vast is the progress, so marvellous the contrast. [In the past] there were numerous independent governing bodies ... there were few public works of magnitude or public buildings of importance, streets were imperfectly made, sparingly lighted, inadequately watched and partially drained.

Forty years of growing municipal government changed all this, [he enthused]. The government of the town is in its own hands, free, unfettered and complete. We have public edifices not unworthy of the place. Our streets are well kept, lighted, drained and watched, the private monopolies of gas and water have ceased to exist, [while] the health of the community is cared for by an efficient sanitary system.

The agents of this change were his friends, who had heeded George Dawson's appeal; instead of abstaining – as in the past –

Men who had made fortunes in the town and acquired leisure, began to feel that they owed to the community a debt of service ... For some years the town has reaped the advantage of this truer view of the responsibility and the duty of individual members of a common society.[366]

This last sentiment might have been borrowed from an R.W. Dale sermon on civic obligation. So, the contours of Birmingham's fortunes in the nineteenth century became established with Bunce's acclaimed *History*, stamping the historian's imprimatur on the achievements of Dawson's civic gospellers.

Some minor modifications to his interpretation have emerged. For example, Thomas Avery, one of the economists who came to recognise the importance of promoting essential sanitary reforms, has recently been rehabilitated, reflecting a new understanding that municipal life before Chamberlain was not unrelievedly small-minded.[367] One might also question Bunce's euphoric conclusion that, 'we now have a representative municipal authority united, active and powerful, linking together parties, sects and classes in one interest'.[368] This prelapsarian vision ignores the acrimony between the parties in general election campaigns, in school board and in council meetings, as well as the resentment at the way that Chamberlain's allies monopolised control of political appointments. In the same year (1878) Bunce wrote these complacent words, *The Times* published a bitter letter from a Birmingham citizen:

> I describe the state of tyranny under which we groan. If a man ventures to call himself a Conservative, he becomes thereby disqualified from serving on the Town Council or the Board of Guardians.[369]

Bunce as both journalist and historian sought to edify and educate Birmingham's citizens. Everything else he contributed to Birmingham public life pursued the same virtuous ends. A deep concern to extend educational opportunity informed all he did. From the mid-1850s he was actively involved in movements to ensure working-class children attended school; to extend literacy among such children; to expand night-schooling in Birmingham to compensate for poor elementary education.[370] He attended the momentous meeting Dixon hosted at his home in 1867 which inaugurated the Birmingham Education Society, newspaper reports singling him out as an active participant in 'considerable discussion'.[371] As we saw, he was a central figure in the National Education League from its inception in 1869. Into his last years he remained involved in education; he was a co-opted governor of King Edward's Grammar school in 1895; he was a long-time trustee of Mason College; and, responding once more to an appeal from Joseph Chamberlain to write 'something lyric, pathetic and emphatic', he was a persuasive advocate for Chamberlain's new civic university in December 1897.[372]

He lived out the Dawsonite injunction that the privileged should endeavour to nourish their fellow citizens spiritually and intellectually. He was president of the Philosophical Institution in 1858 and thereafter a prominent council member of the Birmingham and Midland Institute, notable for his support for ladies' classes. He became its president in 1878 when, under J. H. Chamberlain's leadership, it was near the apogee of its fortunes. His professional literary interest, combined with a passionate belief in the civilising influence of good books, explain his attachment of many years – as a proprietor and then in 1865 as chairman – to the Old Library, a subscription library 'allowing persons to take highest quality literature home to read at their leisure', which ante-dated the municipal free libraries.[373] Inevitably he became closely associated with these too; though not a councillor, he was elected to the free libraries committee in 1870 after a proposal by his friend William Harris, and there he stayed for many years. In 1882 he was honorary secretary of the library restoration fund, raising thousands of pounds for the rebuilding of the reference library after the devastating fire of 1879.

Perhaps inevitably, given his bibliophilic interests and his friendship with Sam: Timmins and George Dawson, he was an early member of Our Shakespeare Club, speaking eloquently at the 300th Anniversary Dinner on 23 April 1864, when he followed on from George Dawson to toast William Shakespeare as 'the opportunity to extend civil and religious liberty all over the world'.[374] Like Dawson and Timmins he conceived the works of Shakespeare, collected in the Memorial Library, as a universal and life enhancing resource for all citizens of whatever class. Friendships fostered among like-minded Dawson disciples were consolidated at the Arts Club, of which Bunce was a founder member in 1873. It 'facilitated the social intercourse of gentlemen professing Liberal politics and who were more or less engaged in public life in Birmingham', at the very time when Liberals were completing their ascendancy in all aspects of public life.[375] No doubt that 'social intercourse' saw discussion of municipal reform as well as of shared literary and artistic interests.

It would be inevitable that some of the conversation in which Bunce engaged would have concerned art. It was a life-long passion. He lectured on 'the nobility and life of David Cox' (Birmingham's foremost artist) to the Birmingham Society of Artists; he commissioned his friend J. H. Chamberlain to build his Edgbaston house 'Longworth' in the latest Venetian Gothic; he was one of a select band, including J. H. Chamberlain, who met John Ruskin in July 1877 at George Baker's Bewdley 'Beaucastle' estate to inaugurate Ruskin's Guild of St George, which set out to recover good design and craftsmanship.[376]

His very first printed contribution was an anonymous letter to the *Midland Counties Herald* arguing for an art gallery and museum in Birmingham.[377] Thereafter he enlisted the columns of the *Post* in the cause. For example, in 1870 he gave generous space to a report of the council's Art Gallery sub-committee which he chaired: after leading a deputation to London's India Museum to purchase choice Indian artefacts he reported that 'as regards form and colour they would be of essential value to Birmingham's manufacturers and artisans … Subsequent discussion pointed to the need for the formation of an Industrial Museum in Birmingham.'[378] Yet no museum or art gallery eventuated through the 1870s because of a lack of public funding, but J T Bunce continued to appeal for one in articles in his paper. It was his persistence which impressed Richard and George Tangye in July 1880. Richard Tangye acknowledged that he had convinced them of 'the great loss the town sustains in the absence of an adequate art collection'.[379] This was a cause of deep satisfaction for Bunce; he boasted in an address at the School of Art a decade later that 'no provincial town has had ampler means of Art instruction than (that provided) by the collections of Birmingham's Municipal Art Gallery'.[380] Thereafter he continued to be prominent on the Art Purchase committee.

Yet it comprised only one half of his prospectus for Birmingham's aesthetic development. For many years he was the civic gospellers' most active critic of the state of art education in Birmingham. On the one hand, reform encompassed extending art teaching into every Birmingham classroom: 'Art must be made a regular part of education. It ought to be a discredit that a student of either sex should leave school without some knowledge of the history of art or of how to draw,' he said in a lecture to the Society of Artists in 1876.[381] On the other, it meant arguing for the building of a new School of Art. Again, he took to his own paper's columns, and again it was Richard Tangye who responded, in November 1881:

In the summer of 1879 you published an article in the *Daily Post* setting forth the great disadvantages the School of Art and Design laboured under for want of suitable accommodation for students and, at the same time, you pointed out how much the town was in need of an Art Gallery. I was much impressed by what you wrote and determined to do my best for supplying the deficiency. A noble Art Gallery is now in the course of erection. I am sure it will be a pleasure and satisfaction to you to be the medium for communicating the enclosed offer to the mayor.[382]

The result was a generous gift for a new School of Art. It allowed the council to set about commissioning Chamberlain and Martin to design an iconic building for the School of Art. Bunce had been a vital intermediary. As later chairman of the Management of the School of Art committee he frequently spoke with great pride of the school's rapid growth, in 1890 contrasting the bad old days:

when 500 pupils occupied ill-ventilated, ill-lighted rooms with the present school, the finest in the country, with ten times the staff, with eleven branch schools, 3,500 students and ... with results [being] the best attained anywhere in the country. No-one could dispute it stood at the head of all the art schools in the UK.[383]

He was responsible for several other notable developments. In 1892 in his School of Art Prizegiving address he announced an extension to the school to accommodate repousse, enamelling, wood carving and terracotta workshops. Here was active support for the headmaster's plans for artists and designers to develop their craft skills in realising their designs. And he positively encouraged the expansion of women's education 'recognising their right to a free, open and equal career', celebrating their national exam success at the school, and 'that it is giving them opportunities of doing the work for which they are showing themselves to be thoroughly fitted'.[384] By a happy chance his daughters Kate and Myra became two of the school's most prominent alumnae.

He also did much to promote art education in schools, presiding over schemes to provide art teaching for the Board schools as well as the King Edward's foundation. He articulated his wider vision for cultivating discrimination in citizens in that same speech in 1892:

Are we not gradually bringing a wholesome influence upon the town generally ... by educating all classes in the knowledge and appreciation of Art directly, and in raising the standards of taste and in the wider diffusion of a knowledge of what it can do to brighten, refine and elevate individual and communal life? An instructed people will refuse submission to sordid cheapness and ugliness in their streets and their homes.[385]

J. T. Bunce believed, as did George Dawson and J. H. Chamberlain, that noble and dignified architecture would help elevate and refine Birmingham's citizens. Like them he thought:

Art must permeate and suffuse the daily life ... there must be public buildings, ample, stately and rich in ornament to dignify public life ... to promote a municipal life nobler, fuller and richer than any the world has ever seen.[386]

Bunce's wide-ranging support for the visual arts was a response to a deeply felt belief in the civilising force of Art and architecture and was central to his enduring achievement; it was just as important as his more widely celebrated legacy as a journalist and historian. In both regards he proved to be one of Dawson's most significant disciples.

Chapter 15

William Kenrick

When he died in July 1919 the *Birmingham Daily Post* concluded that 'to write the life of William Kenrick (1831-1919) would in effect be to write the history of Birmingham during the past half-century'.[387] Of no other individual could this be more truly said, not even of his more famous brother-in-law, Joseph Chamberlain, for Kenrick involved himself in every aspect of Birmingham life. This comprised membership of numerous committees concerned with local and national education, municipal government, working men's sick benefit schemes, nursing and children's charities but – most important of all – it encompassed a range of artistic and intellectual interests, for his special importance lies in his dedication to the aesthetic development of Birmingham and of its citizens.

Born in 1831, a scion of Archibald Kenrick and Sons, the famous West Bromwich cast iron and hollow ware firm, he worked as a director of the family business specialising in commercial management, after he had first graduated from the nonconformist University College in London.[388] Influenced by his own youthful experience in Smethwick and West Bromwich, by Dawson's lectures at the Church of the Saviour, by his membership of a tight-knit philanthropic Unitarian family clique and by his closeness to the dynamic Joseph Chamberlain, he personified the improving instincts of the best of Birmingham's business class. Ideas about how improvement was to be achieved were discussed – among other things – at the Birmingham and Edgbaston Debating Society where he polished his public speaking and where he became president in 1867.

Archibald Kenrick's steady expansion gave him the time and income for that public service. It might have been William Kenrick who G. F. Parker, an American writer, had in mind when, after visiting Birmingham in 1896, he told his readers that 'the foundation of Birmingham administration was the integrity and dedication of these men. Service on the council demanded two full working days each week, chairmen of sub-committees giving four full days, for which they received no remuneration, no expenses, no concessions.'[389] For Alderman Kenrick served on the council and many of its committees across five decades, at the same time as being occupied in national politics as an MP, junior minister and privy councillor.

Few other leaders in nineteenth-century Birmingham made a similar contribution to the implementation of Dawson's ideas on the civic gospel; Kenrick might indeed be thought of as the quintessential Dawson man. On the one hand, he was an invaluable supporter of the municipal revolution instigated by Joseph Chamberlain, the brother of Kenrick's wife Mary. In his wake, Kenrick joined the town council in 1870, and became an integral component of the team which realised Dawson's vision of a better, healthier town. He voted reliably for the revolution in the town's utilities and succeeded his brother-in-law as chairman of the gas committee in 1880, having already done sterling service as chairman of the watch committee (1874-76).[390] Kenrick followed Chamberlain as mayor in 1877, a year after Joseph moved to Westminster as one of Birmingham's MPs. Although he vowed, on assuming office, 'to carry on the recent policy of the Council which was wise, beneficent and economical, as regards to health, welfare and the convenience of its constituents,'[391] Kenrick's mayoralty was marred by the only real controversy of his long and happy career in public service, when he and others of the Chamberlain circle who had put up funds to guarantee the viability of the improvement scheme were accused of private speculation; the criticism proved groundless, but the £5,000 he put down is evidence of his commitment to the civic cause. When it came to making his own assessment of his year of office, tellingly he told those attending a dinner in his honour that his true achievements were the addition of new parks in Hockley and Small Heath, the obtaining of a bill through Parliament the better to utilise Birmingham's disused burial grounds, and the establishment of provident dispensaries throughout Birmingham, all very Dawsonite in his care for the spiritual and physical well-being of the citizens.[392]

On the other hand, valuable though his assistance to Chamberlain's municipal revolution was, his real influence lay elsewhere. William Kenrick had learnt much for himself from his experience as a young man with the summit schools, founded by his family near their factory at Spon Lane in West Bromwich; there among the working-class pupils he discovered a crying need for much more far-reaching educational reform. When George Dixon in 1867 first mooted a Birmingham Education Society to raise money to expand and fund places in Birmingham's schools, William Kenrick attended the inaugural meeting at Dixon's home, along with R.W. Dale, William Temple and other leading figures from the town. And as the realisation grew in 1869 that more was needed, so a campaigning body – the National Education League – was established to agitate for a national, free and compulsory education system; there too we find William Kenrick in the heart of its executive committee. For seven years he helped direct and administer an organisation with over one hundred branches nationally.

He did not confine himself to elementary education. Along with men like William Harris and C. E. Mathews, he fought a long campaign to break open the closed governance and system of admissions at King Edward's Grammar School, with the aim of making it a truly formidable academic institution based on competitive entry for all-comers. Not only was the campaign successful; he then became a long-standing governor of the school as a town council representative. His position there, at the same time as he was directing the expansion of the School of Art, ensured that the two institutions combined in the late 1880s to deliver art teaching throughout the King Edward's foundation, a national first.[393] He also introduced a scheme to provide good secondary education for girls, presiding over the creation of KES High School. In the same vein we find him in a list of shareholders funding the foundation of Edgbaston High School for Girls in 1876. So, he actively worked to live out Dawson's injunction that Birmingham's leaders should dedicate themselves to widening their town's educational opportunities.

Before becoming involved in Birmingham's schools he had already been immersed in the work of the Birmingham and Midland Institute, where he was a member of its council from 1866-77, years which coincided with the energetic impetus to general adult education at the Institute brought about by the new honorary secretary, his close friend J. H. Chamberlain. These two men found they shared a passion for art and architecture and so a remarkably productive partnership grew up.[394] This is partly explained by the fact that William Kenrick was an artist manqué and in his teens he had wanted to enrol at the Academy Schools in London where he would have sat alongside Millais and Hunt; he was gently dissuaded by his father who sensibly asked, 'could you be a good artist, not a mere amateur?'[395]

He then channelled his artistic inclinations into building up his own private art collection, which would include a number of notable examples of Pre-Raphaelite works, and to commissioning J. H. Chamberlain to remodel the Kenrick family house, The Grove in Edgbaston, where the architect applied his passion for Venetian Gothic detailing to create a paradigm of nineteenth-century domestic architecture. Although the house was demolished in 1963, the Harborne Room with its gothic panelling and intarsia wood flooring is still preserved in the Victoria and Albert Museum and reveals 'the creative versatility of its architect and the progressive taste of its patron'.[396] Kenrick's personal enthusiasm for Chamberlain and Martin's work also benefited the town. He was a senior alderman, in a position to press their claims to design a portfolio of municipal projects. Thus it was that the firm planned the extensions of the Birmingham and Midland Institute and of the free library in Edmund Street. It also created the memorial to Joseph Chamberlain, the canopy to George Dawson's statue in Chamberlain Place, and designed the School of Art, the latter only completed after Chamberlain's untimely death.[397]

His particular interest in the visual arts encompassed much more than patronising artists and architects. He wanted to cultivate aesthetic taste and develop latent artistic talent in Birmingham's citizens. In a mayoral speech in 1878, for example, he elaborated on his belief in:

> ... the public good to be derived from the study and love of art [which] must be natural and of universal application. It should be impossible for a workman to produce an article of doubtful and vicious taste. So, they had to get every child taught the elementary principles of form and colour, and they had to establish public art galleries and they had to acquire and lay out public parks and gardens, models of what gardens should be; and they must be accessible.

Much of this prescription for the enhancement of people's lives – in the spirit of Dawson's speech at the opening of the reference library in 1866 – would be realised in his lifetime.[398] Yet what is also striking in that speech is his concern, as an industrialist, to refine the discrimination and craftsmanship of men who Kenricks would be employing.

Steadily from the mid-1870s onwards, his ability to influence the artistic development of the town grew as he came to occupy important positions on key Birmingham committees. From 1874 he was on the managing committee of the School of Art whose studios were located in the Midland Institute; he was its chairman from 1883, and able to finesse the arrangement insisted on by the Tangye brothers whereby the council took over its management on behalf of the town, thereby stealing a march on all its provincial rivals. He was – with many Dawson acolytes – a member of the free libraries committee, which helped realise George Dawson's vision of informing and enlightening Birmingham's citizens. That committee was also responsible for the room in the Central Library which served as an art gallery. Kenrick was a central figure in meeting the need for a larger and more impressive space appropriate to Birmingham's size and status.

In this he was helped by others. J. H. Chamberlain had prevailed on the foremost designer William Morris to serve as president of the School of Art in 1878 and Morris stayed with Kenrick at The Grove on his Birmingham visits, the two men becoming close friends. Morris was well briefed on the town's ambitions as regards the arts and communicated with his friend Edward Burne-Jones, the Birmingham born Pre-Raphaelite painter and designer. The latter recorded that, 'whilst talking with Mr Morris both before and after his visit to Birmingham, we have been much struck with the need there is in that important town for a public Museum of Art. It is not too much to say that without one a School of Art is impossible.'[399]

While Morris and Burne-Jones provided important validation for the project, just as important were J. T. Bunce (through the columns of the *Birmingham Daily Post*) and Richard and George Tangye, but right at the heart of accomplishing the project for the new Museum and Art Gallery was William Kenrick. He was chairman of the gas committee which persuaded the council to agree to giving the municipal gas department the land on which to build much needed offices in 1880. In return it promised the £40,000 required to include an art gallery in the scheme.[400] The profits from Joseph Chamberlain's gas and water socialism were being ploughed back into a project to develop discernment in Birmingham's citizens. The inscription at the museum's entrance, 'By the gains of Industry we promote Art', could not have been more appropriate. So popular was this new gallery when it was opened by the Prince of Wales in 1885 that over one million visitors visited it in its first full year of operation.

William Kenrick then sat alongside six others (including R. F. Martineau, Richard Tangye and Edward Taylor) on the corporation's newly constituted art gallery purchase committee.[401] His influence on Birmingham's outstanding collection of Pre-Raphaelite works was strong from the outset; for example, he persuaded the committee early on to purchase two works by Dante Gabriel Rossetti, one of the founders of the Pre-Raphaelite Brotherhood and, more importantly, he convinced his colleagues to commission Burne-Jones to paint the 'Star of Bethlehem'(1889), a 'blaze of colour and look[ing] like a carol' in the artist's own words, describing his memorable portrayal of the Magi attending the baby in the stable.[402] Birmingham would become the leading centre for Pre-Raphaelite art, partly because its wealthy businessmen responded to the jewel-like colour of the art and partly because the serious moral intent of the artists chimed so well with the earnest desire of the Dawson circle to elevate its citizens. Serious narrative paintings like William Holman Hunt's *The Finding of the Saviour in the Temple* and Ford Madox Brown's *The Last of England* were intended to do just that. Kenrick's influence on Birmingham's artistic taste is clear. It was he who welcomed William Morris to open the first great national exhibition of Pre-Raphaelite paintings in the Municipal Art Gallery in October 1891 and his purchase there of Millais's *Blind Girl* as a gift to the Gallery prompted others to follow, Richard and George Tangye, Joseph Chamberlain and J T Bunce among them. The result was that the town came to own significant examples of the work of William Holman Hunt, Albert Moore, George Watts and Edward Burne-Jones among others.[403]

We have seen that Kenrick was zealous about art education and his chairmanship of the School of Art through the late 1870s gave him a valuable insight into its cramped and dilapidated accommodation. Again J. H. Chamberlain and J. T. Bunce were committed allies, and again – as we have seen in chapter 14 – the Tangyes came to the rescue. With a new art school came reformed governance; the council established a new committee, the Museum and School of Art committee in March 1884. Alderman Kenrick was appointed chairman; its members included those other long-standing supporters of art and design in the town, J. T. Bunce and R. F. Martineau. They, along with the outstanding headmaster Edward Taylor, oversaw remarkable expansion and innovation, but the close understanding between head and chairman was the key to the growing national reputation of the Birmingham School of Art, as was the fact that William Kenrick was, from 1885, a member of parliament and at one time a minister of the Crown.

Every year Kenrick would give a state of the nation address at the School of Art's annual meeting and prizegiving. He had great pride each year in recording dramatic increases in the number of students enrolled; by 1889 there were 3123 registered students and an additional 291 girl students (two of whom would be his daughters, Cecily and Millicent Kenrick). He took evident satisfaction in the extraordinary national success of the School of Art's female students in public exams. For example, at the national Arts and Crafts Exhibition of 1893 58 per cent of prizes for executed design went to Birmingham female students; and in 1901 at the Paris Exhibition, 77 per cent of the prizes for executed design were awarded to Birmingham female students.[404]

Each year he methodically compared the number of Science and Art Department prizes won by Birmingham students with those (invariably lower totals) awarded to candidates from Manchester, Liverpool, Sheffield and indeed London. In 1891 he could boast that in the number of prizes 'the School of Art had never been approached by any other school in the country'. 'It was not simply that Birmingham had improved compared to other schools; it had done so at a greater rate.'[405] Nor was he alone in believing Birmingham to be pre-eminent; in 1900 the annual external examiner's report by William Lethaby stated that:

> The school stands so high as compared with other Art Schools known to me that, if my report were to be mostly comparative, I could say nothing more than that Birmingham stood first, or among the very first, in the kingdom.[406]

Kenrick personally did much to further opportunities in 1884 by setting up a fund of £3,000 to provide scholarships for twelve promising board school pupils, to be known as Kenrick scholars, of whom William Bloye, the famous sculptor, was one. And as chairman he presided over the expansion of free places at the School of Art through the generosity of such as Louisa Ryland and the Tangye brothers. The operation grew year on year: from 1887 advanced students from the King Edward's foundation attended the school for art instruction while the same year saw all board school pupil teachers in Birmingham attending its art lessons. [407] In 1888 he could announce that the city's jewellers and silversmiths had agreed to send apprentices to classes at the School of Art, which Kenrick hoped 'would be an encouragement to employers in the art industries'. Here we again see the industrialist in him, keen that Birmingham manufacturing should benefit from a successful art school.[408]

In 1891 he was able to reveal that the council's consent had been obtained for a large extension to the School of Art. It would enable 50 per cent more students to be accommodated. More importantly, it allowed Edward Taylor to introduce what would be an innovation in art education in Britain to which William Kenrick along with Bunce and R. F. Martineau gave their full-hearted support. In 'a new casting workshop and art studio', Kenrick announced, 'designers might learn something of materials and processes and art workers might receive a more searching and wider training.' For the first time artists could realise their designs, utilising materials which would allow them to make an artefact for themselves. It was particularly apt for a city famed for its metal working. Kenrick's interest in technical education would see him give unconditional support to R. F. Martineau in bringing to fruition his dream of establishing a technical school in Birmingham.[409]

Kenrick's contacts in the art world, especially with William Morris and Edward Burne-Jones, but also his ability to attract household names like Walter Crane and William Holman Hunt to Birmingham, practically benefited the School of Art. Burne-Jones and Walter Crane spent time tutoring students, and William Morris gave lectures and served as an examiner there. Morris and Burne-Jones' influence on Birmingham art was profound – they encouraged the school to develop a curriculum which focused on practical design and on craftsmanship. As a result, the city became an acknowledged centre of the Arts and Crafts movement.

Towards the end of his long life, Birmingham recognised William Kenrick's exceptional service – those 44 years on the Council, and on one or other of its committees, and his time as one of the city's MPs – by granting him the freedom of the city in 1911, the year he eventually surrendered the chairmanship of the School of Art committee. Few of the other original civic gospellers clustering around George Dawson had shown such durability or such versatility; nor did anyone else match his lasting impact on art curation and art education in Birmingham. In a valedictory article in 1919 the *Birmingham Daily Mail* concluded that 'none has done so much for the artistic culture of Birmingham during the last quarter of a century'.[410]

Chapter 16

Robert Francis Martineau

More than most other figures in this book, R. F. Martineau (1831-1909) illustrates the rich associational life of his class in Victorian Birmingham. He belonged to the aristocracy of the town's civic leaders, part of that influential Edgbaston nexus created by intermarriage between the Chamberlain, Kenrick and Martineau families which we find at the heart of much municipal activity in the mid to late nineteenth century. He hailed from the Huguenot Martineau family, who were among the country's Unitarian elite. His uncle was James Martineau, the influential religious philosopher, and his aunt, Harriet Martineau, was the pioneer of sociology in the English-speaking world. From his father – also Robert – he inherited his Unitarian faith, an interest in manufacturing (he directed the family brass cock foundry) and both his political radicalism and sense of civic duty. Robert Snr had 'thrown himself heartily' into the reform agitation of 1830, had led the fight against the payment of church rates, had been a street commissioner (alongside Arthur Ryland) and had then served on the council for twelve years, becoming mayor in 1846.[411]

R. F. (Frank) Martineau is less well known than his brother, Sir Thomas (1828-1893), who by dint of his knighthood, his mayoralty, and his role in the building of the new Victoria Law Courts and the Elan valley reservoir, has been memorialised with a blue plaque and an entry in the *Oxford Dictionary of National Biography*; Frank has not. However, the breadth, and sheer longevity, of his many commitments – and most particularly his service to the extension of intellectual and cultural opportunities in Birmingham – explain why he has a chapter here. When he died in 1909 the obituarists recognised the extent of that participation across over forty years: 'his sympathy with every movement which had for its object the moral, intellectual or physical advancement of his fellow citizens, especially of the poorer classes, was deep and enduring.'[412] On the same lines a contemporary noted that 'he is a thorough Radical, brimful of the doctrine of equality and thoroughly believing that one man is quite as good as another'.[413] In both comments one can discern his strong Unitarian principles.

As a young man he was one of those Birmingham Unitarians becoming 'dissatisfied with the dry bones and thrashed out chaff' dispensed in sermons at the New Meeting, where Unitarians habitually congregated. Many were impressed by a new voice in the town in the mid-1840s, that of the fiery, energetic, young preacher George Dawson at Mount Zion. R. F. Martineau was 'enchanted'. 'Oh! ... this is the preaching I have longed for all my life,' he exclaimed.[414] He would follow – and work alongside – Dawson for the next thirty years, interacting with him at the Midland Institute, at Our Shakespeare Club, in the Education League, at the discussions at the Arts Club and when he attended the preacher's regular evening lectures. His impact on Martineau might be discerned soon after Dawson's death when – in 1878 – Martineau spoke at the Birmingham Free Christian Society to celebrate 'a Church of the people – no hierarchy, no bishops, no church government'. He went on to echo that distinctive strand in Dawson's teaching, the civic duty owed by the wealthy: 'even in Birmingham there were persons who needed to be taught that the business of all was the business of each and that public work was really benevolence on a large scale,' he said.[415] Still, this was not the only religious influence on him; like many prominent Birmingham Unitarians he worshipped at the Church of the Messiah, where he was ministered to by Henry Crosskey. Here Martineau's natural predisposition was reinforced, for Crosskey – who had been taught by James Martineau – saw Unitarianism 'as practical power, a religion of human service'.[416]

There is barely an aspect of Birmingham public life in the second half of the nineteenth century in which R. F. Martineau did not serve in some shape or form. In many areas he was content to lend his support as a committee member, an honorary secretary, or simply as an attendee but the time-consuming nature of his involvement suggests that his career at the family brass works took something of a back seat. Perhaps it helped that he never married. Running right through his adult life was his commitment to the Liberal Party and support for what might be deemed radical causes, starting in 1862 with his organisation of the Birmingham branch of the cotton relief fund to help Lancashire workers suffering from the cotton famine in the American civil war. He was a member of the Birmingham Liberal Association, sat on the committee of 600, represented the party on the town council for over thirty years, and stayed true to it as a Gladstonian Liberal after the Home Rule hiatus in 1886, while his brother abandoned it to become a Liberal Unionist MP in support of Joseph Chamberlain.

He was actively engaged in a number of political causes. He was a leading member of the Peace and Arbitration Society, chairing the local Peace committee meeting in the Friends Meeting House in 1895.[417] It was why he vehemently – and unpopularly – opposed granting the freedom of the city to Lord Roberts, Boer War hero; Martineau deeply disapproved of this South African adventure. Taking his lead from George Dawson, Henry Crosskey and his uncle James Martineau, he was a consistent campaigner for women's rights. In May 1880 he spoke at a meeting of the Birmingham Society for Women's Suffrage when he rather optimistically declared that now 'he had the best hope of our ultimate success', while three years later he was on the platform alongside Josephine Butler to demand the repeal of the invidious Contagious Diseases Act which stigmatised women in the spread of sexually transmitted diseases.[418] He was equally prominent in both encouraging better education for women as well as in supporting their work among Birmingham's poor, this through his championing of the Birmingham Ladies Association for Useful Work.[419]

Like many of his extended family and friends he joined the Edgbaston Debating Society as a young man; by 1868, though he would never become a noted orator in his many roles, he was its vice-chairman, and the press could comment favourably on 'his humorous speech'.[420] Thereafter his range of interests was truly catholic. He was on the committee of the new Birmingham Athletic Club in 1860, appreciating like other Dawsonians the importance of improving the physical well-being of Birmingham's citizens.[421] That concern explains the campaign he successfully fought in Parliament to transform the dangerously unhealthy Park Street burial ground into a salubrious recreational open space, as well as his committee work for the Birmingham and Midland Homeopathic Hospital and his fundraising for Birmingham sanatorium, where he was a founding governor.[422] It also lay behind the lead he gave over many years to the Birmingham branch of the Coffee House company, which aimed to provide a healthy alcohol-free environment for socialising, an alternative to the temptations of the public house. The opening of the 120 bed temperance Cobden Hotel in 1885 consolidated the growing success of the initiative in the town.[423]

His finely attuned sense of public duty led him to heed George Dawson's call for prominent businessmen to offer themselves for municipal service. R. F. Martineau defeated the sitting Conservative in the St Bartholomew's ward and was elected to the council in 1874, borne on a flood tide of Liberal electoral success. Joseph Chamberlain was part way through his municipal revolution and thereafter Martineau (joined two years later by brother Thomas) was a loyal stalwart of the Chamberlain 'party', invariably voting with a sizeable group to support civic gospel policies.[424] Naturally,

Martineau was recruited to one of Chamberlain's pet schemes, that of the town's improvement. So, in 1877 he was a member of the small council delegation deputed to visit – and report on – the improvement schemes in Glasgow and Edinburgh. During the winter of 1878 he was appointed secretary of the council committee charged with distributing relief to the distressed poor suffering in the prevailing depression.[425] He was already recognised as a councillor with a special interest in health and sanitation; in May 1878 he was elected to a committee to form a sanitary supply association for Birmingham at a town hall meeting. The association aimed at diffusing sanitary knowledge, especially that concerning ventilation, drainage and the latest sanitary ware, to householders and house builders.[426] He was on the council's health committee from the 1870s until the early 1890s. As we will see later, his other great conciliar contribution was to matters scientific, literary and artistic.

As for many of the Dawson disciples featured in this book the extension of educational opportunity, the cultivation of taste, of skill and of critical faculties, forms a *leitmotif* running through much of what he did. Early we find him a founder member of the National Education League (in 1869) and a central figure on its executive committee, where he was chairman of the branches committee. He was part of that NEL delegation to 10 Downing Street in 1870 to urge Prime Minister Gladstone to adopt League principles in his education bill. He was the founder of the Sunday Lecture Society established to instruct and inform working people and he was prominent in the Birmingham Selborne Society, which sought to teach urban children to love nature and to reverence the sanctity of animal life. He was on various committees of the British Association for the Advancement of Science. Given that he was the son of the originator of the Edgbaston Proprietary School, established by Robert in protest at the Anglican closed shop of King Edward's School, it was a delicious irony that he should eventually become a grammar school governor. Josiah Mason divined that R. F. Martineau had a deep sympathy for the education of Birmingham's working men and asked him to be a trustee of Mason College. Joseph Chamberlain also discerned that sympathy; however bitter their divisions over the Boer War, Chamberlain was prepared to overlook them and invite Martineau on to the governing council of his new University of Birmingham.

One can also read his many years' membership of Our Shakespeare Club as part of his educational enterprise. Because of the range of his intellectual enthusiasms, it seems very appropriate that he should have given the toast to 'Literature, Science and Art' at the 1869 annual dinner. George Dawson's presidential speech in 1871, when he celebrated that 'the young are studying

William Shakespeare; this little club has done something [to bring this about]', would surely have resonated with the listening R. F. Martineau.[427] Equally, his years of dedication to the Midland Institute form part of his educational legacy. He joined the Institute council as a borough governor in 1874 and remained so until his death in 1909. The linking of Institute and town council in his person was very fruitful for both parties, especially as the town council assumed increasing responsibilities for art and science teaching from the 1880s onwards; needless jealousy and friction was avoided through his diplomatic presence.

Yet it was as the Birmingham and Midland Institute's honorary secretary from 1883, when he took over the reins after J. H. Chamberlain's shockingly early death, that he was at his most significant. He presided over it at the time of its greatest prestige and popularity; in 1905 it had over 2,200 members while it attracted national figures as its president and as its weekly lecturers. He threw himself into its life, speaking at student societies and accompanying the Union of Teachers and Students on its excursions. His obituarist acclaimed a much-loved institutional figure:

The Midland Institute was for many years a second home to him, and his happiest hours were undoubtedly spent within its walls. At meetings of members he would greet them as if they were personal friends, and his face would beam with delight as he watched new students ascend the staircase and guided them to their classrooms.[428]

Martineau himself did indeed treasure the cultivation of a collegial and social education for the working man at the Institute, saying that:

Its object is to furnish a work-a-day university; as one of the chief advantages of a University life is the formation of friendships, so here I trust that our beloved Institute may be the means of bestowing on many of its students the inestimable blessing of the fuller life which comes from pure friendships.[429]

Naturally the Institute had a more serious academic focus too. When he delivered his vice-presidential address on the opening of the Institute's great extension in 1882, designed to meet the growing demand for student places, he talked of

... the desire for the special culture which their classes and lectures gave. From those classes had gone forth every year young men who had carried out in their daily occupation the accuracy of method learned in their scientific training at the Institute.[430]

That allusion to scientific education is apposite. He would become Birmingham's leading figure in the expansion of technical education. When the city council adopted the Technical Instruction Act in 1890, he was the key individual at the Institute who recognised the wisdom of its handing over the Institute's science and metallurgical classes, started in 1885 by George Kenrick, into municipal care. 'The city council could do more than the limited means of the Institute would permit,' he said.[431] He knew that the Institute's industrial department ran at a loss. When in December 1890 the council created a new technical school sub-committee, he was elected its chairman; and when it became apparent that leasing laboratories from the Institute was no long-term solution, he set about mustering arguments for a new technical school building. He visited schools on the continent, and they showed him how far Britain was lagging behind and reinforced his conviction that 'our very existence' was threatened. 'We needed tutored skill to supersede rude force.' Birmingham itself was in danger of losing out to new foreign factories and production methods.[432] Once he was clear what was required, he persuaded the council to purchase land on Suffolk Street and to initiate a design competition.[433] He ushered the completed five storey, 116 room building of brick and terracotta, replete with science laboratories, lecture theatres, metallurgical, carpentry and building construction workshops, to completion in 1895, when it was opened by the Duke of Devonshire.[434] The insights he had gleaned from those continental visits informed the organisation of its technical classes. It became the foremost municipal technical school in the country.

The school confounded its critics ('wittlings who advised (as he put it) that they could solve the housing problem by letting off some of the floors as flats') for such was the demand that soon this huge building was too small to accommodate everyone. Martineau rejoiced that there were day and evening schools where:

Wage earners could expand their mental horizons by learning the truth and seeing the wonders and beauties of science. The school would train a better class of artisan ... effecting a brightening and widening of the lives of individual students.[435]

He recapitulated his belief in the value of technical education when he was guest of honour at various prize-givings in technical schools through the Midlands. One example, at Walsall in 1895, will suffice:

> Besides the commercial advantage which technical education must give
> to the employer, if the technical school enables a studious youth to learn
> something of the science involved in his daily calling (the mechanics of
> the smithy, the physics of telegraphy etc.); besides all this I anticipate that
> it will bring something of joy to the worker also and give to what had
> been the weary drudgery of toil somewhat of the dignity of handicraft.
> [Beyond this I hope] for some to find easy access to the joys of literature
> as well as the wonders of science and through them to attain the highest
> culture of the time.[436]

In that justification for technical education we can see the commercial
concern of a Birmingham manufacturer; but in the solicitude shown for the
working man, in the desire to elevate and instruct, we hear the authentic
voice of the Dawson civic gospeller.

A desire to afford Birmingham people the means to expand their
knowledge and cultivate their literary sensibilities drew many of Dawson's
disciples into the free library movement, as we have seen repeatedly in
this book. R. F. Martineau served the free libraries committee for many
years. He was also associated for some thirty years with organisations
which managed the town's aesthetic provision. He was on the School of Art
committee in 1878 and when the new municipal museum was opened and
a dedicated council committee (the Museum and School of Art committee)
was formed to supervise its management there too we find him from 1883.
He continued as a member through into the new century; he was also a
member of the art purchase committee, alongside J. T. Bunce and William
Kenrick among others.

The School of Art committee was evidently forward thinking. The school's
headmaster Edward Taylor spoke glowingly in 1893 of how 'the School of
Art has thriven under municipal management; I am fortunate to have as
chairman and members of committee gentlemen who are not only interested
in the work of the town but have a knowledge and love of Art'.[437] It had
indeed presided over dramatic change as student numbers had doubled to
3,100 in the five years from 1888 to 1893; Martineau was on the platform to
hear Taylor's encomium of 1893 when the School's much needed extension
was opened. One aspect of the School of Art's development would have
especially resonated with Martineau: that which focused on refining artists'
technical accomplishments. Taylor later explained: 'we were the first school
to link the processes with design, that is we allowed students an opportunity

of working in other materials than paper and clay.'[438] Martineau and other committee members backed Taylor's innovations because they saw the relevance of practical experience for young craftsmen in Birmingham's art-manufacturing industries. These considerations of craft skills were those which in part Martineau's new technical school was intended to address; uniquely he was at the centre of the two municipal committees which were engaged in nurturing the creativity of Birmingham's craftsmen. More striking still, he alone of Dawson's disciples was intimately involved in Birmingham's great educational building schemes from 1880 onwards, encompassing the Birmingham and Midland Institute, the art gallery, the School of Art – and then its extension – and the technical school.

When, with a flourish, he concluded his speech to Walsall technical school hoping '[f]or all, clever or not, through the means of education which are open already – and opening more day by day – that they could live a life with wider interests, wiser aims than has been hitherto possible,' he was rehearsing a familiar Dawson sentiment.[439] Here he was addressing technical students, but he might just as well have been referring to the School of Art pupils, to the thousands who through the Education League had had an elementary education, as well as to the 'poor helpless girls' of the Protesting Dissenters' charity school of which he was a sponsor. For all of them he had expended hour upon hour across the years to increase their educational opportunities. The obituary writers in December 1909 certainly recognised that 'the immense amount of honorary work which he undertook for educational and philanthropic bodies was indeed a labour of love'. For R. F. Martineau there was an unusual degree of affection, for someone 'whose name was a synonym for useful labour for the good of others, quietly and persistently pursued'. He was indeed loyal, clubbable and unselfish in his dedication to Birmingham's service.[440]

Chapter 17

Edward Taylor

'The Birmingham Art School has now introduced into its title the dignified and significant adjective "Municipal",' the *Birmingham Daily Post* announced in its report of the opening of the new building on 14 September 1885.[441] It was the newspaper's editor J.T. Bunce who six years earlier had first suggested that the School of Art ought to become 'a town work'.[442] The School of Art could trace its origins back to the 1820s when the Society of Arts erected a building in New Street where students were taught by poorly remunerated artists. A re-organisation in 1842 led to the establishment of the Birmingham Society of Artists and a separate Society of Arts and Design, which still operated from New Street. Men and women students were taught separately, the number of them rising from 243 in 1844 to 820 in 1858, when new accommodation was provided in the Midland Institute in Paradise Street. Despite these rising numbers 'the School of Art ... lived from hand to mouth. People had to go around begging to get subscriptions to keep it going.'[443] From 1874 the chairman of the committee of the School of Art was J.H. Chamberlain and it is difficult not to believe that from this point on earnest discussions were going on amongst the proponents of the civic gospel in Birmingham to secure a new future for the institution under municipal control. 'What they wanted to do,' Bunce observed, 'was to ensure that every workman in Birmingham whose work was influenced by art – and, in speaking of workmen, he meant workwomen as well – should have the opportunity of a thorough grounding in art that its principles might be applied to the work of the town in the future.'[444]

The idea of linking art with manufacture did not originate in Birmingham in 1885. It had in fact been an ongoing national conversation for half a century, greatly stimulated by the Great Exhibition and soon after by the establishment of the Department of Science and Art at South Kensington. This government department assisted in the formation of Schools of Art across the country. When Edward Taylor (1838-1912) arrived in Birmingham from Lincoln to take up the post of headmaster of the School of Art in 1877, he was already a successful proponent of the idea. He had been the headmaster of the School of Art in Lincoln since its establishment in February 1863. Though he held morning classes for middle-class students – some of whom travelled in from across Lincolnshire and Nottinghamshire in carriages and on the railway – he had made it his great task to recruit working men for evening classes in drawing and painting. Taylor was very proud to have supervised the early training of William Logsdail, who under his tutelage was awarded a gold medal and a scholarship and went to became a well-known artist, but he felt similar pride for the fitters, masons and joiners he recruited and who 'took to art as well as to geometry and machine drawing'.[445] Of the 249 students attending classes in 1874, 179 came in the evening. His success brought Taylor a prize of £40 and, on his departure, he declared himself to be 'quite overpowered' when 230 subscribers presented him with a collection of silverware.[446] He was their 'talented and indefatigable headmaster', and Taylor told them 'he should ever consider the Lincoln School of Art as his own child'.[447]

Born in Hanley on 14 June 1838, Edward Richard Taylor was amongst a few boys – the father of Rudyard Kipling being another – who enrolled in the School of Art in Burslem when it opened in a room in the yard of a pub in 1853. The master was a Birmingham-born glass engraver William Jabez Muckley, but, poorly accommodated and perpetually short of money, the enterprise 'dragged on a miserable existence and finally ceased'.[448] By this point Taylor had enrolled at South Kensington and, equipped with a teaching certificate, was able to take up his post in Lincoln. He was praised, he was congratulated, but fourteen years later still found himself confined to a single room, with a curtain dividing those listening to a lecture and those engaged in drawing and painting. It was not until after he took up his post as headmaster of the School of Art in Birmingham that he discovered that he had exchanged one room for teaching art for another. In 1877 the School of Art was located on the top floor of the Midland Institute. 'To reach it was an awful climb up four or five flights of stairs and the place itself was ill-lighted,' he recalled. 'I told John Henry Chamberlain, who was chairman, that we must get a new school, but his reply was that so little was the interest locally taken in art education that we should not get five pounds towards the cost.'[449] All that, however, was to change when two brothers, who had made their fortunes in engineering, decided to play their part in the transformation of Birmingham.

Those brothers were Richard and George Tangye of the Cornwall Works in Smethwick. Richard Tangye had arrived in Birmingham from Illogen near Redruth in 1852 and was joined the following year by his brother George and soon after by his other siblings. The brothers were a formidable partnership – Richard Tangye complementing his brothers' engineering brilliance with his own brilliance as an entrepreneur. It was he who exploited their success in providing the hydraulic jacks that launched the *Great Eastern* in early 1858. Neither Richard nor George Tangye attended the Church of the Saviour, but they certainly supported wholeheartedly Dawson's civic gospel. It was in the field of art that they chose to make their contribution to Birmingham's remarkable civic progress. Tangye observed that 'while I am fully sensible to the value of an art collection as a means of affording the highest intellectual pleasure, I am also deeply impressed with its absolute necessity in the interest of our material progress and prosperity'.[450] It was the intervention of the Tangyes that secured the building of the Art Gallery and the School of Art in 1885. In both cases, Tangye and his brother provided the impetus to start by offering £10,000 for each project if their financial support was matched by others. At an exhibition Tangye had already privately intimated to Taylor what he planned to do – Taylor's friends thought that he was selling Tangye a painting! Within a month of opening in November 1885 the Art Gallery had been visited by 250,000 people. Dawson would have been delighted.

When an anonymous philanthropist – soon revealed to be Louisa Anne Ryland – matched the Tangyes' offer and Cregoe Colmore provided a site in the centre of the town (worth £15,000) the project was able to go ahead. Its final cost was £21,254, with the Tangyes meeting the overspending. These philanthropists stipulated that the new School of Art should be run by the town council. Taylor was utterly convinced by the arguments for municipal control, remarking that it 'ought to give a higher tone to the School and its work'.[451] Though the members of the existing committee believed that they had the knowledge and competence to run the new institution and found relinquishing their role 'painful' they were in no position to obstruct this plan.[452] Chamberlain sought to assuage their hurt feelings. The new committee of sixteen would include eight original members and eight members nominated by the town council – but with the important proviso that vacancies would subsequently be filled by municipal appointments. J.H. Chamberlain – Tangye's choice as architect – began work on drawings for the new building in January 1882, and died the day that tenders were opened to builders in October 1883. It was left to his partner William Martin to supervise the construction by Sapcote & Sons, with Tangye placing the inscription stone in May 1884.

Built in Gothic style with red brick and stone and terracotta dressings, the School of Art was very much a Birmingham undertaking. Unlike the

Wolverhampton School of Art, which opened in the same year (at a much smaller cost of £8,000), no application was made for financial support to the Department of Science and Art. The first municipal School of Art to be built in Britain, this ornate building was both a testament to Chamberlain's genius and the finest physical expression of the civic gospel. The *Birmingham Daily Post* treated its readers to a very detailed tour of this latest triumph of the town's civic vision, filling its report with such phrases as 'richly designed', 'beautifully designed', 'very beautiful' and 'handsome'.[453] The building was extended by William Martin in 1892-3, enabling another 400 students to be admitted.

Under the direction of Taylor's predecessor David W. Raimbach, the School of Art had concentrated on the teaching of painting. The vision of Tangye and Bunce and, most importantly, Taylor was considerably more ambitious. As well as courses in drawing and painting, there would be classes in geometry, architecture and machine construction, which were 'specially adapted to the requirements of the town and calculated ... to exercise in important and enduring influence alike upon the taste and the prosperity of Birmingham'.[454] For Taylor the School of Art was 'a technical school ... their work should be to develop and direct the mental powers and awaken the sympathies of the pupils'.[455] He was sure that work should not stop with designs but should go on to actually make something. In an early address he cited an example of what he hoped to achieve – nail makers actually producing more ornamental iron work. Through Taylor the influence of the Arts and Crafts movement was to be strongly expressed in the work produced by students at the School of Art.

Each September Taylor – whose office was adjacent to the main entrance – personally supervised the admission of students. The School of Art still provided for the sons and daughters of the Edgbaston middle class. There were elementary art classes for females three mornings a week from 10 am to 1 pm at a fee of 40s per term and advanced art classes two mornings a week from 10 am to 4 pm at a fee of 50s per term. The high fees safeguarded their social exclusion, but not their exclusive access to the study of art. The elementary classes were also offered to artisans over four evenings a week from 7.15 p.m. until 9.15 p.m. at the considerably reduced fee of 7s 6d per term. For those who wished to study architecture there were classes two afternoons a week from 2.30 to 4.30 at a fee of 25s per term and classes three mornings a week from 7 a.m. to 9 a.m. at a fee of only 9s per term.

From the beginning a system of scholarships and free admissions was in place. Louisa Ryland provided £170 per annum to fund fourteen scholarships and over a hundred free places in evening classes. The Tangyes offered a three-year scholarship worth £180; the first recipient was Fred Mason, who was to make a name for himself as an illustrator of books. For those between the ages of 12 and 20 who were employed in the trade, the Birmingham Jewellers' and Silversmiths' Association met half their fees, 95 of them attending the School of Art in 1888. Increasingly manufacturers began to display notices in their works about evening classes offered by the School of Art and encouraged their employees to enrol. Additionally, students who achieved standards of 'good' or 'excellent' in internal examinations were entitled to reduced fees. These arrangements to widen entry were extended over the years.

The reach of the School of Art extended far beyond Margaret Street. Within a few years it was also overseeing the teaching of art in the evenings in ten board schools and additionally the training of masters and pupil-teachers. No other school of art in the country exercised such influence, made possible by its municipal governance. It all amounted to an educational revolution in Birmingham. Local artisans had seen nothing like it. By 1888 2,398 students were being taught at the School of Art or one of its branches; by 1902 the figure stood at 4,163.

A sizeable contingent of young women studied at the School of Art or its branch schools. Amongst these were Myra and Kate Bunce, the daughters of J.T. Bunce. Kate Bunce began to send her paintings – for example, in 1890 'The Minstrel', described as 'a striking figure piece' – to the exhibitions at the Royal Academy very early on.[456] Her paintings, with strong Pre-Raphaelite influences, were to be widely admired. Myra Bunce won prizes for design during her years of study and designed the frames for her younger sister's paintings as well as making jewellery. Georgie Cave France was another notable female student. She regularly won prizes in national competitions organised by the Department of Science and Art – for example, a silver medal for a modelled design for tiles and a bronze medal for a modelled design for a vase in September 1890. The following month, at an exhibition organised by the Armourers' & Braziers' Company in London, she also secured two prizes of £5 each for her designs. Her work was represented at an exhibition organised by the Arts and Crafts Exhibition Society in London in autumn 1893, as was that of other School of Art students Mary Newill, Ida Stubbs and Florence Rudland. These talented young women and others were in receipt of scholarships, and scooped prize after prize for their work – Mary Newill for her designs for stained glass windows, Gertrude Bailey, whose drawings showed 'considerable invention as to quality and range', Elsie Pardoe for her designs for wallpaper, Edith Le Roy for her oil paintings and many more.[457]

In the early years Taylor was assisted by a deputy headmaster F.G. Jackson and a staff of twelve teachers. Amongst them were Jethro A. Cossins and W.H. Bidlake, who took the classes in architecture. Arthur Gaskin and Henry Payne were two of Taylor's own students he recruited to the staff. Arthur Gaskin, who taught drawing and painting, so impressed Taylor that he was appointed before he had completed his own qualification. Gaskin married one of his students, the outstanding Georgie France, and went on to produce woodcut illustrations for William Morris's Kelmscott Press and, jointly with his wife, jewellery. Henry Payne demonstrated in his classes not only how to design but also how to make stained glass windows. He, and subsequently many of his students, supplied the windows for a large number of churches across the Midlands.[458] There were also visiting lecturers, including Whitworth Wallis, the curator of the Art Gallery, C.A. Windle, professor of anatomy at Mason College and Arthur B. Chamberlain, who sought to keep his father's ideas about art alive. Within a month of its opening Edward Burne Jones, who had studied at the old School of Art, visited Margaret Street, meeting a number of students handpicked by Taylor. In later years William Holman Hunt and William Morris were to address the annual gatherings for the distribution of prizes.

In October 1890 Taylor and his staff organised a visit by 300 students to London – for most of them the first time they had visited the capital. It was a long day – leaving Birmingham at 6.15 a.m. and returning at 10. 47 p.m. – and 'in the afternoon it rained pitilessly', but, in different parties, the students were able to visit the National Gallery, South Kensington Museum and the cable factory of Siemens Bros. at Woolwich.[459] At the beginning of the new academic year in September 1895, Taylor threw open the doors of the School of Art so ratepayers could acquaint themselves 'with some of the features of an enterprise so vitally affecting the future of Birmingham'.[460] For a week, from 11 a.m. until 9 p.m., local people wandered from room to room, inspecting the work of the students and being assured by their teachers of its importance. After examining the rooms used for modelling and casting, they left fully aware 'of its intimate connection with the metal trades of Birmingham'.[461]

Taylor himself was a competent and productive painter. His talent, as he himself recognised, was not singular enough for him to make a career as an artist, and from the very beginning he saw himself as principally a teacher of art. There were to be no extended stays in Brittany or Venice for Taylor. According to his own account, he began to paint with serious intent almost by accident – a canon of Lincoln Cathedral provided him with a subject and the painting was accepted for a Royal Academy exhibition.

Taylor was to contribute a number of other paintings to Royal Academy exhibitions. His work was also to be found regularly at the exhibitions of the Birmingham Royal Society of Artists each spring and autumn, and it was favourably reviewed in the *Birmingham Daily Post*. Thus, 'Lincoln from the Witham' in 1878 was deemed to be 'a solid and conscientious study', and of 'Helpmate' in 1886 it was reported that 'Mr Taylor has been especially happy in his light …'.[462] At the Crystal Palace Art Exhibition in 1879 Taylor was awarded a gold medal to the value of £25 for 'The Cloister Well', deemed 'an important and very ably executed work'; and in 1884 William Kenrick bought a painting by Taylor of the interior of the reference library before it was destroyed by fire.[463] That Taylor was an active artist enhanced his reputation amongst those who studied at and supported the School of Art – and his status as headmaster certainly made it easier for him to sell his pictures. After his retirement in June 1903, with a pension provided by the city council, he continued to paint – as well as sell what he called Ruskin Pottery – until he died in Edgbaston nine years later on 14 January 1912.[464]

If Taylor saw his main role as a teacher of art, he did train men who went on to make careers for themselves as artists. A number of his students joined the colony of artists at the fishing port of Newlyn. These men found the fishermen very willing to offer themselves as subjects. Taylor's student William Langley, the son of a tailor, painted many scenes of life at sea and in the harbour. Edwin Harris also spent many years living in Newlyn and, married to the niece of an art dealer, was able to sell his paintings. W.A. Breakspeare was another Taylor protégé who made his way to Newlyn. Amongst many others with whom Taylor remained in contact were Joseph Finnemore, who contributed many illustrations to the publications of the Religious Tract Society, and Florence M. Rudland, awarded a scholarship for book illustration, who had begun to contribute drawings to new editions of Mary Martha Sherwood's children's books *The History of the Fairchild Family* before her death at a young age.

And then there was the working-class lad Oliver Wheatley. At first Wheatley had been able to attend only evening art classes at one of the branch schools, but, after securing a two-year scholarship worth £20 per annum at the School of Art, he went on to win a gold medal for modelling, becoming a designer in the electroplate trade and 'the clever young sculptor' who exhibited in London and Paris.[465] With great satisfaction, Taylor would watch at the School of Art's awards of prizes, a succession of working-class students collecting their certificates for machine drawing, architectural drawing, freehand drawing from memory and designs for tiles, medallions, umbrella stands, bronze lamps, bronze vases and stained-glass windows.

Afterword

George Dawson inspired a generation of leading Birmingham businessmen and professionals; many of them were personal associates who heard him discourse at first hand. They adopted his mantra of bringing 'everything to everybody', which in practice meant opening up educational and cultural opportunity to all citizens, however humble they be. Almost all the men featured in this book joined Dawson in a crusade to provide free elementary education for all; they made Birmingham the acknowledged national centre for educational reform. Just as important was the intellectual development and enculturation of the town's adult population, and Arthur Ryland's initiative in 1854 – that of the Birmingham and Midland Institute – provided intellectual stimulus for scores of inhabitants, as well as specialised technical instruction for apprentices, and those involved in the town's manifold metal-manufacturing activities. By the same token, Dawson and his disciples, men like Sam: Timmins, J. T. Bunce, William Harris and J. H. Chamberlain, convinced of the value of books and of exposure to great art, sought to provide Birmingham's townsfolk with libraries and galleries, where the distilled wisdom and aesthetic creativity of great men might be accessed by all.

This was the genesis of the Shakespeare Memorial Library; in Dawson and Timmins' vision Birmingham would curate a globally important collection of Shakespearean texts and artefacts so that – as Dawson put it – Shakespeare's words might be 'enshrined in the memories and hearts of hard-working men in the town … illuminating the path of the hard-working artisan … and the leaves (on which the words were written) might be turned over by the hardy hands of our own forgemen.'[466] Here indeed was a democratic and egalitarian vision, which began to materialise with the reference library's opening in 1864.

Dawson had been quite as explicit about the seminal importance of cultivating visual discrimination, and men like William Aitken, J. H. Chamberlain, William Kenrick, J. T. Bunce and R. F. Martineau took him at his word. J. H. Chamberlain saw it as his role to inspire fellow citizens with a series of iconic buildings, to generate a consciousness of civic pride;

great Victorian Gothic architecture would contribute to Birmingham's burgeoning sense of itself as the new Florence of the North. Improved artistic education at the School of Art, and at the new technical school, allied to the provision of the opportunity to see improving paintings at the Municipal Gallery, all contributed to the cultivation of a discriminating taste. This hitherto overlooked dimension to the civic gospel has been the focus of a number of the biographies in the foregoing text. The considerable achievement of those civic leaders was recognised beyond Birmingham; in 1887 Alfred St Johnston was writing in London's *Magazine of Art* that 'far from being the centre and hotbed of all that is inartistic and ugly, the Birmingham of today is perhaps the most artistic town in England'.[467]

The men who wrought a revolution in education, and established Birmingham's hegemony in intellectual and aesthetic provision, were extraordinary. The civic gospel involved – as its name suggests – a religious mission, and in earnest pursuit of this civic ideal these leaders evinced a devotion and dedication which involved years of committee work, of public and municipal meetings, as well as an impressive commitment to philanthropic endeavour. Threaded through our story are the generous gifts of the Tangye brothers, of Josiah Mason, of Louisa Ann Ryland, of William Kenrick and a host of others. The figures we have featured here helped summon up what one might call 'the Birmingham moment' when, in the 1890s, the city was both far and wide held up as a model of democratic political organisation, of municipal responsibility and of cultural and aesthetic innovation.

The energy and dynamism which had made Birmingham exceptional began to diminish across the Edwardian era. Many of the men featured in this book, participants in that great civic adventure of the 1860s, 1870s and 1880s, were now dead, and in 1906 a crippling stroke stilled the most charismatic and influential of them all, Joseph Chamberlain. It was left to the aging William Kenrick, William Harris and Frank Martineau to tend the sacred flame of the civic gospel. To an outside observer in 1916, the leader writer of the national *Sunday Chronicle* newspaper, 'Birmingham has receded, and [retained only] a faint glamour around its name.' The point of the article was that 'Neville Chamberlain [Joseph's son] has girded his loins, and something has been done ... and he seeks to regenerate a healthy spirit of municipal ambition. He will make Birmingham anew.'[468] Neville Chamberlain did indeed revive the spirit of Dawson's halcyon days when he became a councillor from 1911, pioneering town planning in England and promoting imaginative slum clearance schemes, while also initiating local health reform. Elected lord mayor in 1916, he founded the only Municipal

Savings Bank in the country, and went a long way to realising his ambition of establishing a Birmingham municipal symphony orchestra. In many ways this was the last hurrah for Birmingham's civic gospel. Neville Chamberlain's departure for Westminster in 1918 removed from Birmingham the most vigorous and resourceful local politician of his generation.

Civic pride and civic governance have steadily receded across the twentieth century, and Birmingham, as with other great Victorian cities like Manchester, Leeds and Newcastle, no longer generates that ferocious, but also creative, local patriotism. Much has changed from the heady days when Dawson and his circle engaged in the transformation of their town. Birmingham is no longer the pre-eminent manufacturing centre, the metal-working workshop for a worldwide Empire; as a consequence, there is not the same level of surplus wealth to be invested by its businessmen in municipal enterprises. The religious zeal among Birmingham's leaders in the nineteenth century directed to improving the lot of others, but that sense of a mission cause, no longer animates as it did. Dawson encouraged the brightest and the best to go into municipal service, and they did. They felt they had a responsibility to make a difference. They could do so because across the mid-Victorian period considerable powers over the local environment, over education and the arts, were vested in municipal authorities. By a cruel irony the first major twentieth-century politician to accelerate the process of centralising powers on Westminster was Neville Chamberlain who, as Minister of Health in the 1920s, introduced the block grants which would – extended through the Thatcher years – see local finance increasingly determined in London. That centralising has surely diminished the sense of accountability for the fate of one's locality.

Tristram Hunt sees a diminution of civic pride as the inevitable result of the emergence of 'an individualistic society with only the loosest of affiliations to nation, region and race, let alone to the city'.[469] Perhaps that also partially explains a change in attitude towards philanthropic endeavour focused on civic projects; whilst philanthropy is, of course, not dead, it is nevertheless the case that across the past century higher government taxes and more large scale projects directed from the centre have fed the expectation that it is national government which will provide. Whilst there is an ongoing debate about the degree to which power can be returned to municipal authorities, it nevertheless seems fanciful to imagine that the degree of initiative and autonomy, the depth of conviction and sense of mission cause shown by George Dawson and his circle can ever be fully replicated in a very different, more complex, multi-racial twenty-first century city.

Appendix:
The Institutions of Victorian Birmingham

Arts Club

Located in New Street, this club was founded for political discussion. J.H. Chamberlain was its chairman.

Birmingham and Edgbaston Debating Society

It was at the meetings of this society, which were often held at the Birmingham and Midland Institute, that many of the civic gospellers made their maiden speeches. The society was very strongly supported, with 255 members in 1869.

Birmingham Central Literary Association

This society, founded in 1856, held debates and published a quarterly magazine, with contributions from its members. The civic gospellers were well represented amongst its membership, which by 1877 stood at 250.

Birmingham and Midland Institute

A committee was formed with the aim of establishing an educational institution for the use of the working class in 1849, but it was not until January 1853 that the Birmingham and Midland Institute was founded. Arthur Ryland was at the fore in this endeavour. With the passing of an Act of Parliament to secure its incorporation in 1854, the foundation stone was laid by Prince Albert in November 1855. Designed by E.M. Barry, the buildings in Paradise Street comprised a lecture theatre, classrooms, laboratories, a newsroom and a museum. For a subscription of one guinea a year, members could join the general department and attend lectures and classes and use the newsroom. For fees of three to five shillings a term, working men could enrol as members of the industrial department and attend classes in science and English Language and Literature. Morning classes catered for females. In 1870 Samuel Timmins added an archaeological section. In January 1879 there were 1,831 members of the general department, 2,617 members of the industrial department and 338 attending the classes for females.

Birmingham Daily Gazette
First published on 12 May 1862, this newspaper cost one penny. A Conservative organ, it had offices in High Street. In June 1886, after addressing a meeting of Conservative supporters, its editor of three years B.J. Grindley collapsed and died.

Birmingham Daily Mail
First published on 7 September 1870, this newspaper cost one halfpenny and had a circulation of 56,000. A Liberal organ, it had offices in Cannon Street. H.J. Jennings was its printer and publisher during its early years.

Birmingham Daily Post
First published on 6 December 1857, this newspaper cost one penny and had a circulation of over 40,000. A Liberal organ, it had offices in New Street. J.T. Bunce was its long-serving editor.

Board of Guardians
The Board of Guardians – 60 in total – met each fortnight in the parochial offices in Paradise Street. W.G. Coulton was clerk to the Guardians and B.J. Carter, a retired naval officer, was governor of the workhouse. The School Board also met in these offices in the 1870s.

Carr's Lane Chapel
The chapel was built at a cost of about £10,000, raised by subscriptions, between July and October 1819. It was refurbished in 1871 and could accommodate 2,000 people. John Angell James and R.W. Dale were, in succession, its celebrity-ministers.

Church of the Messiah
Built on arches over the Birmingham and Worcester Canal, this Unitarian chapel in Broad Street opened, at a cost of £15,000, in January 1862. It could accommodate 600 people. H.W. Crosskey succeeded Samuel Bache as its minister.

Church of the Saviour
Founded by George Dawson, this non-denominational church opened, at a cost of £5,000, in Edward Street in August 1847. John Shakespeare Manton, an original member of the congregation, took part in the cutting of the first sod and noted that Dawson 'digged vigorously.' Dawson's church was noted for its beautiful interior and there was a platform instead of a pulpit. It could accommodate 1,400 people.

Council House
Designed by local architect H.R. Yeoville Thomason, the Council House, with its dome and elaborate decoration, was the most important civic

building. It was erected in 1874-9 and subsequently extended. The town council consisted of 16 aldermen and 48 councillors. The School Board moved its meetings to the council chamber in the 1880s.

Free Hospital for Sick Children

Utilising the building in Steelhouse Lane that had once been occupied by the Polytechnic Institution, this hospital opened in 1862. It was largely the result of the efforts of the doctor T.P. Heslop and C.E. Matthews. Admission was granted on the presentation of a note from two householders. In 1867 a building designed by Martin and Chamberlain to treat out-patients was erected on a site close by and in 1869 the lying-in hospital for poor women in Broad Street was acquired and reconstructed, with a garden laid out at the expense of a benefactor. In 1878, 17,118 children were treated, most of them out-patients.

General Hospital

Opened in Summer Lane in 1779, the General Hospital was funded by subscriptions and the surplus from a triennial music festival. The hospital was extended in 1791 and in 1857, the new wing in the latter year being paid for from the profits of a fete held in the grounds of Aston Hall. By this point the hospital had beds for 240 patients. In 1878 3,041 were admitted to the wards and 11,273 were treated as out-patients. The hospital was transferred to a new site and new buildings in 1897, providing accommodation for 346 patients.

Graham Street Chapel

Erected in 1824 as the Mount Zion Chapel on Newhall Hill – the site was later known as Graham Street – this enormous building cost £11,000 and bankrupted its benefactor. It had been standing empty for a lengthy period when it was purchased by the Baptists in 1827. In 1844 Dawson was appointed minister. His successor departed in 1852 and Charles Vince became minister. He remained in place until his death 22 years later and was a member of the executive of the National Education League and was elected to the School Board. The chapel could accommodate 2,500 people.

Hospital for Women

Opened in the Crescent in 1871, this hospital moved seven years later to a house in Sparkhill owned by Louisa Ryland. Admission depended on family earnings and family size, though those who did not meet the stated criteria were considered by the hospital committee. In 1878 3,141 women were treated, most of them out-patients.

Key Hill Cemetery

Opened in April 1836 by the Birmingham General Cemetery Company, the site extended to eleven acres. With catacombs placed in red sandstone rock, many beautiful monuments and shrubberies and lawns, it became a favourite place for a stroll. A chapel stood in the centre.

King Edward the Sixth's Grammar School

From 1838 this school was located in New Street in an impressive building designed by Charles Barry. The self-appointed body which ran the school was replaced in 1878 by new arrangements which included representatives from the town council. Fees were payable, though there were also a large number of scholarships.

Mason College

Sir Josiah Mason founded this science college in 1875. It cost him £6,000, and was located close to Chamberlain Square. Originally endowed with £200,000, it absorbed the medical faculty of Queen's College in 1892 and was incorporated as a university college in 1896. It became part of the University of Birmingham in 1900.

Philosophical Institution

With origins in the beginning of the nineteenth century, this society was funded by subscribers and purchased premises in Cannon Street, which comprised a lecture theatre, laboratories, a news-room and a museum. Though there were some lectures on literature and music, most were of a scientific nature, with specimens and experiments. With only 68 subscribers and mounting debts, the Philosophical Institution closed in 1849.

Polytechnic Society

Located in Steelhouse Lane, this society provided elementary classes and lectures of a more intellectual nature. However, it struggled for most of its existence. In 1848, only a few years after coming into existence, it was evicted from its premises.

Queen's College

Founded by William Sands Cox in 1828, this college stood in Paradise Street and offered degrees in medicine, theology, law, architecture and engineering from the University of London.

Queen's Hospital

Situated in Bath Row, this hospital opened in October 1841 and provided accommodation for 141 patients. With the support of George Dawson, a committee of working men began, in 1869, to collect funds to enlarge the hospital. The new building was opened in November 1873. In 1878 1,613 were admitted to the wards and 14,220 treated as out-patients.

Royal Society of Artists

Formed in 1821 and from 1829 located in premises in New Street, membership of this society was confined to artists. Each spring and autumn the society held exhibitions.

St. Philip's

Built between 1711 and 1719 on an elevated site, St. Philip's was re-cased in 1859-62, the cost of the work on the south side being met by the sculptor Peter Hollins. The stained glass windows designed by Edward Burne-Jones were installed between 1885 and 1898. St Philip's became a cathedral in 1905.

Society of Arts

This society came into existence in 1821 and sought to promote the talents of local artists. Subscriptions and donations enabled the society to build up a collection of works of art. It held exhibitions in its premises in New Street.

Spring Hill College

This college was founded in 1838 for the training Congregationalist ministers by George Storer Mansfield, with the assistance of his sisters, who gave up their residence, Spring Hill. A building fund set up in 1840 eventually raised almost £20,000 which enabled a much more suitable new building to be opened in Moseley in June 1857. The college had the capacity to recruit over thirty students, who studied theology, philosophy, mathematics, science and Latin, Greek and Hebrew.

The Town Crier

George Dawson and his friends launched this satirical monthly in 1861. It later became a weekly publication and survived until 1903. The *Dart* and the *Owl* were weekly satirical magazines that also circulated in the town.

Town Hall

Built between 1832 and 1834 from designs by Joseph Hansom and Edward Welch, the town hall was first used for the funeral of the magistrate and street commissioner Timothy Smith and subsequently for public meetings, lectures and concerts. It was extended in 1850 and in 1876 decorated with designs by J.H. Chamberlain. The large organ was the property of the governors of the General Hospital. The town hall had seating for 2,600 people, though when benches were removed, 6,000 could be admitted.

Further Reading

The primary and secondary sources on which this study is based are set out in the endnotes. However, we thought it might be useful to the reader who is beginning to explore the story of Victorian Birmingham to draw attention to the main publications:

A. Briggs, *History of Birmingham: Borough and City* (Oxford University Press, London, 1952).

A. Briggs, *Victorian Cities* (Penguin London, 1968)

J. Dixon, *Out of Birmingham: George Dixon (1820-98), 'Father of Free Education'* (Brewin, Studley, 2013)

E.P. Hennock, *Fit and Proper Persons. Ideal and Reality in Nineteenth Century Local Government* (Hodder & Stoughton, London, 1973)

T. Hunt, *Building Jerusalem. The Rise and Fall of the Victorian City* (Phoenix, London, 2005).

P. Marsh, *Joseph Chamberlain: Entrepreneur in Politics* (Yale, New Haven, 1994)

A. Reekes, *Two Titans, One City: Joseph Chamberlain and George Cadbury* (West Midlands History, Alcester, 2017)

A. Reekes, *The Birmingham Political Machine: Winning Elections for Joseph Chamberlain* (West Midlands History, 2018).

S. Roberts, *Dr J.A. Langford (1823-1903): A Self-Taught Working Man and the Sale of American Degrees in Victorian Britain* (Authoring History, Dunstable, 2014)

S. Roberts, *Sir Richard Tangye 1833-1906. A Cornish Entrepreneur in Victorian Birmingham* (Birmingham Biographies, 2015)

S. Roberts ed., *Recollections of Victorian Birmingham* (Birmingham Biographies, 2018).

S. Roberts, *George Dawson and the Church of the Saviour* (Birmingham Biographies, 2020)

S. Roberts & R. Ward eds., *Mocking Men of Power. Comic Art in Birmingham 1861-1911* (Birmingham Biographies, 2014).

R. Ward *City-State and Nation: Birmingham's Political History 1830-1940* (Phillimore, Chichester, 2005)

Notes

1   T. Hunt, *Building Jerusalem* (London, Weidenfeld and Nicolson, 2004) p. 256; J. Moore, *High Culture and Tall Chimneys* (Manchester, MUP, 1824) pp. 95-100.

2   J. Ralph, Article in *'Harpur's Monthly'*, June 1890 pp. 99-110.

3   A. Briggs, *History of Birmingham* volume II (Oxford, OUP, 1952) p. 67.

4   *George Dawson Collection,* Library of Birmingham, volume 21 pp. 1-4.

5   A.W.W. Dale, 'George Dawson,' in Muirhead, J.H., ed. *Nine Famous Birmingham Men* (Birmingham, Cornish Bros., 1909) pp. 105-6.

6   Dale, ibid. p. 100.

7   G. St. Clair, *Shakespeare and other lectures* (London, Kegan Paul, Trench & Co.,1888) p.160; A.E. Reekes, *Speeches that Changed Britain* (Alcester, History West Midlands, 2015) pp. 56-7; for a critical view of Dawson's reference library speech see: A. Green, 'The Anarchy of Empire: Reimagining Birmingham's Civic Gospel' *Midland History* vol.36:2, 2011, pp. 163-74 in which Green argues that 'Dawson's famous statement concerning what a town "should be" may also be interpreted as a tacit form of closure against what it should not be … Dawson's beliefs harbour a subtle declaration about "race".'

8   Wright Wilson, *Life of George Dawson* (Birmingham, Percival Jones, 1905).

9   R.A. Armstrong, *Henry William Crosskey* (Birmingham, Cornish Bros.,1905) p. 261.

10   W. Harris, *The History of Our Shakespeare Club* (Birmingham, Journal Printing Offices, 1903) p. 23.

11   L. Rosenthal, 'Joseph Chamberlain and the Birmingham Town Council 1865-1880', *Midland History* (2016) 41:1, pp. 84-8

12   Ralph, op.cit.

13   *Birmingham Daily Post (BDP)* 20 July 1881.

14   Ibid., 8 March 1870.

15   National Education League Papers MS 4248 (Library of Birmingham); *George Dawson Collection* (Library of Birmingham) volume 15, pp. 189-90.

16   *Inaugural Address by George Dawson, MA, Borough of Birmingham, Opening of the Free Reference Library, 26 October 1866* (Birmingham, E. C. Osborne, 1866).

17   J. A. L. Langford, *The Birmingham Free Libraries, The Shakespeare Memorial Library and the Art Gallery* (Birmingham, Hall and English, 1871), p. 45. Langford is not one of the featured figures in this book, only because he has already been the subject of an extensive study, see S. Roberts, *Dr J. A. Langford (1823-1903), A Self-Taught Working Man and the Sale of American Degrees in Victorian Britain* (Authoring History, 2014).

18   *Inaugural Address* op.cit.

19   *BDP,* 20 July 1881.

20   Museum and School of Art Committee report, January 1888, (Library of Birmingham).

21   Langford, op.cit., pp. 65-6.

22   E. R. Taylor, *Drawing and Design for Beginners* (London, 1893) p. 101.

23   S. Hoban, 'The Birmingham Municipal School of Art and Opportunities for Women's paid work in the Arts and Crafts Movement, 1885-1914,' unpublished PhD thesis, University of Birmingham, 2013, p. 25.

24   K. Gleadle, *The Early Feminists: Radical Unitarians and the emergence of the Women's Rights Movement 1831-51* (London, Macmillan, 1995) p. 130.

25   Hoban, op.cit., p. 10.

26   D. Cannadine, *Victorious Century* (Harmondsworth: Penguin, 2017), figure 32.

27   E. P. Hennock, *Fit and Proper Persons: Ideal and Reality in Nineteenth-Century Urban Government* (Edward Arnold: London, 1973), p. 62

28   Quoted in A.W.W. Dale, 'George Dawson', in *Nine Famous Birmingham Men* p. 90; and in A. Briggs, *Victorian Cities* (Harmondsworth: Penguin, 1990), p. 195.

29   Thomas Carlyle to Jane Welsh Carlyle 9 September 1852 and Thomas Carlyle to John A. Carlyle on the same day. My source for all Carlyle correspondence is the Carlyle Letters Online: https://carlyleletters.dukeupress.edu/.

30   *George Dawson Collection* (Library of Birmingham), vol. 21, pp. 166-7.

31   GDC, vol. 11, p. 36.

32   R. D. Altick, *Writers, Readers, and Occasions: Selected Essays on Victorian Literature and Life* (Columbus: Ohio State University Press, 1989), p. 345, n. 39.

33   G. St. Clair, F.G.S., *Shakespeare and Other Lectures* (London: Kegan Paul, Trench & Co., 1888), p. 342.

34   GDC, vol. 21, pp. 221-4.

35   Dawson, p. 166.

36   T. Hunt, *Building Jerusalem*, p. 356.

37   Dawson, p. 500.

38   Hennock, pp. 172-3; my emphasis.

39   Dawson, p. 431.

40   Dawson, p. 372.

41   A.W.W. Dale, p. 101.

42   Hennock, p. viii.

43   Dawson, p. 389.

44   Quoted in C. Hall, *Civilizing Subjects: Metropole and Colony in the English Imagination 1830 – 1867* (London: Polity, 2002), p. 403.

45   S. Timmins, *A History of Warwickshire* (London: Elliot Stock, 1889), pp. 205-7.

46   *Birmingham and Midland Institute: Address, Delivered at the Annual Meeting of Members 12th January 1874, by Sam Timmins, Esq.* ("The Journal" Printing Offices, New Street, 1874), p. 14.

47   For arguments against the limits and prejudices of George Dawson and the 'Civic Gospel', see C. Hall and A. Green, '"The Anarchy of Empire": Reimagining Birmingham's Civic Gospel', *Midland History* 36.2 (2011), 163-79.

48   T. Hunt, *Building Jerusalem* p. 265; E.P. Hennock, *Fit and Proper Persons* p. 62.

49   P. Marsh, *Joseph Chamberlain, Entrepreneur in Politics* (Yale, USA, 1998).

50   Ibid., p.80; S. Roberts, *Recollections of Victorian Birmingham* (Birmingham Biographies, 2018) p. 20; W. Wright Wilson, *Life of George Dawson* (Percival Jones, Birmingham, 1905) pp. 121ff.

51   Wright Wilson, op.cit., p. 27.

52   *Inaugural address by George Dawson MA,* Borough of Birmingham, Opening of the Free Reference Library, 26 October 1866, (E.C. Osborne, Birmingham, 1866).

53   Speech to the Council, January 13, 1874, quoted by J.L. Garvin, *Life of Joseph Chamberlain* Volume 1 (Macmillan & Co., London, 1932) p. 188.

54   Quoted by J.T. Bunce, *History of the Corporation of Birmingham, Volume ii* (Birmingham, 1885) p. 347

55   See: J.T. Bunce, op.cit.; P. Marsh op.cit; A. Briggs, *History of Birmingham* vol II; E.P Hennock, op.cit.; R. Ward, *City State and Nation, Birmingham's Political History 1840-1940* (Chichester, Phillimore, 2005); A.E. Reekes, *The Birmingham Political Machine* (West Midlands History, Alcester, 2018); J.L. Garvin op.cit.; T. Hunt, op.cit.

56   T. Anderton, *A Tale of One City* (Birmingham, 1900) p. 6.

57   R.W. Dale, 'The Perils and Uses of Rich Men,' in *Week-Day Sermons* pp. 175-6.

58   Speech by Joseph Chamberlain at a dinner given by the Town Council after his election as MP for Birmingham, 9 November 1876, quoted by C.W. Boyd, *Mr Chamberlain's Speeches* vol.1, pp. 71-3.

59   *Birmingham Council Proceedings*, 2 December 1873; 9 June 1874, L34/3 (Library of Birmingham Archives).

60   *Borough of Birmingham, Proceedings on the Adoption by the Council of a Scheme for the Improvement of the Borough* (1875)

61   J.H. Muirhead, *Nine Famous Birmingham* p. 101.

62   Speech at the Annual General Meeting of Severn Street Adult School, 30 November 1874, quoted in C.W. Boyd, ed. *Mr Chamberlain's Speeches* vol. I (London, Constable, 1914) p. 55.

63   Ibid.

64   *BDP*, 21 October 1881.

65   S. Roberts, *Joseph Chamberlain's Highbury – A Very Public Private House* (Birmingham Biographies, 2015) p. 8.

66   E.P. Hennock, *Fit and Proper Persons* (Arnold, London, 1973), p. 172.

67   Letter Joseph Chamberlain to Richard Chamberlain, 10 October 1881, JC 6/1/1, Cadbury Research Library, University of Birmingham.

68   R. Hartnell, 'The Contribution of Art – and of Design – to the Emergence and Establishment of a Civic Culture in Birmingham in the late Nineteenth Century,' (unpublished D. Phil thesis, Birmingham Institute of Art and Design, May 1992) p. 274.

69   Speech by Joseph Chamberlain, 17 June 1874 included in C.W. Boyd, *Mr Chamberlain's Speeches, Volume 1* (London, Constable, 1914) pp. 39-42.

70   Hunt op.cit. p. 356.

71   M. Key, 'Through the Gains of Industry we promote Art; George Dawson's Civic Gospel and the architecture of the Improvement Scheme.' (Open. content, ox.ac.uk, April 2017); Hartnell, R., 'Art and Civic Culture in Birmingham in the Late Nineteenth Century,' *Urban History*, August 1995, Cambridge University Press, pp.229-37.

72   *Six Years of Educational Work in Birmingham; an Address delivered to the Birmingham School Board by the Chairman, Joseph Chamberlain, Esq., M.P. November 2, 1876.*

73   D. Cannadine, 'The Chamberlain Tradition and Birmingham', in *In Churchill's Shadow* (Allen Lane, London, 2002), p. 121.

74   *Pall Mall Gazette*, 1894.

75   Marsh, op.cit., p. 97.

76   J. Chamberlain, *The Forum*, 1892 quoted by T. Hunt, op.cit. p. 265.

77   *BDP*, 26 March 1877.

78   Ibid.

79   T. Martineau, 'Mr Arthur Ryland,' *Edgbastonia 2* (1882), pp. 76-9; In a letter dated 4 July 1850 now in the archives of *Shakespeare Martineau,* the modern iteration of

Ryland's original firm, Arthur Ryland wrote to T Martineau offering a partnership: 'The forming of a partnership I have always regarded as requiring almost as much caution as the selection of a wife …'.

80   Ibid.; These parks were Cannon Hill Park (1873) and Small Heath Park (1876) – see C. Chinn, *Free Parks for the People* (Studley, Brewin Books, 2012) pp. 56-67.

81   *BDP*, 26 March 1877.

82   Ibid., 26 March 1877.

83   Ibid., 29 June 1865.

84   *Birmingham Daily Gazette (BDG)* 20 January 1863.

85   W. Wright Wilson, *Life of George Dawson* (London, Percival Jones, 1905) p. 61.

86   R. Waterhouse, *The Birmingham and Midland Institute* (Birmingham, The Birmingham and Midland Institute, 1954) p. 22.

87   *BDP*, 26 March 1877.

88   W. Hutton, *History of Birmingham* (Birmingham, 1795) p. 127.

89   R. Ward, *City State and Nation* (Chichester, Phillimore, 2005) pp. 16-17; 33-4.

90   A. Briggs, *History of Birmingham* volume II p. 111; D. Fraser, *Power and Authority on the Victorian City* (Oxford, Blackwell, 1979) pp. 96-7.

91   J. A. Langford, *The Birmingham Free Libraries, the Shakespere Memorial Library and the Art Gallery*, (Birmingham, Hall and English, 1871), pp. 5-11.

92   *BDP*, 11 November 1861.

93   A speech by J.T.Bunce at the opening of the new BMI buildings, *BDP*, 21 October 1881

94   R. Waterhouse op.cit, p. 5.

95   Ibid.

96   From a speech made by Arthur Ryland on the occasion of the presentation of his portrait, to hang in the Institute, on 2 July 1860, *BDP*, 3 July 1860.

97   R. Waterhouse, op.cit., pp. 12-13.

98   T. Hunt, *Building Jerusalem* pp. 116-37.

99   *BDP*, 21 October 1881.

100   Ibid.

101   A.W.W. Dale *The Life of R.W. Dale of Birmingham* (London, Hodder and Stoughton, 1898), p. 634.

102   *BDP*, 1 November 1875.

103   A.W.W. Dale, op.cit., p. 52.

104   R.A. Armstrong, *Henry William Crosskey: His Life and Work*, p. 249.

105   *BDP*, 11 December 1876.

106   A.W.W. Dale, op.cit., p. 16.

107   *BJ*, 19 November 1853. Dale continued to support this body for the rest of his life.

108   A.W.W. Dale, p. 54.

109   *Edgbastonia*, vol. VIII, no. 90 (October 1890) for a portrait of Elizabeth Dale. She was president of the Birmingham Ladies' Association for Useful Work.

110   *ABG*, 21 November 1868.

111   A.W.W. Dale, op.cit., p.486.

112   *BDG*, 25 April 1864; *BDP*, 25 April 1864.

113   For thorough discussions of the campaign for educational reform in Birmingham at this time see J. Dixon 'Out of Birmingham: George Dixon (1820-98) (Brewin Books, Studley, 2013), passim; A. Reekes, *The Birmingham Political Machine: Winning Elections for Joseph Chamberlain* (History West Midlands, Alcester, 2018), pp. 22-58.

114   *BDG*, 2 October 1867.

115   *BDP*, 21 April 1870.

116   A.W.W. Dale, op.cit., p. 273.

117   *BDP*, 13 June 1870.

118   S. Roberts, 'John Skirrow Wright: The Benefactor whose Statue was Destroyed', *Birmingham Historian*, no. 33, Spring 2009, pp. 11-15.

119   See M.E.J. Shewell, 'Religious Education in Birmingham Board Schools', in *Educational Review*, XIII (1961), no.2, pp. 133-9.

120   *BDP*, 1 November 1875.

121   Ibid., 22 November 1881.

122   Ibid., 16 December 1885.

123   Ibid., 23 January 1885.

124   Library of Birmingham, MS 1332/1/5, MS 1332/2/1, MS 1366/B/1 for a small collection of letters from Dale; and MS 1332/1/14 for four letters from his wife Nessie. Cadbury Research Library, University of Birmingham, holds 75 letters to Dale from John Bright, W.E. Gladstone, John Morley and Henry Wace.

125   For Charles Clarke see S.Roberts *James Whateley and the Survival of Chartism* (Birmingham Biographies, 2018), pp. 28-43.

126   *BDG* 28 March 1911.

127   *Yorkshire Post* 11 December 1884.

128   *BDG* op.cit.

129   Abbe Sieyes was one of the most important constitutional thinkers during the French Revolution; J.L. Garvin, *Life of Joseph Chamberlain, vol. I* (London, Macmillan, 1932) p234; *Birmingham Daily Mail* 25 March 1911.

130   *BDP*, 22 December 1868.

131   N.M. Marris, *The Rt Hon Joseph Chamberlain* (1900), p. 300.

132   T. Anderton, *A Tale of One City* (Birmingham, 1900) pp. 133-4.

133   W. Harris, *The History of Our Shakespeare Club*, p. 31

134   *BDP*, 14 October 1865

135   A.F. Taylor, 'Birmingham and the Movement for National Education,' (University of Leicester, unpublished PhD thesis, 1960) pp. 251-4.

136   Garvin, op.cit., pp. 256-7; 129-135; see also A.E. Reekes, *The Birmingham Political Machine*, pp. 22-37.

137   J.A. Langford, *The Birmingham Free Libraries* p. 46.

138   W. Harris, op.cit. pp. 6-31.

139   S. Morris, 'Shakespeare's scenes in terracotta,' theshakespeareblog.com/2013/09.

140   *BDP*, 11 November 1865

141   Langford, op.cit., pp. 76-7.

142   *BDP*, 23 May 1866.

143   R.A. Armstrong, *Henry William Crosskey*, p. 261.

144   E.P. Hennock, *Fit and Proper Persons*, pp. 131-8.

145   *BDP*, 21 December 1868.

146   Garvin, op.cit., p. 254.

147   *BDP*, 25 March 1885 (reporting a speech by F. Schnadhorst at the Nechells ward meeting of 23 March 1885.)

148   Garvin, op.cit., p. 251.

149   M. Ostrogorski, *Democracy and the Organisation of Political Parties* Volume 1: England (USA, Anchor Books, 1964) pp. 80-81.

150   F. Herrick, 'The Origins of the National Liberal Federation,' *Journal of Modern History*, Vol. 17, No.2 (June 1945), pp. 124-6.

151   S. Timmins, *A History of Warwickshire*, p. 207.

152   *Illustrated London News* 15 September 1849, p. 190.

153   For the contrast see J. Seed, on Manchester's 'wealthy bourgeoisie ... viewing the artist with apprehension ... for the artist was 'a specimen of humanity unknown to our circle.' 'Commerce and the Liberal Arts: the political economy of art in Manchester, 1775-1860,' Unpublished MS, Roehampton (1985), p. 27.

154   S. Timmins, *The Resources, Products and Industrial History of Birmingham and the Midland Hardware District* (London, Robert Hardwicke, 1866), p. ix.

155   *BDP*, 25 March 1875; 18 August 1880.

156   Ibid.,16 Feb 1872; 12 March 1860.

157   R. Hartnell, 'The Contribution of Art – and of Design – to the Emergence of a Civic Culture in Birmingham in the Late Nineteenth Century,' PhD thesis, Birmingham Institute of Art and Design, May 1992, pp. 76-7.

158   *BDP*, 25 March 1875.

159   *Birmingham Journal* 10 June 1848.

160   *BDP*, 25 March 1875 and 17 November 1853.

161   R.E. Waterhouse, *The Birmingham and Midland Institute* (Birmingham, BMI, 1954) p. 185.

162   Timmins, *The Resources & c.* p. 376.

163   *BDP*, 25 March 1875.

164   Hartnell, op.cit., pp. 49 and 58.

165   Prospectus letter written by Sir Francis Scott on behalf of the workman's committee, 17 April 1858, quoted by Dent, R.K., *The Making of Birmingham* (Birmingham, J.L. Allday, 1894) p. 487.

166   *BDP*, 22 May 1882.

167   Ibid., 22 May 1889.

168   *Birmingham Daily Gazette* 9 January 1868.

169   *BDP*, 24 April 1871.

170   Ibid.,4 April 1871.

171   *BDG* 26 February 1863.

172   *BDP*, 29 March 1879.

173   *BDP*, 6 December 1895.

174   *Aris's Birmingham Gazette,* 29 May 1869.

175   J.T. Bunce, *History of the Corporation of Birmingham,* (Cornish Bros.) p. 211.

176   J.A.L. Langford, *Birmingham: A Handbook for Residents and Visitors* (Birmingham, n.d. Midland Education Company), p. 69.

177   *ABG*, 15 December 1860.

178   Ibid., 13 December 1862.

179   Ibid.

180   Between 1855 and 1865 Mullins became the father of six children.

181   Ibid., 8 July 1865.

182   *BJ*, 16 December 1865.

183 *BDP,* 31 May 1865.

184 Quoted in A. Reekes *Speeches that Changed Britain: Oratory in Birmingham* (West Midlands History, Alcester, 2015), p. 56.

185 *BDG,* 1 October 1868.

186 *BDP,* 4 October 1877.

187 Ibid., 29 April 1869; *BDP,* 1 May 1869.

188 *ABG,* 15 May 1869.

189 *BDP,* 21 August 1869.

190 *BDG,* 29 April 1869.

191 Also see Mullins' contribution to S. Timmins ed. *Handbook of Birmingham* (Birmingham, 1886).

192 *BDG.,* 4 April 1877.

193 *BDP,* 24 April 1874.

194 Ibid.

195 Ibid., 11 December 1877.

196 Ibid., 14 January 1879.

197 Ibid., 13 January 1879.

198 Ibid., 14 January 1879.

199 Ibid.

200 Ibid., 4 November 1881. In 1884 Richard and George Tangye – who did a great deal of business in Australia – bought from the London antiquarian bookseller Bernard Quaritch a copy of the First Folio for the New South Wales Free Library. It was reported in Sydney's *Evening News,* 3 November 1884 that they had paid £136, although the *Northern Territory Times,* 14 February 1885 was probably more accurate when it put the cost at 'close upon £500'. Two pages were missing and had to be supplied in facsimile, but otherwise this copy of the First Folio was in good condition. Oak from the Forest of Arden was used to make the carved box in which the First Folio was placed. Also see the Australian newspapers, the *Daily Telegraph,* 17 February 1885, *Evening News,* 17 February 1885, *Sydney Morning Herald,* 23 April 1923.

201 Ibid., 15 January 1887.

202 Ibid., 16 August 1889.

203 Ibid., 1 June 1900

204 *Handsworth Magazine,* VI, no. 72, June 1900.

205 *BDP,* 24 April 1883 for the final report of a dinner; attendance was beginning to fall off and the dinners were abandoned in 1889.

206 *BDP,* 25 April 1881.

207 Ibid., 25 April 1877, 30 April 1880.

208 Ibid., 25 April 1881.

209 Ibid., 20 April 1880.

210 *BJ,* 21 January 1839, 31 October 1846.

211 Ibid., 1 May 1847 to 11 March 1848 for twenty-eight of these letters.

212 Ibid., 1 May, 29 May, 12 June 1847.

213 Ibid., 14 August 1847.

214 Ibid., 11 March 1847.

215 *BDP,* 27 May 1858.

216 Samuel Timmins died in 1846 and Richard Timmins died in 1850. Edwin Griffiths married into the Timmins family, initially Sam: Timmins' cousin Harriet and then,

after her death in 1855, his cousin Rosa, who died in childbirth in 1860, one year after the marriage. Joseph Timmins died in 1866. Edwin Griffiths died in 1902.

217 Folger Shakespeare Library, Y. d. 4 (176), S. Timmins to J.P. Norris, 5 October 1876.

218 *BDP*, 13 May 1891.

219 *BDG*, 17 November 1870. The chairman referred to was the land agent William Matthews, who had nominated W.L. Sargent as a candidate for the school board. He was successful, but J.A. Cooper was not.

220 Ibid., 18 April 1864.

221 Thomas Hill was headmaster of Hazlewood School in Hagley Road, which was noted for its rejection of corporal punishment. The William Salt Library, Stafford, holds a number of letters written by Timmins in 1894 about the Soho Works.

222 *BDG*, 29 August 1907.

223 According to W. Harris, *The History of the Shakespeare Club*, (*Birmingham Journal* Printing Offices 1903) p. 28 'some of our philosophers were particular as to the quality of their dinner' and so the venue was moved to the Royal Hotel and then the Plough and Harrow.

224 *BJ*, 23 April 1864.

225 For the *Devonshire Hamlets* (1859) see ibid., 17 December 1859.

226 *BDG*, 29 May 1863.

227 Ibid., 20 April 1861.

228 *BDP*, 26 April 1858, 25 April 1868. One member of the club thought it was 'inexcusable' that Dawson did not attribute the idea to Timmins.

229 *BJ*, 23 April 1864.

230 *BDG*, 4 April 1864 for details of some of the donations.

231 *BDP*, 24 April 1874.

232 B. Quaritch to S, Timmins, 8 March 1870, birmingham.gov.uk/directory_record/148744/Bernard_quaritch_letter_1870

233 *BDP*, 24 April 1871. The Shakespeare Memorial Library had earlier acquired a facsimile of the First Folio.

234 Folger Shakespeare Library, Y.d. 4 (173), S, Timmins to J.P. Norris, 29 August 1876.

235 C.M. Ingelby, *Shakespeare's Bones* (Trubner & Co., London, 1883), p. 42.

236 Ibid., April 1873.

237 *BDG*, 13 November 1902.

238 *BDP*, 6 December, 11 December 1876.

239 Ibid., 24 April 1877.

240 Ibid., 27 October 1866.

241 *BDG*, 14 November 1902.

242 *Edgbastonia*, vol. IV, no. 41 (September 1884). For Edwards see S. Roberts *Now Mr Editor! Letters to the Newspapers of Nineteenth Century Birmingham* (Birmingham Biographies, 2015), pp. 8-10.

243 *Edgbastonia*, vol. IV, no. 41 (September 1884).

244 Ibid., 18 November 1902. The inscription on Timmins' headstone reads: 'He loved his books, his home and his friends.'

245 *Birmingham Daily Mail* 31 October 1883, reporting a meeting at the Council House to discuss establishing a memorial to J H Chamberlain.

246 See E.P. Hennock, *Fit and Proper Persons*.

247 'An *Appreciation* by J. H. Chamberlain in 1879' in materials for *The Life of George Dawson* collected by W. Wright Wilson volume 7 MS 3085/7, Library of Birmingham.

248 R. Hartnell, 'Art and Civic Culture in Birmingham in the Late Nineteenth Century,' (*Urban History*, August 1995, Cambridge University Press) pp. 231-3.

249 J. Ruskin, *Seven Lamps of Architecture* (Smith, Elder and Co., London, 1849), p. 1.

250 *BDP*, 20 July 1881.

251 J. Ruskin, *The Stones of Venice* volume II (Smith, Elder and Co., London 1852) Chapter vii, paragraph 47.

252 J. Holyoak 'John Henry Chamberlain' pp. 155-6 in ed. P. Ballard, *Birmingham's Victorian and Edwardian Architects* (Oblong Creative Ltd, 2009).

253 J. Ruskin, *Fors Clavigera* (Letters to British workmen) first published in 1871.

254 S. Eagles, 'Past Masters: George Baker,' www.guildofstgeorge.org.uk; R. Hartnell, 'The Contribution of Art and Design to the Emergence of a Civic Culture in Birmingham in the Late Nineteenth Century,' PhD thesis, Birmingham School of Art and Design, May 1992.

255 W. Morris, *Labour and Pleasure vs Labour and Sorrow: Address in Town Hall* (Birmingham 1880), later published in *The Collected Works of William Morris, with an Introduction by his daughter May Morris*, vol.22, *Hopes and Fear for Art, Lectures on Art and Industry* (London 1914) p. 28.

256 Quoted by E. Fernie in 'Modernity Unbound: Birmingham, Shakespeare and the French Revolution,' in *Actes des congres de la Societie Francaise Shakespeare*, 37/2019 (Societie Francaise), p. 3.

257 *BDP*, 24 October 1883.

258 R.E. Waterhouse, *The Birmingham and Midland Institute* (BMI, Birmingham, 1954) p. 13.

259 *BDP*, October 21 1881. Speech by Joseph Chamberlain on the occasion of the opening of the new BMI buildings.

260 *Report of the Council to be presented at the Annual Meeting January 1884* (BMI).

261 Waterhouse, op.cit., p. 71.

262 *Inaugural Address by George Dawson, M.A.*, Borough of Birmingham, Opening of the Free Reference Library, 26 October 1866 (Birmingham, E. C. Osborne, 1866).

263 *BDP*, 24 October 1883.

264 For details of the funeral *BDM* 27 October 1883; for Joseph Chamberlain's tribute, *BDP*, 01 November 1883.

265 W. Harris, *The History of Our Shakespeare Club*, p. 33.

266 Dawson, G., *Shakespeare and other Lectures*, preface by George St Clair (London: Kegan Paul, Trench & Co., 1888).

267 *Institute Magazine*, November 1892, Vol. VI., (Birmingham: Cornish Brothers, 37, New Street, 1894) p. 33-5).

268 *Gloucester Journal*, 4 July 1857.

269 *Phonetic Journal*, 19 September 1891, p. 596.

270 *Birmingham Faces and Places*, September 1892.

271 *Institute Magazine*, op. cit.

272 Simpson, D., 'Marie Bethell Beauclerc', *Oxford Dictionary of National Biography*; for Beauclerc's desire to mark Dawson's birthday after his death, see S. Roberts *George Dawson and the Church of the Saviour* (Birmingham 2020), p.22.

273 Watts, R., 'The Policy and Practice of Enlightened Education', *Birmingham: The Workshop of the World,* eds., C. Chinn & M. Dick, (Liverpool: Liverpool University Press, 2016), pp. 199, 212.

274 *BDP,* 12 October 1887

275 *Institute Magazine,* op. cit.

276 *BDP,*12 October 1887

277 'Our Portrait Gallery: Miss Marie Bethell Beauclerc', *Phonetic Journal,* 19 September 1891.

278 *BDP,* 10 August 1892

279 *The Institute Magazine,* op. cit.

280 R. A. Armstrong, *Henry William Crosskey LL.D., F.G.S.: His Life & Work* (Cornish Bros., Birmingham, 1895), pp. 247-51. Crosskey was awarded the degree of LLD by the University of Glasgow in 1882. He was the first Unitarian minister to receive such an honour.

281 Ibid., p. 305

282 Ibid., p. 5

283 Ibid., p. 261.

284 *BDP,* 11 February 1886.

285 Armstrong, p. 16.

286 Ibid., pp. 17-18

287 Ibid., p. 21

288 Ibid., 24.

289 Ibid., pp. 58-9.

290 R.Armstrong, p. 155, 188. Library of Birmingham, UC 2/3/8/3, Minute Book of the Visiting Committee, 1877-84 provides a great deal of detail about the families who attended the the Church of the Messiah.

291 See, for example, *The Memory of George Dawson* (1876) and *A Citizen of No Mean City: Discourse in the Church of the Messiah, Birmingham, in Memory of Alderman (Thomas) Phillips* (1876). Copies of these, and other, sermons can be found in the Library of Birmingham.

292 *BDG,* 17 December 1869. Library of Birmingham, UC 2/11/2/3, Minute Book of the Home Mission provides much information about the operation of the Sunday School.

293 Ibid., 8 December 1869.

294 Ibid.; *BDP,* 6 September 1873.

295 Ibid., 2 December 1876.

296 *BDG,* 2 September, 21 November 1870.

297 *BDP,* 1 February 1877.

298 Ibid., 1 February 1879.

299 Ibid., 1 February 1877.

300 Ibid., 5 October 1888.

301 Ibid., 9 April 1883, 5 October 1888

302 Ibid., 5 December 1879.

303 Ibid., 12 February 1881.

304 Armstrong, p. 297.

305 Ibid., 6 December 1871.

306 Ibid., 18 March 1873

307 Quoted in H.Plant, 'Ye all one in Christ: Aspects of Unitarianism and Feminism in Birmingham c. 1869-1890', in *Women's History Review*, 9:4,(2000), p. 735. This article offers an excellent discussion of the contribution Crosskey and the Church of the Messiah made to the feminist cause in Birmingham.
308 Armstrong, p.393
309 *BDP*, 23 February 1881.
310 Plant, p. 727.
311 Armstrong, p. 257.
312 Armstrong, pp. 388-9
313 *BDP*, 12 February 1885.
314 Ibid., 26 October 1875.
315 *County Advertizer and Herald for Staffordshire and Worcestershire*, 7 November 1874.
316 See J.A. Langford, *Birmingham: A Handbook for Residents and Visitors* (Midland Education Co., Birmingham, 1879); *ABG*, 17 September 1827, 3 August 1829, 9 October 1830.
317 *BJ*, 28 February 1846.
318 Ibid.
319 Ibid.
320 *BDP*, 5 October 1860.
321 Ibid.
322 Ibid. See ibid., 12 October 1860 for a description of the music at Mount Zion being 'almost unendurably bad'.
323 Ibid., 15 November 1870.
324 S. Roberts, *Recollections of Victorian Birmingham* (Birmingham Biographies) p. 43.
325 Ibid.
326 See A.W.W. Dale, *The Life of R.W. Dale of Birmingham* (1898), p. 403; *Birmingham Journal*, 27 October 1866 which records simply 'The Rev. Charles Vince also responded'.
327 *BDP*, 24 July 1
328 *BDP*, 2 March 1870.
329 *BDG*, 13 April 1870.
330 *BDP*, 2 April 1895.
331 Ibid., 25 March 1870.
332 Ibid., 19 January 1870.
333 Ibid., 2 March, 25 March 1870
334 Ibid.
335 *BDG*, 14 December 1870.
336 *BDP*, 1 August 1872.
337 Ibid., 2 March 1870. Also see ibid., 1 November 1878 for a denial from C.A. Vince to an accusation that his father had ever abandoned this position.
338 Ibid., 6 November 1873.
339 *Lancaster Gazette*, 7 November 1874.
340 *BDP*, 18 November 1891. Her eldest son Charles A. Vince was one of those who addressed the meeting – for whom see A. Reekes, *The Birmingham Political Machine*, pp. 169-71,
341 *Birmingham Faces and Places*, 1 September 1888. Jaffray retired in December 1893; the paper was carried on by John Feeney.
342 *BM*, 7 January 1901.

343 See *BDP*, 21 August 1862, 2 February, 6 October 1864. From these investments he derived annual dividends of 10-15%.

344 S. Roberts, *Now Mr Editor! Letters to the Newspapers of Nineteenth Century Birmingham* (Birmingham, 2015), pp. 1-7 for the early history of the *Birmingham Journal.*

345 *BDP*, 17 March 1886.

346 *BDG*, 1 August 1867.

347 See obit., *BDP*, 25 March 1875.

348 J.T. Bunce, *History of the Corporation of Birmingham* (Birmingham, 1885), p. 239.

349 See S. Roberts, *Sir Richard Tangye 1833-1906: A Cornish Entrepreneur in Victorian Birmingham* (Birmingham Biographies, 2015), pp. 26-8.

350 *BM*, 8 October 1883.

351 Allsopp, 3,629; Jaffray, 2,692; Maj: 937.

352 *BDP*, 17 March 1886.

353 *BDG*, 9 January 1901. Library of Birmingham, MS 1784/3 for a collection of papers relating to John Jaffray.

354 S. Hoban, 'Bunce, John Thackray,' *Oxford Dictionary of National Biography* 2004-16; H.J. Hanham, *Elections and Party Management* (Sussex, The Harvester Press, 1978) pp.109-13.

355 H.R.G. Whates, *The Birmingham Post 1857:1957* (Birmingham, The Birmingham Post & Mail Ltd., 1957) pp. 80-81.

356 *BDP*, 8 July 1868; 7 November 1868; 22 April 1886.

357 A.F. Taylor, 'Birmingham and the Movement for National Education,' (University of Leicester, unpublished PhD thesis, 1960) pp. 251-2.

358 *BDP*, 2 and 3 December 1870.

359 Ibid., 16 January 1873.

360 Ibid.,19 and 21 November 1873.

361 W. Harris, *History of Our Shakespeare Club*, p.40; Cadbury Research Library, Letter J. Chamberlain to J.T. Bunce, March 1873 JC 5/8/7.

362 Quoted by S. Koss *The Rise and Fall of the Political Press in Britain* (London, Hamish Hamilton, 1981) p. 219; p. 240.

363 Letter J. Chamberlain, to Bunce, J., JC 5/8/59, Cadbury Research Library.

364 Quoted by E.P. Hennock, *Fit and Proper Persons*, p. 322

365 J. Bunce, *History of the Corporation of Birmingham* vol.2 (Birmingham, Cornish Bros., 1885) pp. xxvi, xxxii

366 J. Bunce, *History of the Corporation of Birmingham* vol.1 pp. 352-4

367 R. Ward, *City State and Nation* p. 52.

368 Ward., p. 351.

369 Quoted in an article by J. Chamberlain in 'The Caucus,' *The Fortnightly Review* November 1878.

370 He acted as secretary to a meeting at the Willis Rooms in May 1857 chaired by Prince Albert on early schooling, *Salisbury and Winchester Journal*, 30 May 1857; he awarded prizes for reading at the Birmingham Education Association prizegiving – the organisation was concerned with improving school attendance and literacy, *BDP*, December 1859; he attended a conference on evening schools in South Staffs *BDP*, 27 February 1861.

371 *BDG* 14 February 1867.

372 Letter Joseph Chamberlain to Bunce 6 December 1897 JC 5/8/123.

373 *BDP*, 11 December 1873.

374 Ibid., 24 April 1864.

375 W. Wright Wilson, Notes for the *Life of George Dawson* (George Dawson Collection vol.7, Library of Birmingham) MS 3085/7

376 *BDG* 11 November 1876; R. Hartnell, *Pre-Raphaelite Birmingham* (Studley, Brewin Books, 1996) pp. 60, 65-77.

377 Hoban, op.cit.

378 *BDP*, 21 June 1870.

379 S. Davies, *By the Gains of Industry – Birmingham Museums and Art Gallery 1885-1985* (Birmingham, 1985) p. 20.

380 Speech at Prizegiving for Birmingham School of Art, 17 February 1892 in Birmingham School of Art Addresses 1892-1912, Library of Birmingham, L54.1.

381 *BDP*, 1 December 1876.

382 J.T. Bunce, *History of the Corporation* vol.2 p. 248.

383 Speech by Bunce at the retirement of the curator of the School of Art, John Gough after fifteen years' service 12 October 1890 *BDP*, 13 October 1890.

384 School of Art Prizegiving speech, 17 February 1892.

385 Ibid.

386 Quoted by D. Cannadine, 'The Bourgeois Experience as Political Culture. The Chamberlains of Birmingham,' in M.S. Micale and D. Dietle (eds) *Enlightenment, Passion and Modernity* (USA, Stanford, 2000) p. 151.

387 *BDP*, 1 August 1919.

388 R. Church, 'The Kenrick family,' *Oxford Dictionary of National Biography* (Oxford, OUP, 2004).

389 G.F. Parker, 'An Object lesson in Municipal Government showing how public affairs are conducted in the City of Birmingham,' *The Century Magazine* Vol. LIII, No.1, November 1896, New York, p. 83.

390 L. Rosenthal, 'Joseph Chamberlain and the Birmingham Town Council 1865-1880', *Midland History* (2016) 41:1, pp. 71-95.

391 *BDP*, 21 February 1878.

392 Ibid., 11 November 1878.

393 Ibid., 14 September 188.

394 R. Hartnell, *Pre-Raphaelite Birmingham* (Brewin Books, Studley, 1996) p. 39.

395 C. Debenham, *Recollections,* an unpublished MS c. 1910, quoted by Hartnell, R. 'The Contribution of Art and of Design to the Emergence and Establishment of a Civic Culture in Birmingham in the late nineteenth century', Unpublished PhD thesis, Birmingham Institute of Art and Design, May1992, p. 259.

396 Ibid., p. 264.

397 J. Holyoak, 'John Henry Chamberlain,' pp. 178-9 in ed. P. Ballard, *Birmingham's Victorian and Edwardian Architects* (Oblong Creative Ltd., 2009).

398 *BDP*, 21 February 1878.

399 G. Burne-Jones, *Memorials of Edward Burne-Jones* Volume II (Macmillan, London, 1912) pp. 99-100.

400 *BDP*, 20 July 1881.

401 J.T. Bunce, 'Local Governing Bodies,' in *Handbook of Birmingham* (Birmingham, Hall and English, 1886) p. 9.

402 Hartnell, *Pre-Raphaelite Birmingham* p. 84.

403   Ibid,. p. 87.

404   *BDP*, 13 September 1889; S. Hoban, 'The Birmingham School of Art and Opportunities for Women's paid work in the Arts and Crafts Movement 1885-1914,' unpublished PhD thesis, University of Birmingham, 2013; J. Swift, 'Birmingham Art School, its Branch schools and Female students, 1880-1900,' in ed. B. Tilson, *Made in Birmingham: Design and Industry 1889-1989* (Brewin Books, Studley,1989), pp. 49-64.

405   *BDP*, 18 September 1891

406   Quoted by Hoban, op.cit. from the Examiner's Report 1900, prepared for members of the management sub-committee, Birmingham Municipal School of Art management sub-committee minutes 13 February 1900.

407   *BDP*, 16 September 1887

408   Ibid.,14 September 1888

409   Ibid.,18 September 1891

410   *Birmingham Daily Mail*, 31 July 1919.

411   J. Martineau, 'The Martineau Family in Birmingham 1828-2014' (unpublished private paper 2016 in the possession of A. Reekes).

412   *BDP*, 16 December 1909.

413   E.P. Hennock, *Fit and Proper Persons* (London, Edward Arnold, 1973) p.100, note 63.

414   R. Watts, 'Education, Civic Service and Social Reform in Birmingham – The Martineau Connection' (*The Martineau Society Newsletter*, No. 40, February 2017) pp. 8-11. She is quoting from William Henry Ryland (ed.), *Reminiscences of Thomas Henry Ryland*, (Birmingham: The Midland Counties Herald Limited, 1904), pp. 137-8.

415   *BDP*, 9 April 1878.

416   R.A. Armstrong, and E.F.M. MacCarthy, *Henry William Crosskey* p. 221.

417   *BDP*, 12 October 1895.

418   Ibid., 27 October 1880; 10 October 1883.

419   Ibid., 4 April 1884.

420   Ibid., 4 July 1868.

421   Ibid., 7 July 1860.

422   Ibid., 23 February 1878; *BDP*, 27 February 1869.

423   Ibid., 21 January 1885.

424   L. Rosenthal, 'Joseph Chamberlain and the Birmingham Council, 1865-1880,' *Midland History* 2016 41:1 pp. 71-95.

425   *BDP*, 30 April 1877; 27 December 1878.

426   Ibid.,16 May 1878.

427   Ibid.,24 April 1869; 24 April 1871.

428   R.E. Waterhouse, *The Birmingham and Midland Institute 1854-1954* (Birmingham, The Birmingham and Midland Institute, 1954) pp. 163-4.

429   Ibid., p. 121.

430   *BDP*, 10 January 1882.

431   *BDP*, 24 February 1890.

432   *BDP*, 7 December 1892.

433   Ibid.

434   Ibid.14 December 1895.

435   *BDG* 18 December 1909.

436   *Walsall Advertiser* 28 December 1895; the self-same arguments appeared at the Dudley Technical School Prizegiving recorded in *The County Advertiser and Herald for*

Staffordshire and Worcestershire 10 November 1898.

437   Speech at the opening of the School of Art 10 October 1893 reported in *BDP,* 11 October 1893.

438   Taylor quoted by R. Hartnell, 'The Contribution of Art and of Design to the Emergence and Establishment of a Civic Culture in Birmingham in the late nineteenth century,' unpublished PhD thesis, Birmingham Institute of Art and Design, 1992, p. 166.

439   *Walsall Advertiser,* 28 December 1895.

440   *BDG,* 18 December 1909.

441   *BDP,* 12 September 1885

442   Ibid., 22 September 1885.

443   Ibid., 31 January 1882.

444   Ibid., 22 September 1885.

445   *BDG,* 7 December 1907. William Logsdail was the son of a clergyman at the cathedral. His work was first shown at an exhibition of the Royal Academy in 1877. He spent much of his early life in Venice, having travelled there with another of Taylor's pupils Frank Bramley. He painted a portrait of Taylor.

446   *Lincoln Gazette,* 7 April 1877.

447   Ibid., 27 January, 7 April 1877.

448   *Staffordshire Sentinel,* 12 October 1907.

449   *BDG,* 7 December 1907; reptd. In S. Roberts, *Recollections of Victorian Birmingham* (2018), pp. 61-3.

450   Quoted in S. Roberts, *Sir Richard Tangye* (Birmingham Biographies) pp. 27-30.

451   *BDP,* 22 September 1885.

452   Ibid., 31 January 1882.

453   Ibid., 12 September 1885. See A. Foster, *Birmingham* (Yale University Press, 2005), pp. 69-73.

454   *BDP,* 12 September 1885.

455   Ibid., 13 September 1889.

456   Ibid., 2 May 1890.

457   Ibid., 25 July 1891.

458   R. Albutt, 'Henry Payne: Stained Glass Work at Birmingham School of Art', historywm. com/file/historywm/e04-a16-henry-payne-32430. Pdf.

459   *BDP,* 28 October 1890.

460   Ibid., 3 September 1895.

461   Ibid.

462   Ibid., 28 March 1878, 29 March 1886.

463   Ibid., 25 April 1879.

464   *BDP,* 17 January 1912 for obit. Taylor is buried in the churchyard of St. George's, Edgbaston.

465   Ibid., 18 September 1891, 11 April 1900.

466   Quoted by E. Fernie in 'Lost Prophet' an essay in the *Revolutionary Players* series, published by History West Midlands in 2019.

467   A. St Johnston, 'The progress of art in Birmingham,' in *The Magazine of Art* (London 1887).

468   *Sunday Chronicle,* November 1916.

469   T. Hunt, *Building Jerusalem,* p. 362.

Index

Aitken, William 12
    contribution to industrial crafts 58,
        62-3
    Dawson and 146
    education provision 13-14, 58-62
    working life and skills 56-8
Albert, Prince Consort 39, 60
Allday, Joseph 117
Allday, Thomas 36
Alldritt, William 65
Archibald Kenrick and Sons 123
Arnold, Matthew 23
art galleries *see* Birmingham Art
        Gallery
art school *see* Birmingham School of
        Art
Arts and Crafts movement *see* Morris,
        William
Arts Club 11, 12, 25, 119, 149
Aston Hall 60, 61, 111, 151
Avery, Thomas 27, 37, 53, 68, 117

Bailey, Gertrude 143
Baker, George 83, 119
Barry, E. M. 64
Beaucastle, Wyre Forest 83, 119
Beauclerc, Marie Bethell
    reporting 86, 88-9
    early life 86-7
        and death 90-91
    Shorthand Writers Association 90
    teaching 88, 89-90
Bidlake, W. H. 144
Birmingham and Edgbaston Debating
        Society 49, 72, 123, 133, 149

Birmingham and Midland
        Homeopathic Hospital 133
Birmingham and Midland Institute 21,
        105
    building 39, 81-2, 149
    classes, departments, lecturers 11,
        13-14, 39-40, 58, 73, 89, 90
    science and metallurgical classes
        136
    founding principles 29, 37-9, 89
    members 59, 83-4, 110, 118, 125,
        135-6
Birmingham Architectural Society 52
Birmingham Art Gallery 64, 126, 144
    acquisitions 111
        Pre-Raphaelite collection 127-8
    campaign for 15, 85, 109-10, 119-
        20, 126-8
    committees 52, 61, 111, 127
    funding 82
    new building 12-13, 80-81, 111, 141
    see also Birmingham School of Art
Birmingham Art School *see*
        Birmingham School of Art
Birmingham Athletic Club 133
Birmingham Central Literary
        Association 149
Birmingham Chamber of Commerce
        62
Birmingham Council House 15, 21-2,
        30, 31, 68, 150-51
Birmingham Daily Gazette 150
Birmingham Daily Mail 130, 150
Birmingham Daily Post 34, 35, 50, 58,
        108, 109, 111, 123, 142, 145,
        150

Bunce as editor 11, 109, 114-16, 119-20
Birmingham Daily Press 50
Birmingham Education Society 44, 118, 124-5
Birmingham Free Christian Society 132
Birmingham Jewellers' and Silversmiths' Association 143
Birmingham Journal 109
Birmingham Law Society 33
Birmingham Liberal Association (BLA) 41, 45, 49, 53-4, 93, 96-7, 105, 112-13, 115-16
  and National Liberal Federation (NLF) 54-5
Birmingham Library (Old Library) 65-6
Birmingham Morning News 88
Birmingham municipal council (1838) 35-6
Birmingham Natural History and Microscopical Society 100
Birmingham Philosophical Institution 37-8, 58, 118, 152
Birmingham Philosophical Society 100
Birmingham Reference Library
  chief librarian *see* Mullins, John Davis
  committees 66, 77, 105, 110, 119, 126, 137
  fire (1879) 64, 68, 76, 77, 82, 119, 145
  and legislation 36, 38, 51-2
  opening (1866) 14, 23, 26, 29-30, 66, 85
Birmingham Religious Education Society 45-6
Birmingham School Board 16, 26, 27, 96-7, 99, 106-7, 115-16, 151
  commissioning of new schools 31, 81
  denominational competition 45-6, 72-3
  see also education legislation; National Education League

Birmingham School of Art 16, 120-21
  building 22, 62, 82, 142
  committees 83, 85, 128, 137-8
  core principles 15-16, 142
  Kendrick's work 125, 126-7, 128-30
  origins 17, 139
  Taylor's headmastership 139-45
  see also Birmingham Art Gallery
Birmingham Selborne Society 134
Birmingham Society for Women's Suffrage 88-9, 98-9, 133
Birmingham Society of Artisans 61
Birmingham Society of Arts 39, 61-2, 139, 153
Birmingham Town Hall 21, 36, 39, 43, 59, 72, 83, 98, 134, 153
Birmingham Women's Suffrage Society 88-9, 98-9, 133
Board of Guardians 118, 150
Breakspeare, W.A. 145
Briggs, Asa 6
Bright, John 49, 53, 105, 112
Builder's Industrial Society 34
Bunce, John Thackray 41, 56
  and Chamberlain, J. H. 83-4, 85
  educational reform 51, 115-16, 118-19, 139
  literary and artistic interests 15, 52, 65, 74, 119-22, 128, 129, 137
  newspaper editorship 11, 109, 114-16, 119-20
  politics 115-16
  role in civic gospel 114, 116-18
  on Ryland 33, 34, 35, 39-40
Bunce, Kate 16, 143
Bunce, Myra 143
Burne-Jones, Edward 127-8, 144, 153
Butler, Josephine 16

Camm, Florence 16
Cannadine, David 31
Carlyle, Thomas 93-4
Carr's Lane Chapel 41, 43-5, 47, 71, 150
Chamberlain, Arthur 95, 144

Chamberlain, J. H. 19, 127
  on art 15
  building designs 81-2, 125-6
  Dawson's influence on 79-80, 82,
    83
  tributes to 85
Chamberlain, Joseph 56, 102, 123,
    124, 128, 134, 147
  and Bunce 115-16, 118
  and Chamberlain, J. H. 79, 82
  and Dale 46
  and Dawson 21, 25-6
  educational reform 14, 16, 25-6, 28-
    30, 95
    participation 34, 40, 44, 45, 51
  monument 19-20, 126
  municipal revolution 9, 26-8, 127,
    133-4
    art and design 15, 30-32
    'gas and water' socialism 11-12,
      22-3, 27-8
    philanthropy 68, 76
    politics 54-5
Chamberlain, Neville 147-8
Church of the Messiah 11, 25, 29, 95,
    96, 97, 99, 100-101, 150
Church of the Saviour 11, 35, 41, 43,
    50, 88, 91, 123, 150
civic gospel, historical overview
  19th century 9-17
  20th century 147-8
  Dawson's vision 10, 23-4
  Ruskin's influence 80-81
Cole, Henry 30
Collings, Jesse 13, 27, 62, 96
Collyer, Robert 89
Cossins, Jethro A. 144
Council House 15, 21-2, 30, 31, 68,
    150-51
Cox, David 119
Cox, William Sands 152
Crosskey, Hannah 95, 97-100
Crosskey, Henry 150
  biographical details and church
    ministries 93-5, 99-100
  education provision 90, 92, 95-100

  interest in science and geology 97-
    8, 100
  Unitarianism 132

Dale, A. W. W. 10, 28
Dale, Elizabeth 43
Dale, Robert
  church ministry 150
  and Dawson 41-2
  educational reform 44-7, 96
    Education Bill (1870) 44-5
    School Board work 45, 107,
      115-16
  municipal responsibility 11, 24, 27,
    46
Dawson, George 65, 73, 78, 116
  and Beauclerc 88-91
  and Chamberlain, J. H. 79-80, 82,
    83
  and Chamberlain, Joseph 21, 25-6
  church ministry 11, 22, 49, 88, 103-
    4, 132, 150
  civic gospel 10, 23-4
  and Dale 41-2
  death 77
  educational reform 10-11, 26, 29-
    30, 50-51, 84
    Birmingham Education Society
      44, 118, 124-5
  and John Jaffray 109
  library campaign 14-15, 36-7, 50,
    67
    opening speech (1866) 14, 26,
      66, 85
  personal objective and intent 20-21,
    42
  politics 16, 41, 49-50, 88-9
  and Ryland 35
  Shakespeare's influence on 20, 52,
    74-5, 77, 134-5, 146
  statue 19-21
Dawson, Susan 88
Delius, Nicolaus 76
Dickens, Charles 38
Downing, William 78
Dyos, H. J. 23

Edgbaston Debating Society 49, 72, 123, 133, 149
Edgbaston High School for Girls 15, 125
Edgbaston Proprietary School 70-71, 134
education legislation 9, 26, 27
    Education Bill (1870) 13, 44-5, 96, 106
    Free Libraries Act (1850) 38, 51-2
    Free Libraries and Museums Act (1855) 36, 38
    see also Birmingham School Board; National Education League
Edwards, Eliezer 78
Eginton, Francis 58

Feeney, John Frederick 109, 115
Fernie, Ewan 20, 171
Fine Arts' Prize Fund Association 109-10
Finnemore, Joseph 145
France, Georgie Cave 143, 144
Free Hospital for Sick Children 37, 111, 151
Free Libraries and Museums Act (1855) 36
Free Reference Library see Birmingham Reference Library

Garvin, J. L. 48, 49, 54
Gaskell, Elizabeth 93
Gaskin, Arthur 144
'General View of Birmingham' 19-22
General Hospital 111, 151, 153
Graham Street Chapel see Mount Zion Chapel
Grammar School Association 50
Great Exhibition (1851) 60
Griffiths, Edwin 72
Grindley, B.J. 150

Harris, Edwin 145
Harris, William 11, 116, 119, 147
    on Chamberlain, Joseph 85
    Dawson and 49-50

educational reform 13, 34-5, 50-51
    library campaign 51-2
    literary and artistic interests 52, 111
    municipal work 52-3, 147
    political legacy 48-9, 53-5, 115
Harrison, William Jerome 97
Hartnell, Roy 80
Hennock, E. P. 20, 23, 25
Henshaw, F.H. 100
History of the Corporation of Birmingham 116-18
Hollins, Peter 153
Holyoake, George Jacob 94
Hospital for Women 111, 151
Hunt, Tristram 148
Hutton, William 35

Jabet, George 65
Jackson, F. G. 144
Jaffray, Hannah 113
Jaffray, John 51, 75, 102, 115
    artistic interests 109-11
    civic work 108
    Dawson and 109
    early life 108-9
    and death 113
    hospital work 111-12
    politics 112-13
Jaffray, William 'Citizen' 108
James, John Angell 42-4, 71, 150

Kenrick, Caroline 99
Kenrick, George 136
Kenrick, Timothy 95
Kenrick, William
    artistic interests/municipal projects 15, 125-30
    education provision 62, 128-9
    civic work 13, 123-4, 147
    mayoralty 124, 126
    educational reform 124-5, 129
Key Hill Cemetery 78, 91, 151-2
King Edward's Grammar School 50, 114, 118, 125, 129, 134, 152

Langford, J. A. 15, 34, 49, 51, 52, 65
Langley, William 145
Lapworth, Henry 100
London Society of Arts 30

Martin, William 62, 64, 81-2, 120-21,
    126, 141-2, 151
Martineau, Harriet 131
Martineau, James 94
Martineau, Robert Francis 49
    Dawson and 132
    education provision 13-14, 15-16,
        34, 39, 62, 134-8
        technical education 129
    family and biographical details
        131-2
    municipal service 111, 133-4, 147
    politics 16, 132-3
Mason College 62, 144, 152
Mason, Fred 143
Mason, Josiah 59, 114, 134, 147, 152
Midland Institute see Birmingham and
    Midland Institute
Miller, Rev. Dr 36
Morris, William 16, 58, 83, 127-8,
    129-30, 144
Mount Zion Chapel 22, 35, 102, 103-6,
    151
Mullins, John Davis 12, 102
    early life 64-5
    and death 69
    librarianship 14, 64, 65-9
    reference library catalogue 69

National Education League 9, 13, 26,
    27, 44, 49, 51, 90, 93, 106, 115,
    134
    tenets and leadership 95-6, 124-5
    see also Birmingham School Board;
    education legislation
National Liberal Federation 54-5, 116
National Society for Women's
    Suffrage 16, 98
Newill, Mary 143
Norris, Joseph Parker 76

O'Neill, Arthur 43
Osborne, E. C. 36, 51
Osler, Caroline 99
Osler, Follett 95
Ostrogorski, Moisei 54
Our Shakespeare Club 50, 52, 59, 70,
    74-8, 85, 119, 132, 134-5
    see also Shakespeare Memorial
        Library; Shakespeare's
        influences

Pall Mall Gazette 31
Payne, Henry 144
Perry Barr Institute 89
Philosophical Institution 37-8, 58, 118,
    152
political associations see Birmingham
    Liberal Association (BLA)
Polytechnic Society 38, 71, 152

Queen's College 152
Queen's Hospital 111, 152
Queen's College 152

Raimbach, David W. 142
Ralph, Julian 12
Reed, Thomas 90
Roden, W. T. 76
Rogers, Henry 43
Royal Society of Artists 145, 153
Rudland, Florence 143, 145
Ruskin, John 58, 62, 80-81, 82-3, 85,
    119
Ryall, John 71
Ryland, Arthur 14, 109, 110
    contribution to the civic gospel 33-4
    Dawson and 35
    educational reform 13, 34-5, 37-8,
        96
        library campaign 36-7
    municipal work 35-6
        mayoralty 36-7
    philanthropy 82
    professional reputation 34
Ryland, Louisa Anne 141, 143

Schnadhorst, Francis 54
School Board *see* Birmingham School
    Board
School of Art *see* Birmingham School
    of Art
School of Design 39, 62
Shakespeare Memorial Library 14, 21,
    22, 67-9, 74-6, 77, 82, 83, 108,
    113, 146
    see also Our Shakespeare Club;
        Shakespeare's influences
Shakespeare's influences 44, 93
    on Dawson 11, 20, 52, 74-5, 77,
        134-5, 146
    see also Our Shakespeare Club;
        Shakespeare Memorial
        Library
Society of Arts 39, 61-2, 139, 153
Spring Hill College 43, 153
St George's Institute 58
St. Philip's Cathedral 15Street
    Commission 36
Street, James Christopher 89
Stubbs, Ida 143
Sturge, Eliza 16, 88-9
Sunday Lecture Society 134

Tangye, Richard and George 111, 120,
    126-8, 129, 140-41, 142-3, 161
Taylor, Edward
    Birmingham School of Art project
        83, 137-8, 140-45
    at Lincoln School of Art 139-40
    paintings 144-5
Taylor, William and Caroline 89

Timmins, Samuel 13, 111, 149
    character 78
    Dawson and 24, 71, 76
    early life 70-72
    and death 78
    library campaign 14, 68
    literary works 77
    public speaking and teaching 40,
        72-3, 84, 96
    Shakespeare Club and Memorial
        Library 70, 74-8, 146
    steel toys business 72
    Town Crier, The 50, 153

Vince, Charles 11
    church ministry 104, 151
    early life and death 102-3, 107
    politics and educational reform 51,
        104-7

Wallis, Whitworth 144
Watts, Ruth 90
Wheatley, Oliver 145
White, William 28
Windle, C.A. 144
women's social position 16-17, 75, 88,
    98-9, 121, 133
    Birmingham Women's Suffrage
        Society 88-9, 98-9, 133

Yeoville Thomason, H. R. 21-2
Yorkshire Post 48
Young Men's Christian Association 43

About the Authors

Andrew Reekes was a scholar of Exeter College, Oxford. He was Sub-Warden at Radley College, and formerly Head of History at Tonbridge, Cranleigh and Cheltenham Colleges. He was a Chief Examiner and school inspector as well as running two Prep Schools. He has completed postgraduate research at the University of Birmingham and is the author of *The Rise of Labour 1899-1951* (1991), *Speeches that Changed Britain: Oratory in Birmingham* (2015), *Two Titans, One City: Joseph Chamberlain and George Cadbury* (2016) and *The Birmingham Political Machine: Winning Elections for Joseph Chamberlain* (2018).

Stephen Roberts holds honorary positions as Associate Professor and Senior Fellow at, respectively, the Australian National University and the University of Birmingham. He has written extensively about the Chartists and is the author of *Radical Politicians and Poets in Early Victorian Britain: The Voices of Six Chartist Leaders* (1993) and *The Chartist Prisoners: The Radical Lives of Thomas Cooper (1805-1892) and Arthur O'Neill (1819-1896)* (2008) and the editor of *The People's Charter: Democratic Agitation in Early Victorian Britain* (2003) and *The Dignity of Chartism: Essays by Dorothy Thompson* (2015). He has also written a series of short books about Victorian Birmingham: see www.birmingham-biographies.co.uk.

Ewan Fernie is Chair, Professor and Fellow at the Shakespeare Institute, University of Birmingham. He is Director of the major, lottery-funded 'Everything to Everybody' Project, which aims to revive the world's first great Shakespeare library, founded in nineteenth-century Birmingham by Dawson and his circle, with people and communities across the contemporary city. Fernie's latest books are *'Macbeth, Macbeth'* (with Simon Palfrey, Boiler House Press), *New Places: Shakespeare and Civic Creativity* (edited with Paul Edmondson, The Arden Shakespeare) and *Shakespeare for Freedom: Why the Plays Matter* (Cambridge University Press). The book he's currently writing aims to offer a new perspective on the cultural legacy of the nineteenth century in general, and on nineteenth-century Birmingham in particular, and is titled *The Dirty History of Hope*.

Nicola Gauld is a Project Manager at the University of Birmingham, currently working on the 'Everything to Everybody' project. She studied History of Art at the University of Aberdeen and attained a PhD in 2006. Since then she has worked on a number of exhibitions and community engagement projects. She has worked for the University since 2014 and was the Coordinator of the Voices of War and Peace WW1 Engagement Centre from 2014 to 2020. Nicola is the author of *Words and Deeds: Birmingham Suffragists and Suffragettes 1832-1918*, published by History West Midlands in 2018, to celebrate 100 years of women's votes.